Therapeutic Communities

Therapeutic Communities
Series editors: Rex Haigh and Jan Lees

The Therapeutic Community movement holds a multidisciplinary view of health which is based on ideas of collective responsibility, citizenship and empowerment. The tradition has a long and distinguished history and is experiencing a revival of interest in contemporary theory and practice. It draws from many different principles – including analytic, behavioural, creative, educational and humanistic – in the framework of a group-based view of the social origins and maintenance of much overwhelming distress, mental ill-health and deviant behaviour. Therapeutic Community principles are applicable in a wide variety of settings, and this series reflects that.

An Introduction to Therapeutic Communities
David Kennard
Therapeutic Communities 1
ISBN 1 85302 603 4

Therapeutic Communities

Past, Present and Future

Edited by Penelope Campling and Rex Haigh

Foreword by John Cox

Therapeutic Communities 2

Jessica Kingsley Publishers
London and Philadelphia

Grateful acknowledgement to Geoffrey Pullen for permission to reproduce Table 18.1 on p.226, from his paper 'Street: The Seventeen Day Community' originally published in *International Journal of Therapeutic Communities 2*, 1982, pp.115–126.

First published in the United Kingdom in 1999 by

Jessica Kingsley Publishers Ltd,
116 Pentonville Road,
London N1 9JB, England
and
325 Chestnut Street,
Philadelphia, PA 19106, USA.

www.jkp.com

Library of Congress Cataloging in Publication Data

Therapeutic communities : past, present and future / edited by
Rex Haigh and Penelope Campling.
p. cm. -- (Therapeutic communities : 2)
Includes bibliographical references and index.
ISBN 1-85302-614-X (hc. : alk paper)
1. Therapeutic communities. I. Haigh, Rex, 1957– .
II. Campling, Penelope, 1958– . III. Series.
RC489.T67&47 1998

British Library Cataloguing in Publication Data

Therapeutic communities
1. Therapeutic communities
I. Haigh, Rex II. Campling, Penelope
362.2

ISBN 1-85302-614-X hb
ISBN 1-85302-626-3 pb

Printed and Bound in Great Britain by
Athenaeum Press, Gateshead, Tyne and Wear

Contents

Part III: Specialist Communities

Part IV: The Future

This book is dedicated to everybody who knowingly
or unknowingly contributed to it: our families, especially
Nicky and Steffan, our friends and colleagues,
our teachers and our patients

Foreword

This book is most timely and indeed long overdue. Its publication coincides poignantly with the 50th Anniversary Celebrations of the National Health Service which, like the TC movement was forged out of the smouldering ashes of the Second World War. The book is a necessary reminder for a wide international readership – including psychiatrists – that community mental health services, if they are to survive and flourish need to retain their core humanistic values enunciated so clearly by Bion, Main and Maxwell Jones.

Many of their successors, who now include Penelope Campling and Rex Haigh, were also psychiatrists yet their message was to all mental health professionals as well as users. They have challenged us to think community and so to re-establish those ingredients necessary for care in the community to remain therapeutic – whether such care is provided by mental health resource centres, roving community psychiatric nurses, multi-professional teams in primary care or by residential therapeutic communities.

I very much hope therefore that the influence of this book will not be restricted only to those working in residential therapeutic communities – although it will provide valuable information for these individuals – but it will also reach those working in hard pressed acute admission units as well as in generic mental health day hospitals.

The theory and practice of large group work, the ability to flatten the hierarchy yet to ensure firm leadership, and the recognition that our patients and residents are sometimes better able to assist each other than health professionals, are important insights. The TC approach, which acknowledges an appropriate degree of autonomy and responsibility of residents for their own behaviour, is a necessary antidote to a paternalistic protocol-driven approach which has characterised so much recent mental health legislation.

Psychiatric services are almost stifled by excessive top-heavy edicts from anxious managers, politically vulnerable politicians and sadly at the present time by somewhat demoralised health professionals. The radical and alternative strategies for patient care that come across from the contributors to this book are the life blood for any renewal of community psychiatry.

We do not regret the closure of the large asylums but the reader will be reminded that the TC movement which changed the management structure of these large institutions has not only survived but is very much alive and kicking. It is now time for therapeutic communities to come in from the cold and again to play their part in revitalising the theory and practice of contemporary community care.

John Cox
Keele University, Staffordshire
Royal College of Psychiatrists, London.

Introduction

Penelope Campling and Rex Haigh

This book is about therapeutic communities – the vision, the ideas, the work and the people involved. It is a book for those who work with people, who believe that growth and development is an essential part of being human, and that the capacity to care well for each other is a measure of our humanity.

Sadly, this ethic has been denigrated in the 1980s and 1990s, and it is no wonder that therapeutic communities and the values they uphold have seemed so deeply unfashionable. Thus we have had to keep alive difficult and conflicting ideas such as democracy, permissiveness, communality, the inherent value in work, the importance of self-reflective open communication, mutuality and interdependence at a time when society has been divided as never before. Striving for compassion, humanity and common sense in the field of mental health has been very difficult: corrupted by individualism and inequality, short-termism, fragmentation and alienation, and subtle but powerful policies of social control. This has been set in a culture of pervasive cynicism which makes it feel that these degradations are inevitable, unchallengeable and impossible to change.

This book is the second in a new series about therapeutic communities, which has evolved out of discussions in the Association of Therapeutic Communities. The first is a new edition of David Kennard's *Introduction to Therapeutic Communities* (1998), which presents the basic ideas of TC history and practice in a straightforward way. This volume aims to take those basic ideas and develop them using a variety of authors, different theoretical frameworks and various settings. We have invited a wide range of contributors: young and old, professors and trainees, the established and the emerging, from the capital and from the provinces. This was a deliberate attempt to paint a picture of the diversity and colour within the movement. Inevitably, it means that some people with wise and important things to say have been left out.

Future books planned for the series include some which will go into more detail and depth about subjects raised in this volume: paradigms of research, psychologically sophisticated models of community care, the expanding role of day units, the visionary origins of institutional child care in TCs, the growth of TCs in the criminal justice system and details of projects elsewhere in the world.

The last book published in this country with a similar remit to this one was written nearly twenty years ago (Hinshelwood and Manning 1979). It is extraordinary reading it now, that a book with such an eclectic range of ideas and such passion and wisdom about the life-giving potential of human relationships, should have made so little impact on psychiatry and social policy in general. Unfortunately, the tide was already turning – and the time between this book and its predecessor has been, in many senses, 'wilderness years' for the TC movement, with many communities closing, and others left lonely and struggling to survive.

However, the move to strengthen the spirit of community is gathering momentum (Etzioni 1995). It may be that the election of a new government in the UK both reflects and will effect a change in the unfavourable climate. Certainly, there is a desire to bind society together, to create employment, to invest in education and the NHS. On the other hand, much has been lost, and as yet there has been little understanding or analysis of the depth of alienation, inequality and social disruption. These conditions breed abuse, isolation and neglect, but there has been little compassion preached for the group of alienated children and adults from whom many users of TCs are recruited.

Another important feature of British society in the 1990s, and one that has made it difficult for therapeutic communities to survive, is short-termism. The corrosive effects on British industry and services of putting short-term gain before long-term investment has been frequently compared with more successful economies (Hutton 1995). This has direct parallels with unwillingness to invest in definitive treatment programmes (such as therapeutic communities) rather than patch together care which solves immediate problems but denies the potential for growth, and leads to meagre long-term prospects of leading a more fulfilling life. Examples abound: the fashion for brief cognitive-behavioural therapy and powerful new antidepressants can be equally seen as a reflection of society's values as a result of 'evidence-based medicine'. In the wider health service, measures of 'success' such as finished consultant episodes, purchaser efficiency index and efficiency savings have resulted in quicker turnaround, but not necessarily better treatment, for available resources. Some of the proposed changes to the NHS (DoH 1997) look encouraging. It is to be hoped that these shifts towards longer-term strategies, greater collaboration and more involvement in decision-making by key stakeholders, particularly users, will be reflected in the world of mental health.

It becomes increasingly difficult, as the twentieth century draws to a close, to imagine what the future will be like because the pace of change is so rapid. Maybe many people's experience of the world is becoming 'borderline', with little experience of the safety of stability, of core identity or of attachment to fixed points. Our therapeutic community patients often experience this to an extreme. They have had so little that is good and solid in their lives, so much betrayal and change, that many of them cannot imagine surviving until the next day: they have little sense of identity or their own continuity. Many of them are preoccupied with the thought of death and don't expect to wake up in the morning. Often their suicide attempts try to put an end to this crippling uncertainty, the chronic disabling pain of everyday living. Profound insecurity like this will continue to need intensive long-term therapy, and we should be extremely cautious of any attempt to make us shorten or dilute the service we offer. Therapeutic communities, after all, are about rescuing patients from short-term maladaptive 'fixes' to their problems and futile crisis intervention from professionals.

Risk management is another managerial fad imported into psychiatry, talked about as if it is a new discovery rather than something that has always been inherent in good practice. At its most extreme, risk is enumerated and evaluated with a shallowness or hollowness that is breathtaking. No understanding of 'why' is attempted, the inner world and experience of patients is not considered, and an interview can be reduced to following an arithmetical algorithm based on actuarial calculations of probability. It is probably no accident that it could be better done by a computer: the essence of care, compassion and humanity is lost. Professional and therapeutic relationships are where risk is contained through understanding – and the discomfort, intimacy and anxiety that entails. Therapeutic communities are good at containing risk, but – like the centipede asked if it remembers how to walk – might lose it if called on to describe it!

Many of us in psychiatry are particularly worried about its changing focus away from therapy and towards *control*. Indeed, a high order of social control is now imposed through mechanisms like the supervision register, supervised discharge and care programme approach (CPA). Although they were developed as a means of improving standards, and ensuring that those who were genuinely dependent and needy were properly cared for, they seem like a road to Hell paved with good intentions. As well as taking up so much time that few professionals in mental health have space left to develop therapeutic relationships with patients, they directly undermine the open-minded thinking that any sort of care based on relationship and understanding demands. The relationships are set up in terms of control and planning: 'we will arrange this meeting for you so we can sort out what is best'. Dependency is unwittingly encouraged, autonomy is undermined and psychiatrists can be made to feel legally responsible for their patients' thoughts, feelings and actions – all without the resources, practical ability or moral right to control them. Although TCs often thrive on adapting to adversity, and many have incorporated these procedures in as democratic a way as possible, having to collude with such policies in order to survive is a measure of how deep the blaming, defensive and paranoid culture – from which we try to help our patients escape – has become.

However, wilderness years are a stimulus for reflection and for distilling out what is of lasting importance. The first part of the book attempts to return to our roots; to the Northfield Experiments in Chapter 1, the social psychiatry movement in Chapter 2 and the evolving psychoanalytic and group analytic influences on our work for Chapters 3 and 4. We have also included Chapter 5 on the development of therapeutic community ideas within the nursing profession, which have been at the heart of the movement but largely overlooked.

In the second part, we look at practice itself, the art of translating ideology into the medium of our working relationships. As models of the mind, of the group and the working of systems, become more sophisticated, our practice is informed and developed. At the same time, there must be space for all involved to explore and discover for themselves what is mutative and of real value. These chapters cover crucial aspects of our work: the problem of engaging our patients and then facilitating their separation (Chapter 6); the managing of boundaries and maintaining a safe therapeutic environment (Chapter 7); the issue of consent in therapy and the potential for abusing power and re-traumatising patients (Chapter 8); an illustration of the turbulent processes in a typical community group (Chapter 9), and finally the opportunity for creative therapies to nurture potential and uncover repressed energies (Chapter 10). As most of us practise an integrated psycho-social approach, we chose these general themes, rather than separating out psychotherapy and sociotherapy. We also considered a chapter from a user perspective, but hope that this will be the focus for a further book in the series.

Many of these general approaches are further explored in Part 3, where different types of therapeutic communities are described. Part of the legacy of the wilderness years has been a process of redefinition, with therapeutic communities emerging to be clearer about their objectives and more specific about whom they can help. Most of the surviving therapeutic communities within the NHS work with adults suffering from personality disorder, which is the subject of the first contribution, Chapter 11. However, Chapter 12 on the Eric Burden Community in Oxford, and Chapter 13 about the work of community housing and therapy in the field of community care, remind us that therapeutic communities can also support and enrich the lives of the mentally ill. Another niche has been established within the penal system: Chapter 14 describes how therapeutic communities can be set up and developed inside the obvious confines of a prison. Sadly, few therapeutic communities for children and adolescents have survived the inclement climate since the 1970s. Chapter 15 is the last contribution in this part: it is wise and optimistic about the difficulties and opportunities that a therapeutic community perspective can contribute to residential care for the young.

The therapeutic community movement runs deeper than a definable treatment method or organisational structure. The vision extends beyond setting up and developing units for specific types of people in specific settings. Many people working in this field feel passionate about the need for a fundamental change in the way we conduct professional relationships. For example, as the information revolution rolls on, technical advances in computers and media reduce personal contact. Through so much interaction with machines, human agency can be denied, uncertainty is not tolerated and relationships are often reduced to a predetermined ritual. At a different level, global communications and the degradation of the environment present a more pressing need than ever before for human kind to work together co-operatively and non-competitively.

In the final part of the book, we look to the future and our influence on a wider network of caring professionals and therapeutic and supportive organisations. If the movement is to play a significant part in the worlds of psychiatry, social services and allied organisations, there needs to be a continuing and creative dialogue with leaders in the professions, managers and policy-makers. This requires us to be proactive, confident and clear about what we can offer; but also eager to learn from other models and perspectives, willing to question ourselves, and search for ways to do things better.

Training has an important part to play in sharing our vision and expertise and ensuring that staff in therapeutic communities practise to a high standard. Most important, we need to develop a training process that is consistent with therapeutic community principles, a process that allows for interpersonal discovery and growth. We need a training culture that celebrates difference and avoids the indoctrination and infantilising that can be a feature of both medical and psychoanalytic training. For Chapter 16, we visit the Open Psychotherapy Centre in Athens, where such a training has evolved well ahead of anything in this country. This is a good example of why international links are so important. We have much to learn from one another, a truth that is further elucidated in Chapter 19, on European therapeutic communities.

A broad-based and rigorous research effort also has a vital role to play in the future, if the process of 'reinvention', emphasised in several chapters, is to move us forward – expanding our perspective and creativity, as well as deepening our understanding of what we already know is fundamental. The second chapter in this part (Chapter 17) gives a broad-based overview of research that has been done in TCs, and likely directions of development. Chapter 18 makes the case for more therapeutic communities within the NHS, using arguments that appeal to health service managers and economists.

The final chapter gives an overview of the qualities inherent in a therapeutic community. It seems likely that an increasing number of young people are growing up in an alienated insecure world with profound emotional problems. They will desperately need the experience of being part of a group, and citizens in a community, if they are to achieve emotional integrity and overcome their destructiveness. This chapter describes how a therapeutic milieu can be enacted in practice. It is an example of the creative interplay between theory and practice which is such an important feature of our work. There is no place for the equivalent of 'armchair socialists' in our movement, for the ethos embedded in the theory extols us to roll our sleeves up and get involved. If we want it, the 'living-learning' experience is all around every one of us. We offer this book in the hope that it facilitates this 'living-learning', 'learning-living' experience, which must engage us all.

REFERENCES

Department of Health (1997) *The New NHS: Modern, Dependable.* London: DoH.

Etzioni A (1995) *The Spirit of Community.* London: Fontana, originally published in the USA, 1993.

Hinshelwood, R.D. and Manning, N. (1979) *Therapeutic Communities: Reflections and Progress.* London: Routledge and Kegan Paul.

Hutton, W. (1995) *The State We Are In.* London: Jonathan Cape, revised and updated 1996.

Kennard, D. (1998) *Introduction to Therapeutic Communities.* London: Jessica Kingsley Publishers.

PART I

Our Roots

CHAPTER 1

A Momentous Experiment
Strange Meetings at Northfield
Tom Harrison

EDITORS' INTRODUCTION

Tom Harrison is consultant in rehabilitation psychiatry in the Northern Birmingham Mental Health Trust. He is interested in the care of those with long-term severe and enduring mental illness, in particular psychological approaches to their problems, including psychotherapy and a therapeutic community ward.

His desire to improve the lot of those with schizophrenia and his particular concern to address their role within society, has led to active involvement with the Royal College. He is presently secretary of the Rehabilitation Section and a member of the Public Education Committee.

His interest in the Northfield experiments spring from a long-nurtured involvement in therapeutic community ideas working at John Connolly Hospital between 1976 and 1980 and later at Hollymoor Hospital where the events took place. He is at present researching for an MD and writing a book on the subject.

INTRODUCTION

Between 1942 and 1948 Hollymoor Hospital, in Birmingham, was taken over for use by the British Army to treat soldiers suffering from psychoneurosis. During this time two attempts were made to investigate how a total institution might transform itself into a coherent whole to implement the rapid and economic return of these men into the army as effective soldiers. These events, known as the 'Northfield Experiments', inaugurated the therapeutic community movement in the United Kingdom.

> One of the biggest, costliest experiments in psychodynamics. (Rickman 1945a)

When Wilfred Bion and John Rickman faced the enemy at Northfield Military Hospital they began to turn psychiatry upside down. They had to fight a battle against neurosis, and the troops that they had to rally to assist them were the 'sick' soldiers themselves. They forged an alliance with the patients in order to defeat the problems of mental ill-health. The full impact of this decision has yet to be fully grasped. The story of their campaign, and of others in the Second Northfield Experiment, is a continuing source of insight and inspiration.

The importance of the Northfield Experiments extends into many areas, particularly psychotherapy. Most famously, working with an early form of systems theory, the workers there began to examine how lower and higher order social systems within the institution interacted. Main described their attempts to weld all of these into a single, mutually enabling, task orientated organisation as the 'Therapeutic Community' (Main 1946, 1984). Of equal importance was the fact that they implemented entirely new methods of group psychotherapy. These included dealing with the reality of 'here and now', making the examination of members' interrelationships the centre of therapy, allowing the psychodynamics to reveal themselves, and working with the group transference. Leadership was another focus, and Bion's modus operandi clearly prefigured Tom Peters' observations on 'Management by Wandering About' (Peters and Austen 1985). Finally they examined their obligations as therapists in a time of national emergency. Main expressed this in characteristically blunt terms referring to some of the other psychiatrists at Northfield: 'they wanted to go on treating people, but it was inappropriate in war. They wanted to pursue this selfish interest of theirs when there were bloody great issues to be solved' (Main 1984). It was better to enable a man to operate as an effective soldier, rather than cure all his neurotic problems. How many psychiatrists, or other professionals, even today, are aware of their social responsibilities beyond treating individual patients?

Any account of the Northfield Experiments is incomplete without understanding the influence of social psychology during the Second World War. From this distance in time it appears inconceivable that an institution so imbued in 'Bull' as the British Army, could ever have given rise to such apparent indiscipline as a 'Therapeutic Community'. Yet it did so, not once; but three times, if Maxwell Jones' work at Mill Hill is included. Military psychiatry evolved rapidly, not least under the influence of ideas proposed by John Rickman. He had been proselytising about the psychological challenges of the impending conflict long before the outbreak of hostilities.

These experiments did not 'come out of the blue'; but emanated from a ferment of ideas among military psychiatrists and psychologists; many of whom constituted the 'invisible college' that eventually evolved into the Tavistock Institute of Human Relations (Main 1977).

Unfortunately the full history has yet to be written, and this chapter can only give a brief glimpse of the strategies and tactics deployed.

THE IMPORTANCE OF MILITARY PSYCHIATRY: 'THE GREATEST UNPLEASANT SURPRISE'

> The greatest unpleasant surprise of the war for medical men was the importance of psychiatry and psychology. And yet so inconstant, evasive, or preoccupied are the majority of men that this greatest lesson can be disputed, evaded, and soon forgotten. (Gregg 1947)

It is a well-ignored fact that psychiatrists and psychologists had an enormous impact on how the military functioned in the Second World War. This was despite the fact that early on in the war many of them persisted in their peacetime tendency of treating the individual in isolation, rather than appreciating that all people are inextricably entangled within the society that they lived. This latter perception lay at the heart of how the Tavistock Group of doctors saw their military roles. They recognised that the soldier relies on the group of people he is with to survive and has to subsume his own wishes to fit in with the greater good. Under the influence of Kurt Lewin's theories on social psychology they transformed the army's functioning in areas as disparate as personnel selection, leadership, morale, delinquency, resettlement of prisoners of war, and battle school training. It also stimulated psychiatrists to recognise the value of groups for treating their patients.

THE IMPORTANCE OF THE INTERPERSONAL IN OFFICER SELECTION: 'TO BEFRIEND THE MEN AND BEDEVIL THE ENEMY'

Of most direct relevance to the Northfield Experiments were the War Office Selection Boards, affectionately known as 'Wosbies'. From 1939 there was increasing alarm about the apparent lack of potential candidates for officer training. Traditional methods of appointment relied on a 10 to 20 minute interview that was largely concerned with the background of the candidate, such as which school they went to. As a result up to 50 per cent dropped out of officer training.

In 1940 the Leaderless Group Test was added to the selection procedure. This has commonly been attributed to Wilfred Bion, however Vinden painted a more complex picture. When Colonel Delahaye, president of the pioneering Edinburgh selection board, was accompanying a test group past a stack of granite blocks he spontaneously ordered them to take the top block off the stack, without nominating someone to take charge as had been done previously. He then recounted his observations to the psychologist and psychiatrists in the team, including Bion and Trist (Vinden 1977).

In the established form of the tests the candidates went through a series of unstructured group interactions including: a discussion, outdoor practical task solving and an inter-group game. These assessed four skill areas: exploration, competition, co-operation and discipline. Initially they sized each other up and gave a short account of themselves, followed by a free group discussion. Next each man had the opportunity to exercise his leadership skills through short practical tests. Then the progressive group task, characteristically carrying a heavy and awkward load over a series of obstacles, illustrated their ability to co-operate when under physical stress. The final test demonstrated the individual's willingness to identify himself with the group decision, and to accept a role assigned to him in a competitive game with another group (Research and Training Centre 1944).

The board personnel acted as observers, without interfering in any way. Bion's account, even if he was not the progenitor, is important as it established both the rationale of the process and his own mode of thinking. He saw the tests as a framework in which the selection staff could observe the candidate's ability to consider the needs of those he was with, while under stress himself. It wasn't success in the apparent task that mattered; but the way that the person maintained his personal relationships while in a real life situation of fear of personal failure and hope for achievement (Bion 1946). 'If a man cannot be a friend of his friends, he cannot be the enemy of his enemies' (Bion 1948, p.88).

Rickman held similar views. The psychiatrist's role was to assess the individual's capacity for compassion; because an officer needs to be someone 'who will befriend his men as well as bedevil the enemy' (Rickman 1943, p.97). They had to be able to remain objective even when the stresses in the group became threatening, so that they could encourage hostile impulses to be directed against the foe, and friendly ones to strengthen morale in their own unit (Rickman 1943).

The social role and 'adaptability to persons' were central to the officer's job. Leadership should engender the confidence of the ordinary soldier under stressful situations. This was achieved by attending to such apparently trivial matters as sorting out pay problems, demonstrating concern for each individual's welfare, and ensuring that he knew that if he was wounded or killed he would be properly attended to. Poor social skills meant that he would be insensitive to his men's needs. A distinction had to be made between the technical proficiency of the potential officer, whether he *could* do his job, and his behaviour, in other words, whether he always *would* (Research and Training Centre 1944, p.3).

The passivity and receptiveness, of the observer/psychiatrist in these selection procedures was directly replicated in the work of Rickman and Bion at Northfield. Their understanding of the group process took account of the individual's role in promoting group cohesiveness or disruption. The selection boards were thus a particularly important stage in the advancement of group therapy during the war and significantly influenced the work at the hospital.

THE IMPORTANCE OF REHABILITATION: 'AS THE OCCUPATION OF THE SOLDIER IS SOLDIERING THE BEST OCCUPATIONAL TREATMENT SHOULD BE SOLDIERING ACTIVITIES'

From the start of the war Rickman concerned himself with the rehabilitation of psychologically traumatised soldiers. Within three days of its outbreak he had outlined a strategy for promoting their recovery. Known as the Haymead's Memorandum, it became an early blueprint for military psychiatric units (Rickman 1939).

He considered that rapid treatment and effective, appropriate occupational therapy, were central to success. The aim was to prevent the development of chronic problems by getting the soldier as quickly as possible to the 'stage of resolution' when he was able to resume social interactions, recognise his responsibilities, regain self-confidence and then return to his duties. It was essential to divert the individual's energy from 'inward neurotic brooding' to external activities including work and normal life (Rickman 1939). Occupational therapy had a central role and was to be carried out in a unit near the treatment centre, enabling a graduated transfer from hospital to normal routines. Crucially this form of therapy was to be appropriate to the role of a soldier, i.e. military training of one sort or another.

Today it is difficult to recognise how radical this approach was. Psychiatrists before the war either worked solely in the large asylums, where their main concern was with severe and long-standing mental illness, such as schizophrenia, or were psychotherapists treating paying patients over long periods of time with psychoanalysis. There were few, if any, who had any relevant experience.

Rickman then moved to Wharncliffe Hospital in Sheffield, where he was able to carry out his plans more effectively, with the help of Sergeant-Major Bryant, who ran the Rehabilitation and Training Centre. This latter individual set up a system of 'para-military training' which included appropriate military exercises. These were combined with psychiatric testing of the patient's ability to manage in different situations, assessing their discipline, spontaneity, self-confidence and physical fitness. Psychiatric progress could thus be evaluated alongside improvement as a soldier (Rickman 1941).

By 1941 the unit's fame had spread to Eliot Slater, at Mill Hill Hospital. He was sceptical about the effectiveness of such a system to improve the outcomes of soldiers with neurosis; but acknowledged that the positive expectations could only be beneficial. He also described the new concept of occupational therapy as consisting 'of the widest possible application of the principle that, as the occupation of the soldier is soldiering, the best occupational treatment should be soldierly activities'. These included physical training, route marches, grenade practice, classes in map-reading, strategy and signalling (Slater 1941).

This compares with Slater's own hospital where there were various occupational therapy workshops including: rug-making, basket and leather work, weaving, painting, and embroidery. In 1940 Trist met a 'large punch-drunk ex-boxer, now in the Guards, forlornly carrying an absurd peacock painted on glass' (Trist 1985). Bion acidly described this as: 'helping to keep the patients occupied – usually on a kindergarten level' (Bion 1946).

Slater's greatest tribute was that of imitation, he arranged for a young psychiatrist to set up the rehabilitation centre at Mill Hill. This was Dr Maxwell Jones who went on to develop his own form of therapeutic community there, and embarked on his subsequently prolific career in the field.

Rickman was probably not treating his patients in groups at this time; but Bion and he were thinking about how all the relationships and activities of the hospital could be used in a therapeutic manner. Bion outlined these thoughts in the Wharncliffe Memorandum, a document that is now lost (Bridger 1990a; Trist 1985). Rickman's attempt to put these ideas into practice was resisted by the medical and administrative staff of the hospital and as a result its implementation was delayed until he arrived at Northfield.

THE IMPORTANCE OF SOCIAL SYSTEMS: 'THE SOLDIER IS NOT CHIEFLY A MILITARY FIGURE; HE IS PRIMARILY A SOCIAL FIGURE'

Main, when describing the events at Northfield, was at pains to emphasise that they were only a small part of what was happening in the army as a whole. He considered that the real creativity and intelligence lay with the 'Tavistock Group': psychiatrists who had worked at the Tavistock Clinic and other sympathetically minded individuals (Main 1984; Sutherland 1985, p.85). With the backing of the Adjutant-General, Lieutenant-General Sir Ronald F. Adam, this group formed a powerhouse of innovation and change within the British Army. Without their commitment, support and vision Main feared that the army psychiatric services would have been left to others who wanted 'to treat casualties' only.

This grouping, while never exclusive, tended to cultivate each other. When working with Trist and Wilson in the first Civilian Resettlement Unit, an ex-Northfield officer-patient related that they were very friendly to him; but that he was aware of their mutual understanding and co-operation (Mr K., 1994).

They shared a mutual interest in social psychology and the practical application of psychoanalytic thinking. Rickman emphasised the importance of object-relations theory, and was applying this to conceptions of group working in lectures given in 1938 (Rickman 1938, 1941). Sutherland was familiar with the work of Fairbairn in Scotland, whose emphasis on early childhood relationships accorded closely with the concepts of field theory. This latter was propounded by an American social psychologist, Kurt Lewin, and was a precursor to systems theory. He considered that psychology should identify underlying laws of behaviour that could be applied to all situations. 'The thesis of general validity permits of no exceptions in the entire realm of the psychic, whether of child or adult, whether in normal or pathological psychology' (Lewin 1935, p.24). The forces that determine activity did not exist within the individual alone, but included responses to the social environment. In physics the stone does not propel itself towards the earth; but is subjected to the gravitational pull that is exerted from without. 'Only by the concrete whole which comprises the object and the situation are the vectors which determine the dynamics of the event defined' (Lewin 1935, pp.29–30). These insights were used to examine social situations and analyse the range of forces operating at lower and higher level systems.

NORTHFIELD HOSPITAL: A WILDERNESS OF BRICKS

Hollymoor Hospital was a traditional late Victorian asylum. Typically, it consisted of a series of large open wards connected by long and seemingly endless corridors, which could accommodate a maximum of 800 patients. It was set in attractive grounds, originally a farm, in a close proximity to the larger Birmingham asylum called Rubery Hill Hospital. Rayner Heppenstall described it as 'a small brick wilderness being engulfed by the red brick rash of Birmingham as it extended southward' (Heppenstall 1953, pp.86–87). He drew attention to its most famous landmark, regularly referred to by all who know the area, the water tower which can be seen for miles around.

The military authorities divided the hospital into two. The eastern wards were named after British queens and acted as a medical and treatment wing, with 200 beds. In the other half, with the wards named after kings, the training wing had 600 beds. The soldiers undergoing rehabilitation wore normal battle dress with a blue epaulette; but those in treatment had to wear 'the blues'. This consisted of 'a white flannelette shirt, a red tie, a pair of socks and bright blue jacket, waistcoat and trousers' (Heppenstall 1953, p.88). This uniform made them easily identified by the local population, and the target for abuse such as 'skrim-shankers' and worse (Foulkes 1948; Mrs H. 1989). When they visited the local public houses they attempted to hide it under long army coats (Mr S. 1997; Mrs H. 1989). One reason for this vilification, apart from prejudice about nervous disorder, was the fact that the patients were not subject to the same rationing restrictions as the civilians and thus had good food including regular meat (Markillie 1993).

The military hospital was established in 1942 and came at the end of a long chain of therapeutic interventions for soldiers. It was set up with the explicit purpose of returning soldiers suffering from neurotic disorders to military service, and incorporated many of the principles laid out earlier by Rickman and Bion. However, not all the staff fully understood their role and it was characteristic that early on some patients received six months of intensive psychotherapy only to be discharged from the army thereafter (Mr A. 1990).

Many of the soldiers were of high calibre, and indeed had won medals for bravery (Bridger 1990; Harrison and Clarke 1992). The range of disorders being treated included enuresis, hysterical conversion disorders, anxiety states, post-traumatic stress syndrome, bereavements and personality difficulties. The treatments ranged from electro-convulsive therapy to individual psychotherapy (Harrison and Clarke 1992).

THE FIRST EXPERIMENT: 'A SCALLYWAG BATTALION'

Rickman came into this mélange, at the end of 1942, to take over a small 16-bedded medical ward. Here he inaugurated daily group discussions for the whole ward. These examined issues of living in a group situation in the 'here and now'. The army is primarily a communal living environment, in which each soldier depends on his comrades for survival. By exploring difficulties in relationships in such a direct way they were learning to understand the nature of their obligations, and the responsibilities and pleasures of such mutual reliance (Bion and Rickman 1943). In particular, Rickman was interested in how individuals handled aggression in either a group disruptive or cohesive manner (Rickman 1938).

Bion joined early in 1943 to take over the training wing. After facing the initial frustrations of day-to-day trivial demands he considered how he should tackle the problem of treating the individuals under his command. He looked at the unit as a whole, rather than remaining concerned with individual problems. As an ex-tank commander in the First World War he had a clear understanding of what his overall task was: to enable as many men as possible to return to active service. The enemy to be overcome was their psychoneurosis and its disruptive nature. He concluded that he was in charge of a 'scallywag battalion' that needed to develop its own sense of discipline.

On a daily basis, during the midday parade, he brought the soldiers together to examine their contributions to living communally, and their wider responsibilities in a time of war. He encouraged the men to evaluate themselves and the activities they were engaged in. After an initial period of anarchy the next few weeks began to show a demonstrable improvement in their attitudes, as they started to assume a sense of self-discipline (Bion and Rickman 1943). However, a dispute between them and their commanding officer led to the experiment being terminated abruptly (Bridger 1990a).

What had been learnt from this experience? The first and most important message for those who followed was that such dramatic changes in one part of the system had to be accompanied by attention to the higher-order systems. Bion and Rickman were viewed with some suspicion by the other psychiatrists, who quite clearly did not understand what they were up to (Lewsen 1993). Moreover, they had not satisfactorily explained what they were trying to achieve to their commanding officer.

The positive lessons concerned how the group therapy was run. Three particular tactics appeared to be entirely new. First, was the lack of direction that the therapists gave the members. Unlike other contemporaries such as Foulkes, who at this time, while claiming to be non-directive actually started the sessions with a mini-lecture unaware of the influence this had (Foulkes 1948, pp.72 and 86). Second, was their emphasis on the reality confrontation in the 'here and now'; unlike the contemporary who announced to his patients that they could 'say what you like here, for within these four walls we are not in the army!' (quoted in Rickman 1945b). Last, was the importance of exploring the social intra-group tensions, rather than using the group as a form of mass personal analysis. This has often been misunderstood, but is a crucial aspect. In an environment which relied on individuals working together, any activity that undermined this destroyed the cohesion of the whole. For many present-day therapists some of these conceptions are commonplace; however, it was at Northfield that they were first put into practice.

THE SECOND EXPERIMENT:
'THE-HOSPITAL-AS-A-WHOLE-WITH-ITS-MISSION'

Sigmund Foulkes arrived at Northfield within a month of his predecessors' departure. He had 'discovered' the group transference a year earlier while working in Exeter (Foulkes and Lewis 1944). His initial attempts at group therapy on the ward were tolerated rather than encouraged, until the arrival of Dennis Carroll as the Commanding Officer in March 1944. This man's role has been overlooked in most accounts. He brought with him knowledge of a previous 'therapeutic community' approach in a unit for the rehabilitation of young men with difficulties in social adjustment called the Hawkspur Camp. Here, in the 1930s, a number of teenagers had the opportunity to explore their relationships in a camp that they themselves built. Carroll, through the Institute for the Scientific Treatment of Delinquency, was noted as a source of inspiration for this experiment (Wills 1967, p.9).

Other psychiatrists interested in group therapy began to work there and by the time Harold Bridger was asked to take over the training wing, he was informed by Ronald Hargreaves that there were all sorts of interesting 'groupy things' going on (Bridger 1990b). Bridger had recently read an account of the Peckham Experiments. This was an attempt to set up a health centre, where families joined a club that provided advice about how to remain healthy, rather than treatment for illness (Pearse and Crocker 1943). The lure was the use of a swimming pool. When he arrived he considered his role as 'social officer', and, replicating the swimming pool, he established a social club. Initially this consisted of him sitting in an empty ward with a table and a chair, with the sign 'Hospital Club' on the door. Attracted by the notice, a number of inquisitive soldiers came in, looked around and left again. Finally, an angry deputation accosted him, demanding to know why he was wasting time sitting in the middle of an empty room. The discussion that followed led to the group forming the first social club committee (Bridger 1990b; Main 1977).

In parallel, he initiated other tactics to create a sense of the 'hospital-as-a-whole': teaching staff about social therapy, promoting ward discussions on the wider environment, and changing the culture from one of prescription to one of enabling creativity (Bridger 1990a). From this began the Second Northfield Experiment proper. Foulkes moved from being a ward-based doctor to a peripatetic group therapist, initiating discussions spontaneously in the Art Therapy Hut, or resolving conflicts with the hospital band. The central concept was 'the-hospital-as-a-whole-with-its-mission'; a single organism working towards the central task of enabling men to rediscover their abilities (Bridger 1985). Consequently, the flourishing of creativity led to the rebirth of the hospital newspaper, drama, music, a range of work training and the first industrial placements in the local car factory. The patients even wrote a booklet on the work of the hospital to give to new arrivals.

Tom Main, later to be director of the Cassell Hospital, arrived a year later, and spent a short while alongside Bridger. He observed of the latter's work: 'The best group therapy here, is I think, done in the functional groups, over which Bridger watches. True there is no discussion in them of a set-piece type but there is a reshuffling of interpersonal relationships and there are crises about the function and relating deficiencies of members' (Main 1945, unpublished letter). He took over one of the two treatment wings and found that there was a great deal of indiscipline, inappropriately excused by the psychiatrists as being a consequence of illness. He set about tackling the lower- and higher-order systems in order to create a whole institution that was realistic and therapeutic. He discussed with the commanding officer what they were doing on a daily basis. He extended Bridger's work in the training wing to the medical wards under his management. In particular, he inaugurated a system of ad hoc groups to examine crises; to discover what had gone wrong and how to resolve it. It was during this time that he coined the term 'The Therapeutic Community' (Main 1977).

When Main left, a couple of years after Bridger, the community began to disintegrate. This was the result of rapid staff changes and a loss of a sense of direction.

AFTERMATH

It is difficult to enumerate all the outcomes of these heady experiences. Most directly the Northfield Experiments influenced the formation of the Civil Resettlement Units for Prisoners of War. Foulkes continued to develop his theories of small group therapy and formed the Institute of Group Analysis. A number of other influences were less overt. Some therapeutic communities were inspired by Northfield; but the influence of Maxwell Jones tended to overshadow the earlier and more complex model.

There are still profound lessons to learn. The sense of social responsibility of practitioners was thrown into sharp relief by the exigencies of war. However the return to treatment on an individual basis in peacetime has left a legacy which is only just being undone. Most families of individuals who have experienced severe mental illness complain bitterly of professional neglect of their needs. Psychiatrists' avoidance of the media may have contributed to their patients being pilloried on an almost daily basis. It is only since the mid 1980s that the Royal College of Psychiatrists has begun to take on the role of public education seriously.

The social role of people who have experienced mental ill-health has too often been grossly neglected. Rehabilitation for many years was seen as a very poor relation to the glamour of acute psychiatry. The idea that the task of treatment in psychiatry is to enable people to function meaningfully in society, rather than cure their disease, continues to be alien to many practitioners. Work, and the role of occupational therapy in preparing for this, is consistently one of the last issues to be considered as part of the therapeutic tool kit. Interestingly, rehabilitation and the therapeutic community having been part of the same process at Northfield, and at Mill Hill, became divorced, such that in 1970 the two procedures could be compared, and contrasted, in their therapeutic efficacy for people with severe and enduring mental illness (Wing and Brown 1970).

Most of all, it is only recently that the incredible reserve of creativity that people with mental illness have is beginning to be recognised again, along with their rights to form a treatment alliance, rather than being passive recipients of a prescription.

RECOMMENDED FURTHER READING

A number of participants in the Northfield Experiments have written about their experiences. The first was Bion and Rickman's joint paper published in 1943 (Bion and Rickman 1943). This is a densely written paper that contains an enormous amount of information once the background is understood. A little known set of papers (by Main, Bridger, Bion, Foulkes and others) were published by the Menninger Clinic and illustrate a lot of the activities and attitudes (*Bulletin of the Menninger Clinic* (1946) 10, 3). These have recently been republished in *Therapeutic Communities* with a number of commentaries (*Therapeutic Communities* (1996) 17, 2 and 3).

Foulkes wrote two main accounts of his time at Northfield (Foulkes 1948, 1964). The earliest provides some particularly vivid images of the hospital and its patients. However some details have not been confirmed by other participants. Tom Main also gave his own views in a paper entitled 'The concept of the therapeutic community: variations and vicissitudes'. This gave an account of some of his army experiences and his stay at the hospital.

Perhaps the most objective account comes from Harold Bridger, whose views do not always agree with the other accounts (Bridger 1985, 1990a). Finally the present author has written two papers; the first, written with David Clark, is an attempt to illustrate some of the background, and the second is a brief review of their relevance and importance even today (Harrison 1996; Harrison and Clark 1992).

REFERENCES

Bion, W.R. (1946) 'The leaderless group project.' *Bulletin of the Meninger Clinic 10*, 77–81.

Bion, W.R. (1948) 'Psychiatry at a time of crisis.' *British Journal of Medical Psychology 21*, 81–90.

Bion, W.R. and Rickman, J. (1943) 'Intra-group tensions in therapy.' *Lancet* 678–681.

Bridger, H. (1985) 'Northfield revisited.' In M. Pines (ed) *Bion and Group Psychotherapy*, 87–107. London: Routledge and Kegan Paul.

Bridger, H. (1990a) 'The discovery of the therapeutic community: the Northfield experiments.' In E.L. Trist and H.A. Murray (eds) *The Social Engagement of Social Science*. Vol. 1. London: Free Association Books

Bridger, H. (1990b) Interview with author (unpublished).

Foulkes, S.H. (1948) *Introduction to Groupanalytic Psychotherapy: Studies in the Social Integration of Individuals and Groups*. London: Heinemann.

Foulkes, S.H. (1964) *Therapeutic Group Analysis*. London: George Allen and Unwin.

Foulkes, S.H. and Lewis, E. (1944) 'Group analysis: a study in the treatment of groups on psycho-analytic lines.' *Journal of Medical Psychology 20, 1*.

Gregg, A. (1947) 'Lessons to learn: Psychiatry in the First World War.' *American Journal of Psychiatry 104*, 217–220.

Harris, H. (1949) *The Group Approach to Leadership-Testing*. London: Routledge and Kegan Paul.

Harrison, T.M. (1996) 'Battlefields, social fields and Northfield.' *Therapeutic Communities 17*, 145–148.

Harrison, T.M. and Clark, D. (1992) 'The Northfield experiments.' *British Journal of Psychiatry 160*, 698–708.

Heppenstall, R. (1953) *The Lesser Infortune*. London: Jonathan Cape.

Lewin, K. (1935) 'The conflict between Aristotlean and Galilean modes of thought in contemporary psychology.' In K. Lewin (1935) *A Dynamic Theory of Personality*. New York: McGraw-Hill.

Lewsen, C. (1993) Interview with author (unpublished).

Main, T.F. (1945) Letter to John Rickman, in Rickman Archive of the British Psychoanalytic Society (CRR/F20/35, unpublished).

Main, T.F. (1946) 'The hospital as a therapeutic institution.' *Bulletin of the Meninger Clinic 10*, 66–70.

Main, T.F. (1977) 'The concept of the therapeutic community: variations and vicissitudes.' *Group Analysis 10* (Suppl.), 2–16.

Main, T.F. (1984) Interview with author (unpublished).

Markillie, R. (1993) Interview with author (unpublished).

Montgomery, B.L. (1946) 'Morale in battle.' *British Medical Journal 2,* 702–4.

Mrs H. (1989) Interview with staff (unpublished).

Mr A. (1990) Interview with ex-patient (unpublished).

Mr K. (1994) Interview with ex-patient (unpublished).

Mr S. (1997) Interview with ex-patient (unpublished).

Pearse, I. and Crocker, L. (1943) *The Peckham Experiment. A Study in the Living Structure of Society.* London: Allen and Unwin.

Pines, M. (ed) (1985) *Bion and Group Psychotherapy.* London: Routledge and Kegan Paul.

Peters, T. and Austin, N. (1985) *A Passion for Excellence: The Leadership Difference.* Glasgow: Fontana/Collins.

Research and Training Centre (1944) *Part 2 – The Method of Leaderless Groups,* from R.T.C. Memorandum No. 5., 'The work of the military testing officer at a War Office selection board (O.C.T.U.s)', Ref R.T.C./Inf/2. In Foulkes Archives, Wellcome Institute of Contemporary Medical Archives. (PP/SHF/1.11.1).

Rickman, J. (1938) 'Uniformity or diversity in groups.' Paper based on two public lectures which were delivered in March 1938, sponsored by the Institute of Psycho-Analysis (ed P. King, undated). Unpublished, in possession of P. King.

Rickman, J. (1939) Haymeads Memorandum, Rickman Archive of the British Psychoanalytic Society (CRR/F14/07, unpublished).

Rickman, J. (1941) 'A case of hysteria – theory and practice in the two wars.' *Lancet 1,* 785–786.

Rickman, J. (1943) 'The influence of the "social field" on behaviour in the interview situation.' Unpublished paper written by Rickman while working as a Major on a War Office selection board during 1943–1944. In possession of P. King.

Rickman, J. (1944) Letter to S.H. Foulkes, in S.H. Foulkes Archives, Wellcome Institute Contemporary Medical Archives Centre.

Rickman, J. (1945a) Letter to S.H. Foulkes, in S.H. Foulkes Archives, Wellcome Institute Contemporary Medical Archives Centre.

Rickman, J. (1945b) Contribution to the discussion of Dr W.R. Bion's paper on 'Intra-group tensions in therapy: their study a task of the group' given to the Medical Section of the British Psychological Society, 19 December 1945. In Rickman Archive of the British Psychoanalytical Society.

Slater, E. (1941) Report on visit to Wharncliffe Emergency Hospital, 13 and 14 January, 1941, Rickman Archives of the British Psychoanalytic Society.

Sutherland, J.D. (1985) 'Bion revisited: group dynamics and group psychotherapy.' In M. Pines (ed) *Bion and Group Psychotherapy.* London: Routledge and Kegan Paul.

Trist, E. (1985) 'Working with Bion in the 1940s: the group decade.' In M. Pines (ed) *Bion and Group Psychotherapy.* London: Routledge and Kegan Paul.

Trist, E. and Murray, H.A. (eds) (1990) *The Social Engagement of Social Science.* Volume I: *The Socio-Psychological Perspective.* London: Free Association Books.

Vinden, F.H. (1977) 'The introduction of War Office Selection Boards in the British Army: a personal recollection.' In B. Bond and I. Roy *War and Society, 2.* London: Croom Helm.

Wills, W.D. (1967) *The Hawkspur Experiment: An Informal Account of the Training of Wayward Adolescents.* London: George Allen and Unwin.

Wing, J.K. and Brown, G.W. (1970) *Institutionalism and Schizophrenia.* London: Cambridge University Press.

CHAPTER 2

Social Psychiatry
The Therapeutic Community Approach
David Clark

EDITORS' INTRODUCTION

David Clark qualified in medicine in 1943 and after three years in the army, trained in psychiatry at Edinburgh and then at the Maudsley. During this time, he undertook a personal psychoanalysis, trained as a group analyst with S. H. Foulkes and became interested in the sociology of mental hospitals - and the possibility of using the hospital environment to help patients towards recovery. In 1953, he went to Fulbourn Hospital, Cambridge, as Medical Superintendent and worked there until his retirement in 1983. He has published a book about the work (Clark 1996).

Although he is best known for unlocking the doors and applying the 'therapeutic community approach', he was also responsible for setting up a number of 'therapeutic communities proper' in the hospital. One of these, Street Ward, is referred to by Geoff Pullen in Chapter 12.

In this chapter, David Clark reviews the ideas that influenced the therapeutic community approach and describes the implementation of social psychiatry, before going on to reflect on the reaction against liberalisation in psychiatry since the 1970s.

It is interesting that morale in the profession has dropped dramatically over this time, and recruitment (of both psychiatrists and nurses) has become an increasingly urgent problem. It is worth considering how this might be related to the increasingly inflexible and sterile roles that are currently expected of staff.

THE 'THERAPEUTIC COMMUNITY APPROACH'

The British therapeutic community movement is rightly seen as rising from the wartime work of Foulkes, Bridger, Main and others at Northfield, and of Maxwell Jones at Mill Hill and Dartford. All these pioneers were dealing with servicemen, mostly with psychoneurotic, depressive or psychosomatic disorders. But there is another strand to the story of British social psychiatry that should not be forgotten, the work in the old lunatic asylums with psychotic patients, later to be described as 'the therapeutic community approach' (as opposed to the 'therapeutic community proper'). For a number of years – from the 1950s until the 1970s – this was what many psychiatrists meant by the phrase 'social psychiatry' and this was what brought visitors from all over the world to see what was being done in British psychiatry.

The notion was best formulated in a World Health Organization Report (WHO 1953) which was written by an international panel chaired by Kraus of Groningen and led by T.P. Rees of Warlingham Park Hospital, Surrey and Sivadon of Paris. Its full title was 'The Third Report of the Expert Committee on Mental Health'. It considered various subjects such as the prevalence of mental disorders and patterns in community mental health services but the most striking part was that dealing with 'essential mental hospital provisions'. They spoke of the importance of the atmosphere of the hospital.

> The most important single factor in the efficacy of the treatment given in a mental hospital appears to the Committee to be an intangible element which can only be described as its atmosphere, and in attempting to describe some of the influences which go to the creation of this atmosphere, it must be said at the outset that the more the psychiatric hospital imitates the general hospital as it at present exists, the less successful it will be in creating the atmosphere it needs. Too many psychiatric hospitals give the impression of being an uneasy compromise between a general hospital and a prison. Whereas, in fact, the role they have to play is different from either; it is that of a therapeutic community. (pp. 17–18)

They spelled out the constituents of this atmosphere and italicised the following:

(1) Preservation of the patient's individuality

(2) The assumption that patients are trustworthy

(3) That good behaviour must be encouraged

(4) That patients must be assumed to retain the capacity for a considerable degree of responsibility and initiative

(5) The need for activity and a proper working day for all patients.

They finally said that:

> The creation of the atmosphere of a therapeutic community is in itself one of the most important types of treatment which the psychiatric hospital can provide. (pp. 17–18)

The fundamental premise of social therapy was that for people spending a long time in a medical institution the way that they lived, the work they did, their personal relationships, the regime and its rewards and punishments, were more important for their ultimate rehabilitation than the medication or medical treatment they might receive.

UNLOCKING THE DOORS

All these recommendations may seem obvious and commonsense today but in the early 1950s they were revolutionary. At that time mental hospitals were closed, prison-like institutions, full of locked doors, where all patients were regarded as unreliable and unpredictable and many as suicidal or escapist so that the main effort of staff was devoted to control, to anti-suicide precautions, to counting patients, to sudden searches for 'contraband' (tools, money, matches etc.) The general belief among both nurses and doctors was that the asylum had always been like this and always would be. The squalid degraded and brutalised life of the old mental hospitals has been often described and it is to be hoped it is not necessary to recall those days in detail yet again. I have however depicted these situations myself in my retirement interview (Clark 1986) and in my historical account of Fulbourn Hospital, Cambridge (Clark 1996). The ideas of the reformers as expressed in the WHO report were seen as impracticable, idealistic and a distraction from 'real doctoring' – insulin coma therapy, electroconvulsion therapy, leucotomy and other medical treatments fashionable at that time.

The WHO report set down what was already being worked on by a group of British pioneers, notable among whom were T.P. Rees of Warlingham Park Hospital, Croydon, George McDonald Bell of Dingleton Hospital, Melrose, and Duncan MacMillan of Mapperley Hospital, Nottingham. One of their first policy moves was to open the locked doors of the hospitals – Dingleton in 1948, Warlingham and Mapperley in the early 1950s. This caused great controversy among British psychiatrists. *The Lancet* ran a series of articles and major debates were held by the Royal Medico Psychological Association. But behind the open doors was a programme of activity – especially work – for all patients and the development of trust and initiative for the patients – in-patient clubs, self-governing wards etc.

ROOTS IN 'MORAL THERAPY'

Some of these ideas – such as Full Activity – were not new, as Rees pointed out in the RMPA Presidential Address entitled 'Back to moral treatment and community care' (Rees 1957). The great nineteenth-century fathers of hospital psychiatry Tuke, Pinel, Browne and Conolly had all stressed the importance of work, rewards and warm relations in their institutions. But the pioneers of the 1950s went further, in particular pushing for the opening of ward doors and eventually of whole hospitals. Their work was widely applauded and copied throughout the country. It was an exciting time. Through the 1950s and 1960s the task of liberalising the old institutions won praise and public support. The rehabilitation programmes, sheltered workshops and halfway houses began to move many long-term patients out of hospitals. A flow of American psychiatrists came across to see our achievements and attempted to apply some of the ideas to the State Hospitals in the USA, some of which had fallen into a disgraceful condition after wartime neglect.

During the same immediate postwar period, the work of Maxwell Jones at Belmont and of Main at the Cassel, developing what were called therapeutic communities, was becoming widely known and studied. There was much cross-fertilisation between the reforming mental hospitals and the small face-to-face communities. I was in touch with all these trends and felt that there was confusion about the term 'therapeutic community'. I therefore proposed in a talk given in 1964 that we should differentiate the 'therapeutic community proper' – the small face-to-face units as developed by Maxwell Jones and Main and the 'therapeutic community approach' applied to the whole of a large institution (Clark 1965). I also spoke of how things in the mental hospitals of Britain were at that time.

We may remind ourselves of the position now in 1964 in Britain. There has been a striking change in the mental hospital scene; most ward doors in most hospitals are unlocked and the patients are able freely to come and go through them. A number of mental hospitals are fully open-door, though many maintain one or two locked wards. Most patients are occupied and instead of sullen, surging hordes in the airing courts one now finds workshops and industrial units. The level of work varies, but a fair number of patients are engaged in skilled work for industrial firms, reasonably well paid. Aided by a change in the law the amount of legal liberty available for patients has changed dramatically, where before the majority of patients were certified, now nearly all are 'informal'. Although a substantial proportion of patients are compulsorily admitted to hospital, the number under compulsory long-term detention is very small, varying between 2 and 10 per cent through the country. Rehabilitation is actively encouraged, many hospitals have patients going out to work and many long-stay patients have been successfully discharged from hospital. A striking corollary of all this is a fall in the total number of psychiatric patients in British mental hospitals. The peak number of patients was in 1954 when there were 152,000 patients in psychiatric hospitals; the most recent figures for 1962 showed that there were 131,500 patients in corresponding accommodation. This is the first time for a century and a half that there has been, during peacetime, a sustained fall in the total number of people in psychiatric institutions. I think that the development of the therapeutic community approach and the adoption of active rehabilitation and discharge policies in psychiatric hospitals has been a major contributing factor to this decline. (p.949)

Implicit in this piece was my belief at that time that the principles of social psychiatry and of the therapeutic community approach in mental hospitals had been generally accepted by the majority of psychiatrists and by the general public. For the ten years, into the 1970s, this seemed to be true.

THE 1970s TO 1990s

The following decades have shown a different picture. Some gains of the therapeutic community approach have remained. Most patients have informal status and are free to come and go within hospital. Most ward doors are still open. Sheltered workshops, halfway houses and group homes abound. But the heart has gone out of the liberalisation of mental hospital life and it is relevant to consider why. Now in the late 1990s there is little talk of social therapy in psychiatric hospitals or units. There are very few therapeutic communities proper in the National Health Service. The therapeutic community approach is seen as an incident of psychiatric history like the insulin coma units of the 1940s. Why has this happened? I believe there are a number of reasons.

The in-patients in psychiatric units are different nowadays. The therapeutic community approach was developed to help the mental hospitals of the 1950s, vast institutions containing hundreds of patients, many of them sturdy middle-aged people with not much residual mental disorder who were trapped in a dreary institutional setting. These people responded well to the new opportunities. They enjoyed the improved life. They had sufficient social skills to operate self-government policies and even therapeutic communities proper. They worked in sheltered workshops. They moved out to sheltered housing and group homes. After rehabilitation they functioned quite well socially. The psychiatric units of the late 1990s contain few such people. Many patients are recently admitted, still confused. The long-stay patients who still remain are much more severely handicapped. There are fewer people who would benefit from a vigorous therapeutic community approach.

The management structure of the psychiatric services has changed greatly. Psychiatric units are often linked with general hospitals. This means that management is in the hands of administrators trained in running general hospitals where patients are short-stay, and severely ill. They view patients as passive recipients of medical skill and nursing care. They see little point in developing a therapeutic atmosphere. In the 1950s medical superintendents had great power; a determined innovator could change the whole social structure of a hospital, especially if backed by an understanding hospital management committee. Now no one has such power; the pressures are for conformity with the bureaucracy, with accounting and maximising revenue.

Public attitudes towards the mentally disordered and their keepers have changed markedly. In the 1950s there was enthusiasm for the dismantling of old oppressive institutions. There was support for the opening of asylum doors and favourable publicity. In the 1960s there was public interest and media enthusiasm for experiments such as Belmont, Villa 21, and Kingsley Hall. Now attitudes are different. There is media publicity for violent incidents with frequent portrayal of the schizophrenic as a dangerous homicidal madman. There is constant pressure for more locking up of patients and for building secure units. The emphasis is often on strengthening security and preventing incidents rather than on helping individuals to emerge from confinement.

The British psychiatric profession too, seems to have changed both in its public image and in the way it operates. During the Thatcher years social workers and psychiatrists were frequently pilloried and criticised. Public enquiries scapegoated individuals and institutions calling for greater control and greater 'responsibility'. The profession has reacted in various ways. There is an increased tendency to identify with the general hospital and its staff. In the journals the articles are about new and differing drugs or else about 'predicting dangerousness'. Few psychiatrists nowadays have the power to rearrange their patients' wards; perhaps very few want it. There are no figures like T.P. Rees or George McDonald Bell, willing to challenge cautious officials in order to improve their patients' lives.

The therapeutic community which started in psychiatric hospitals and was led by psychiatrists has now almost vanished from those hospitals. Therapeutic communities are now to be found in small independent units, halfway houses, special schools, probation hostels, 'concept houses'. It may be because the idea is too revolutionary for a fossilised bureaucracy such as the National Health Service of the 1990s. A unit in which patients govern themselves, where they criticise consultant psychiatrists, where they challenge insensitive managers, is too much to be tolerated.

FULL CIRCLE?

The era of the therapeutic community approach in mental hospitals, of liberal humane management, of open doors, of freedom of patients and self-government was perhaps a transient phenomenon. It occurred while society was moving from custodial to community management of chronic mental disorder and it was an effective and humane way of rehabilitating the masses of institutionalised moderately psychotic people. Although tolerated for a few decades, it proved too challenging for a National Health Service dominated by omniscient doctors and economising managers.

However, as T.P. Rees pointed out in 1956 certain principles have been known for two centuries. If mentally disordered people are gathered in an institution run by doctors and nurses, that 'hospital' can easily sink into custodial nihilism with institutionalisation and often neglect, squalor and brutality. There is always scope for social therapy, for the therapeutic community approach, for giving the patients freedom, trust, responsibility and rehabilitation. It seems likely that as the current phase passes and as patients accumulate in the secure units, social therapy and moral management will be discovered again.

REFERENCES

Clark, D.H. (1963) 'Administrative psychiatry 1942–1962' *British Journal of Psychiatry 109*, 178–201.

Clark, D.H. (1965) 'The therapeutic community, concept, practice and future.' *British Journal of Psychiatry 111*, 947–954.

Clark, D.H. (1986) 'In conversation with David Clark.' *Bulletin of the Royal College of Psychiatrists 9*, 42–49 and 70–75. Reprinted in Wilkinson (ed) 1993 *Talking About Psychiatry.* London: Gaskell.

Clark, D.H. (1996) *The Story of a Mental Hospital: Fulbourn 1858–1983.* London: Process Press.

Rees, T.P. (1957) 'Back to moral treatment and community care.' *Journal of Mental Science 103*, 303.

World Health Organization (1953) *Expert Committee on Mental Health: 3rd Report.* Geneva: WHO.

CHAPTER 3

Psychoanalytic Origins and Today's Work

The Cassel Heritage

R. D. Hinshelwood

EDITORS' INTRODUCTION

Bob Hinshelwood's interest in therapeutic communities started in the 1960s, partly from a personal revulsion with standard psychiatry. It was also from a political interest in experimenting with new forms of egalitarian and anti-authoritarian forms of social organisation. The influence of R.D. Laing was powerful and exhilarating at the time of 'swinging London'. The TC was one of the new ideas that was around about how to run the world differently. Other people involved were equally enthusiastic believers in the power of the human spirit.

His interest in trying to understand the most mysterious of all things in the universe — what makes people tick — led him to become a psychoanalyst and writer of a number of books (Dictionary of Kleinian Thought; Clinical Klein; What Happens in Groups; Therapy or Coercion: Does Psychoanalysis Differ from Brainwashing?). He also established two professional journals (International Journal of Therapeutic Communities and the British Journal of Psychotherapy), and formed his own publishing company, Artesian Books.

He is now Professor of Psychoanalysis at the University of Essex, but until last year was an NHS consultant — most recently as Clinical Director of the Cassel Hospital. He is currently Chair of the Association of Therapeutic Communities. His continuing interest in TCs is motivated by his fascination with psychoanalysis beyond the consulting room, his drive to establish a human environment rather than a technological procedure and his affinity with like-minded colleagues dedicated to human ideals in the face of monetarism and its impersonal efficiencies.

This chapter shows how TCs grew out of psychoanalytic ideas. It is testament to the fact that psychoanalysis is relevant to understanding how people live their lives in the real world.

Psychoanalysis is the founding idea of therapeutic communities. The unconscious in human experiencing, and the transference, are the foundations of psychoanalysis and of the therapeutic community as well. Blended, at various times, with the social psychology of Kurt Lewin (de Board 1978) or with the Systems theory of Bateson (Bateson 1956, p.39), and others (for instance, Janssen 1994; Munich 1983), the therapeutic community has remained nourishingly attached to its roots.

It was with the coming of the Second World War and the desperate need in Britain to develop novel ideas, that a psychoanalytic practice of the hospital itself came about. The therapeutic community idea can be precisely placed to 1942 in Birmingham (Bridger 1990). The Northfield experiment began with a venture that lasted six weeks (Bion and Rickman 1943). It ended in failure but was so inspiringly novel that the entire staff of the hospital made efforts to adapt, refine and explore the new idea.

It evolved in the rehabilitation wing. Major W.R. Bion with the help of John Rickman who had been Bion's analyst before the war, took the view that rehabilitation needed the men to practise forming a high-morale fighting group again. Bion, the medical officer in charge, announced that the enemy was neurosis: 'I became convinced that what was required was the sort of discipline achieved in a theatre of war by an experienced officer in command of a rather scallywag battalion' (Bion and Rickman 1943, p.12). Officers and men alike joined in a common project. Bion was perhaps the only member of the medical staff who had seen operations in a theatre of war; he had been a tank commander in the First World War. He had set out to lead an attack on neurotic defences by his scallywags as a *group* in high morale. He stressed the *whole* wing as the patient and as the instrument of treatment, the aim being 'the education and training of the community in the problems of interpersonal relationships' (p. 15).

This emphasis on learning was the focus for another experiment in using the social setting as a therapeutic agent. Maxwell Jones' cardiac syndrome unit, at Mill Hill, was for soldiers who were invalided because of vague chest pain that they believed originated in the heart. Jones (1952) set up lectures and seminars to teach the soldiers that such pain felt in the chest did not come from the heart at all. He found that group discussion and group activity had a strong therapeutic effect in diminishing the complaint.

After the war both Bion and Jones went into psychoanalysis with Melanie Klein, and under this influence, both developed their ideas, though in different ways. The engagement in a group learning process has become a core feature of therapeutic communities. It is the group activity as much as the learning one which is crucial – although it seems that the group activity has to be of a learning kind.

Northfield was the moment when the application of psychoanalysis to a social setting first began to develop a method. Though the initial experiment was terminated by the military authorities, the ideas survived under Bion's successor, T.F. (Tom) Main. He realised that the problem with the first experiment was that the whole social system needed to be included in the range of thought about what would be therapeutic (Main 1946). He conceived the whole hospital as a therapeutic agent. Like Bion, Main was not yet a psychoanalyst but also went on to become one after the war. Then, in 1946, he became Director of the Cassel Hospital which he reorganised as a therapeutic community on psychoanalytic lines

S.H. (Michael) Foulkes was already a psychoanalyst when at Northfield, but belonged to an older generation. Trained in Germany, he brought a very different background of psychoanalytic thought. By training, he opposed the thinking of Melanie Klein, but nevertheless he was interested in social processes and how to apply psychoanalysis.

Interestingly, Foulkes had studied experimental psychology, and its German form, gestalt psychology. Gestalt psychology however influenced the British psychiatrists at Northfield too, but through a quiet different route. They had been influenced by Kurt Lewin's work in America during the 1930s but this had been a direct attempt to apply gestalt psychology, in which Lewin had trained in Germany before his exile in America. Thus Foulkes and the British had a common ground, though indirectly, in German experimental psychology. Both inherited the notion of the 'group-as-a-whole'.

Foulkes, less interested in pursuing theoretical differences, set his mind to the way the psychoanalytic method could be applied. The core feature of the individual method is free association, and he sought to establish a group equivalent of frank exchange. He called it a 'communication matrix', and began to work it out in the communication matrix of the Hospital (de Mare 1983).

Many therapeutic communities are or have been aligned with these psychoanalytic origins. But, currently, most explore the importance of systems theory. This chapter is restricted in this respect, and concerns itself with the inspiration from current psychoanalysis. The foremost influence of psychoanalysis on the therapeutic community has perhaps been the Cassel Hospital during and after Main's period there (1946–1976).

So much for history.

PRINCIPLES IN PRACTICE

Many aspects of the contemporary practice of a therapeutic organisation derive from these psychoanalytic origins:

- Insightful learning is itself a curative force in overcoming personal resistance and neurosis.

- The state of the organisation is kept under continuing examination, analysis and renewal.

- Frank communications are freed up among all members, staff and patients.

These intentions remain deeply embedded in therapeutic community practice some fifty years later. Some of these principles are potentially at variance with each other, particularly, the person's individual learning versus examination of the therapeutic organisation and the contriving of a free communication system versus the study of resistances. These contradictions come from the early efforts to apply psychoanalysis to a social setting (see Rapoport 1960 for his discussion of contradictions between therapeutic community principles), but to an extent, they are also internal contradictions within psychoanalysis itself. And in so far as psychoanalysis keeps on evolving under the pressures towards greater consistency so the therapeutic community lives in its shadow as we strive for a coherent practice.

Psychoanalysis continues to inform the practice of the therapeutic community, but more in terms of its understanding of social settings than directly in terms of psychoanalytic practice as it has evolved in the consulting room. I shall consider these continuing contributions under the headings 'internalisation', 'epistemophilia', and 'responsibility, guilt and the depressive position'.

INTERNALISATION

Like any form of therapy, if the therapeutic community has any influence on its members, it must do so in some deeply personal or internal way. Of course in any therapy, the client is expected to take away inside him/herself new knowledge and new understanding, especially about himself. This is called insight. However, there is a special influence that the therapeutic community might expect to have on the internal state of mind of its members. We might distinguish the external world of the community from the internal world of the person. Clearly both are interconnected. Many patients, who are sufficiently disturbed to need in-patient care (or even in a daycare setting), will have an internal world which is fragmented and deeply split apart with inconsistent and conflicted attitudes and behaviour. These near-psychotic personalities (sometimes diagnosed with a borderline and narcissistic label) have a profound disturbance of the internal organisation of their minds, or of their selves.

When a number of such people with internal disorganisation are gathered in one institution, they are likely to have an impact on the organisation of the institution itself. Equally, the state of organisation of the institution will have a reciprocal impact on the internal state of its members. In short, poorly organised institutions will risk enhancing the internal disorganisation of their severely disordered members, who in turn will tend to dismantle and disturb the organisation of the institution. From this psychoanalytic point of view, they mutually influence each other. A depressive patient, with an internal world composed of despair and emptiness, can easily fill those around him, his community, with similar feelings. Likewise, a demoralised community can enhance the internal despair of its depressed members. The continuum between a state of mind and the state of the organisation has been described by Jaques

(1955). This correspondence has been stressed recently by the notion of the organisation in the mind (Armstrong 1997; Hirschorn 1995).

This reciprocal to-and-fro effect is well known, and expressed psychoanalytically in terms of the processes of 'projection' – the members' projection of their disturbance into the community around them – and 'introjection' when they internalise the state of organisation of the community. There is therefore potential – a therapeutic potential – for the organisation to be sufficiently well maintained for disturbed people to take into themselves a strong sense of being together in themselves. And a potential for an anti-therapeutic effect when the community disturbance becomes ingrained into the community and can then be internalised to support the patient's own internal disturbance (further discussed in Chapter 7).

This way of thinking comes directly out of contemporary psychoanalytic ideas deriving especially from the school of British object-relations (Fairbairn 1941; Klein 1946; Winnicott 1958). It has been exploited in the work of many therapeutic communities, but perhaps most explicitly at the Cassel Hospital (Hinshelwood and Skogstad 1998; Kennedy, Heymans and Tisehier 1987). The three steps of projection, community reactions to the projection, and re-introjection have recently been detailed clinically by Santos and Hinshelwood (1998).

EPISTEMOPHILIA (CURIOSITY)

The love of knowledge, and its derivative, curiosity, is often severely hampered in therapeutic work, especially with more disturbed people. It is of importance that such a mental function is kept in play. Insight into oneself is the clearest example of this function occurring in a therapeutic setting. Often the community itself has to represent the drive to enquire, while the members are initially mentally maimed in this sense.

There are specific and important aspects at the level of the social setting. A community that fails to enquire into its own functioning runs the risk of many deleterious consequences. Notably, it becomes cut off in any adaptive way from what is happening around it: it fails to react to changes in its umbrella funding organisation, in the pattern of its referrals, in the climate of opinion about communities or therapy (the Magic Mountain syndrome described by van den Langenberg and de Nastris in 1985). In addition it becomes ossified in its routines. A lack of vigour and an allegiance to procedures for their own sake take over from a full community life. It becomes a pale version of itself. Its own demise often comes swiftly, and always unexpectedly.

The life of a community must be a process of constant regeneration and renewal. This does not mean merely changing things from time to time, though that might help. Tom Main (1967) described a process of ritualisation in therapeutic communities, resembling the more familiar institutionalisation in large mental hospitals. Main's contribution is that the community must establish and sustain a specific culture – a 'culture of enquiry' (Main 1967; Norton 1992). This is rather like the process in a psychoanalysis itself which has to sustain a constant enquiry. The analytic couple need to continually address the question: 'What is going on between us?' Thus they address the unconscious aspects of the transference and the counter-transference. This enquiry is a bedrock attitude of psychoanalysis since Freud's work on dreams in which he believed an enquiry into the unconscious was therapeutic.

In the practice of psychoanalysis, we now distinguish sharply between the emotional relationships (loving and hating), which are part of any authentic relationship, and the specifically enquiring curiosity that psychoanalysis nurtures. Bion, later, referred to these as relationships characterised by 'L' (for loving), 'H' (for hating), and by 'K' (for knowing and being known) (Bion 1962). The last of these is the characteristically psychoanalytic relationship.

So too, in residential care institutions. Enquiry into the state of the community is, in a way that is not too far-fetched, the equivalent of this characteristic 'K' attitude towards the transference and counter-transference. The community state may veer from severe rigidity and ossification, as Main described, to fragmented disorganisation. Or alternatively, a more flexible growth enhancing state (Hinshelwood 1987) may be attained. It is that flexible, adaptable state which will reverberate therapeutically with the internal state of the individuals, countering their disintegration or rigidity.

Main described what happens to this kind of adaptive flexibility. Community procedures are developed by a flexible approach to the real problems that crop up all the time when people are living together. Such reality-based solutions to problems are then handed on from one generation to another. They change however in this intergenerational passage, to become 'the way things are done' – they ossify and become rigid and unthinking. Memories of why they are done this way are forgotten often quickly, and a moral tone – 'We do it this way' – takes over from the original practical one. In psychoanalytic terms, Main says that the particular procedure changes its residence from the ego to the super-ego. In community terms it stops being a realistic solution to become an (often enforced) unthinking ritual. The way of coping with this potentially lethal process (terminal for the community as well as deadly for the personalities in the community) is to sustain a process of thinking about the way things are done. If we can continually ask: 'What is the problem that this is a solution to?', then the respect for reality can be re-energised (further discussed in Chapters 7 and 8).

Simple though this sounds, the difficulty is that the forces which result in this drift into unthinking and unrealistic ritual are unknown (i.e. unconscious) ones. One of the problems that has recently been noticed is that the culture of enquiry may itself become ritualised (Griffiths and Hinshelwood 1995; Levinson 1996). Vigilance is not sufficient, we must keep vigilance over vigilance itself. Consequently, we must accept that the dynamic interplay in a community between rigidifying processes and enquiry into reality problems is going to swing continually one way and the other between both polar states of the community. And these swings in the level of enquiry must become a prime focus of communal curiosity.

RESPONSIBILITY, GUILT AND THE DEPRESSIVE POSITION

The Cassel Hospital is most noted for its structure in which individual psychoanalytic psychotherapy is conducted within the context of a living-together community of some fifty patients. This dual track approach keeps the individual work rather separate from the community, but it also allows more specific psychoanalytic thinking about the community itself as a tool of therapy. In this section I want to describe the unique thinking which has given rise to the community practice. This work is a psychosocial practice (or psychosocial nursing). It is founded on the idea that patients and staff live and work together – though the roles may differ. This rules out any form of psychoanalytic practice. Raising issues to a level of conscious insight with words has a very secondary place. Of primary importance is the relationship that occurs between the patient and nurse in working on ordinary things and playing in ordinary ways. And this relationship is mediated in different ways: not primarily verbal, it is from *actions* that new and therapeutic experiences arise.

Actions in work and play are important in a different way from words. Actions directly affect the quality of life of the community for good or bad. Basing the life of the community on the work and play of the patients involves a recognition by staff of the patients' healthy self, and conveying an attitude that allows it to speak out. It is crucial that all staff recognise that patients, however disturbed, are also capable of functioning in quite ordinary and helpful ways. Often patients are regarded as wholly sick, and their capacities are overlooked. Psychoanalytically this is regarded as a form of splitting when only one side of the person is acknowledged. With many disturbed people it is quite evident that they can move between states of disturbance and of helpful normality. This may occur abruptly, which is often unsettling to staff and others and certainly arouses a sense of personal instability in the patients themselves.

The aim of the work in the community is to support this healthy side within the context of everyday life – the 'work of the day' (James 1987; Kennedy 1987). Thus the patient and the nurse work together in different roles. The patient is regarded as capable of carrying considerable degrees of responsibility provided they get enough initial support and the nurse works alongside to offer that support (Barnes, Griffiths, Old and Wells 1997). The work of the day, as it is termed at the Cassel, comprises quite ordinary activity like cleaning the bedroom, but also significant responsibility such as helping to cook supper for all, to quite major responsibilities that include managing a work team or a leisure activity, chairing meetings, caring for each others' well-being and providing a rota of support for those in crisis. For the families who come to the Cassel much effort is devoted by patients to enable the parents to be supported sufficiently to explore new ways of caring and parenting the children. Most prominent is the work of preparing practically for separation – not just leaving the hospital eventually, but every weekend when patients are expected, if possible, to go to their homes.

All this can feel a heavy responsibility, and responsibility is a powerful source of guilt. This kind of human experience is known as the depressive position in which a person feels he has responsibility for the state of someone else. His own aggressive phantasy life often leads to the experience of others as being damaged by himself. While people do in reality hurt each other, these phantasies tend to be of a very much greater degree of violence, and truly of a phantasy intensity. It can then be difficult for more disturbed people to sort out the reality of what they have done and what they have phantasised.

In terms of community practice, responsibility is the key concept. So many fragmented disturbed people feel their lack of personal resources have ebbed away with their fragmented selves, and their capacity to put right what they think they may have done seems to them so puny. Much that is required from them seems to represent an overwhelming task. In the place of responsibility there looms failure and usually guilt. Psychoanalytically this scene is an internal one in which a harsh slave-driving conscience, or super-ego, berates the person, in an internal replica of an external abuse which the person has usually encountered. The slightest failing means failure, writ large. The ferocity of their own expectations, coupled with their sense of depletion in themselves, is an explosive mixture. They break into states of mind and behaviour which is intolerable for everyone. Their worst fears of themselves are confirmed. A life of such circular defeat is frequently ended early and often brutally. So, work must always be in the context of a supporting relationship. Psychoanalytically this represents a necessary concrete external support that the patient can eventually internalise. The result aimed for is internal support to a sense of personal well-being.

Often there is a history from childhood of unreliable adult supports, frequently abusive ones. Through the same process of internalisation, many patients have in the past resorted to alarming behaviour that leads to, and intends, horrific self-harm. Such self-abuse, clearly related to childhood abuse at the hands of another, is required to be given up in the community. Instead a substitute is demanded of them: that is, to talk to others, to talk about their feelings and desperation. In other words the expectation is that turning to new relationships of support (eventually to be internalised) will gradually take the place of symptoms and dangerous behaviour.

The community is thus a network of relationships for support and being supported. All patients are expected to play a part as both supporter and supported and this is to some extent true of staff. The work of the day thus carries a maximum degree of responsibility drawing on the support that is available everywhere. If abuse as a child leads to self-abuse as an adult, then supportive understanding can lead to self-support, a greater confidence and a greater understanding of one's resources and limitations.

The conceptualisation at the Cassel is to interrupt the cycles of abuse, through the intervention of a non-abusive supporter working alongside. To this end, support to carry on the work of the day is relentless. Patients are encouraged to continue with their work, their management of their team, their chairship, etc. in the face of these crippling states of guilt and failure. Thus there is a form of literal 'working through' that does not focus directly upon pathology and symptoms, but demands and supports the functioning side of the person.

CONCLUSION

This chapter has reviewed three ways in which psychoanalysis has given new impetus to thinking about, and working in, a therapeutic community. The Cassel Hospital has been pre-eminent in pioneering the application of psychoanalysis. But its style and structure has evolved in ways which are not typical of all therapeutic communities. Nevertheless, the recasting of the work that we do in terms of psychoanalysis allows a continual reconceptualising of the therapeutic community. The need to be on guard for tired ritualistic practices – and even tired theory – is very great in the therapeutic community, as the processes of ritualisation and institutionalisation can take a community towards an unthinking, antitherapeutic practice. It is not generally understood in residential care that the practice has to be rethought every day. This is a gift the therapeutic community can make to the rest of psychiatry, residential and daycare.

I have tried to demonstrate that a modern approach to therapeutic communities may require a confidence to continually question ourselves, to embark with our patients on the approach road to the depressive position and to evolve a psychoanalytic theory of action. None of this is easy, and as always in the past, the therapeutic community requires an openness in both staff and patients to the state of their internal worlds. In some ways, working in a therapeutic community is an intensely professional activity, and in some ways it is the most naturally human relationship with each other.

The therapeutic community is a practice in its own right, and proudly so. It retains its links with its roots but not slavishly. There are many influences on it today: group analysis, systems theory, management practice, political and financial pressures, the demands and needs of psychiatry. The psychoanalytic root remains too as a continuous fertile source of inspiration for practice and for theories.

REFERENCES

Armstrong, David (1997) 'The "institution in the mind".' *Free Associations* 7,1–14.

Barnes, E., Griffiths, P., Old, J. and Wells, D. (1997) *Face-to-face with Distress.* London: Butterworth Heineman.

Bateson, G. (1956) 'Towards a theory of schizophrenia.' In G. Bateson (1972) *Steps Towards an Ecology of Mind.* New York: Chandler.

Bion, W.R. (1962) *Learning from Experience.* London: Heineman.

Bion, W.R. and Rickman, J. (1943) 'Intra-group tensions in therapy: their study as the task of the group.' *Lancet 2*: 678–681. Reprinted (1961) in W.R. Bion, *Experiences in Groups.* London: Tavistock.

de Board, R. (1978) *Psychoanalysis of Organisations.* London: Tavistock.

Bridger, H. (1990) 'The discovery of the therapeutic community.' In Eric Trist (ed) *The Social Engagement of Social Science.* London: Free Association Books.

Fairbairn, R.D. (1941) 'A revised psychopathology of the psychoses and psychoneuroses.' In R. D. Fairbairn (1952) *Psychoanalytic Studies of the Personality.* London: Routledge and Kegan Paul.

Griffiths, P. and Hinshelwood, R.D. (1995) 'A culture of enquiry: life within a hall of mirrors.' Paper given at the ISPSO Symposiurn, London, July 1995.

Hinshelwood, R.D. (1987) *What Happens in Groups.* London: Free Association Books.

Hinshelwood, R.D. and Skogstad, W. (1998) 'The hospital in the mind: the setting and the internal world.' In Julia Pestalozzi, Serge Frisch, R.D. Hinshelwood and Didier Houzel (eds) *Psychoanalytic Psychotherapy in Institutional Settings.* London: Karnac.

Hirschorn, L. (1995) *The Workplace Within.* Cambridge, MA: MIT Press.

James, O. (1987) 'The role of the nurse/therapist relationship in a therapeutic community.' In Roger Kennedy, Anne Heymans and Lydia Tisehier (eds) *The Family as In-Patient.* London: Free Association Books.

Janssen, P. (1994) *Psychoanalytic Therapy in the Hospital Setting.* London: Routledge.

Jaques, E. (1955) 'Social systems as a defence against persecutory and depressive anxiety.' In Melanie Klein, Paula Heimaun and Roger Money-Kyrle (eds) *New Directions in Psychoanalysis.* London: Tavistock.

Jones, M. (1952) *Social Psychiatry.* London: Tavistock.

Kennedy, R. (1987) 'The work of the day.' In Roger Kennedy, Anne Heymans and Lydia Tischler (1987) (eds) *The Family as In-Patient.* London: Free Association Books.

Kennedy, R., Heymans, A. and Tisehier L. (1987) (eds) *The Family as In-Patient.* London: Free Association Books.

Klein, M. (1946) 'Notes on some schizoid mechanisms.' In *The Writings of Melanie Klein.* Volume 3. London: Hogarth Press.

van den Langenberg, S. and de Nastris, P. (1985) A narrow escape from the Magic Mountain? *International Journal of Therapeutic Communities 6*, 91–101.

Levinson, A. (1996) 'The struggle to keep a culture of enquiry alive at the Cassel Hospital'. *Therapeutic Communities 17*, 47–57.

Main, T.F. (1946) 'The hospital as a therapeutic institution.' *Bull Menninger Clinic 10*, 66–70. Reprinted (1989) in T.F. Main, *The Ailment and Other Psychoanalytic Essays.* London, Free Association, 7–11.

Main, T.F. (1967) 'Knowledge, learning and freedom from thought.' *Australia and New Zealand Journal of Psychiatry 1*, 64–71. Reprinted in *Psychoanalytic Psychotherapy 5*, 49–78.

de Mare, P. (1983) 'Michael Foulkes and the Northfield Experiment.' In Malcolm Pines (ed) *The Evolution of Group Analysis*. London: Routledge.

Munich, R.(1983) 'Suicide on an in-patient unit: a sociotherapeutic view.' *International Journal of Therapeutic Communities 4*, 196–211.

Norton, K. (1992) 'A culture of enquiry – its preservation or loss.' *Therapeutic Communities 13*, 3–25.

Rapoport, R. (1960) *Community as Doctor*. London: Tavistock.

Santos, A. and Hinshelwood, R.D. (1998) 'The use at the Cassel of the organisational dynamics to enhance the therapeutic work.' *Therapeutic Communities 19*: 29–39.

Winnicott, D.W. (1958) *Through Paediatrics to Psychoanalysis*. London: Tavistock.

CHAPTER 4

Group Analytic Ideas
Extending the Group Matrix into TCs
Davey Rawlinson

EDITORS' INTRODUCTION

Davey Rawlinson trained as a psychiatric nurse between 1989 and 1992. He found his way to Winterbourne Therapeutic Community when it was a rather unusual ward at Fair Mile Hospital in Oxfordshire. He has subsequently undertaken the Sheffield University group analytic training at Turvey Abbey in Bedfordshire and become an adult psychotherapist at Winterbourne House. This has been the home of Winterbourne TC since 1995, and it is a group-based NHS district psychotherapy service, where the day-TC is the treatment offered to people with particularly intractable or deep-seated problems.

In this contribution he explains, in simple and down-to-earth terms, some of the ideas that come from Foulkes' group analysis and how they are relevant in the clinical work of a TC which practises in a group analytic way.

THE ORIGINS OF GROUP ANALYSIS

In 1940, S.H. Foulkes brought together a group of patients in the waiting room of his private practice in Exeter and encouraged them to talk in each other's company, and 'free associate' together. This was the birth of group analytic psychotherapy. His arrival at Northfield Military Neurosis Centre three years later sparked the 'second experiment', following Bion and Rickman's earlier efforts to establish and observe a group approach on one of the rehabilitation wings.

Foulkes was a psychoanalyst, trained in Germany and influenced by gestalt psychology: at Northfield it was his method to place as much emphases on patients' social nature as on their instinctual drives. In his paper in 1966, Foulkes writes 'Those familiar with Gestalt psychology will find no difficulty understanding that the whole is more elementary than the parts.' In applying this to his group approach, he found that the group provided an ideal backdrop against which the individual could be seen. Patients would re-enact neurotic conflicts in their relationships within the group, which provided multiple transference relationships for the group to work with.

Foulkes' main contribution to group analysis was his concentration on small group psychotherapy, which he described as being with between five and ten patients. However, many other developments have grown from the group analytic approach – including organisational applications, large groups, staff groups and certain types of therapeutic community. This chapter will cover some basic concepts of group analysis and then illustrate their application in a TC.

GROUP ANALYTIC CONCEPTS

Through his treatment technique, Foulkes developed a series of factors specific to group analytic situations: *mirror reactions, condenser phenomenon* and *socialisation*. One of his best-known concepts is the *group matrix* which offers considerable insight in understanding the idea of 'the group as a whole'. This will be explained in more detail later.

In the *mirror reaction*, patients see parts of themselves in other group members. This happens through their sharing of thoughts, feelings and behaviour. Foulkes describes this process as not only a projective mechanism but also acknowledges identification as a feature (1964). When it takes place, patients may then be able (or be helped) to recognise the qualities they see in others as aspects of themselves, and hence re-own projected feelings. This leaves them more self-aware and less isolated and fearful.

The *condenser phenomenon* describes the pooling of collective unconscious feelings within the group, and it is observed though the use of symbols and symptoms. In the group situation, relief can be found by hearing other members bring up issues which may be difficult for the individual to mention themselves.

Having a forum where they can feel less isolated by being heard and hearing others, at a level of some depth and often out of conscious awareness, is of great therapeutic benefit. The same process is also sometimes referred to as *resonance*. A simple example would be where somebody has decided to leave a group and is discussing it: this may put another member in touch with painful feelings which are based on a loss of an important person when they were small, which might never have been fully accepted or grieved for. In powerful emotional moments in groups, several members may experience this sort of resonance simultaneously.

Foulkes describes *exchange* as a therapeutic factor specific to groups. He comments on how a patient is more likely to take in something said by a fellow group member than by the therapist, in the same way that children can accept some things from other children which they may have not been able to take from their parents. This is particularly important in TCs, where members may come with profound mistrust of professionals or those in authority. Early on in somebody's time in a group, they may well experience more 'give and take' among their peers; they will be able to accept confrontation and challenge much more readily from fellow group members than from therapists.

> Barbara was a TC member with a history of early and persistent childhood sexual abuse by several members of her family, and a long catalogue of serious incidents of deliberate self-harm. Almost immediately after her case conference she started to feel very untrusting of staff. She saw them as persecutory, and any feedback was distorted and experienced as punishing and rejecting. On one particular occasion, having bought a bag of razor blades with the intention of cutting herself, she presented them to the staff asking them to dispose of them for her. In the community meeting, members congratulated her on stopping herself from self-harming and therefore doing something different. She appeared to feel warmth from the group, but when a therapist suggested that she herself should dispose of the blades as a way of taking further responsibility, she was devastated, feeling that the staff had rejected her attempts to ask for help. Any further interventions from staff were experienced as attacking. We were at an impasse. If the community could not contain her distress and find some resolution, the staff felt she would leave the group and harm herself. The members in the group came forward offering support and positive feedback. They suggested that at breaktime, she could go to the pharmacy, with the support of some members, and hand the razors in. The sense that other people could be genuinely concerned for her and keen to help her marked a change in her response. She accepted their offer and later was able to say how moved she was by their caring.

The 'basic law of group dynamics' is a foundation stone of group analytic theory, and it summarises how individuals' deviation from social and cultural norms, together with those individuals' healthy elements, combine to promote movement from regressed and disorganised functioning, towards progression and coherence:

> The deepest reason why these patients can reinforce each other's normal reactions and wear down and correct each other's neurotic reactions, is that collectively they constitute the very *Norm* from which individually they deviate. (Foulkes 1964, p.29)

For example, in TCs we often refer to patients who are at risk of 'acting out' their distress in a dramatic manner, perhaps cutting themselves or losing their temper and throwing something. There are also patients who 'act in', directing all this overwhelming rage inwards and presenting with severe depression, anxiety or psychosomatic symptoms. In a group setting, such extreme ways of coping will tend to move towards the norm, and become modified as patients learn from each other and articulate the underlying feelings in the 'network of relationships'. Foulkes comments on the process by which this is done: 'working towards an ever more articulate form of communication is identical to the therapeutic process itself' (1964). In therapeutic communities there are many levels on which this can happen, and opportunities for it to do so.

Foulkes' optimistic view of groups is somewhat at odds with the way in which Bion's (1959) observations of group process have been used. Bion described groups in which regression was pronounced and the main task was to work with the 'basic assumptions': dependency, fight–flight and pairing. Foulkes' therapy groups are in 'work group' mode, and he paid little attention to the darker and more destructive forces which occur.

However, more recent group analytic writing has started to consider these areas. Nitsun (1996) has described the 'anti-group' as the destructive aspect of groups that threatens integrity and therapeutic development. It is present in all groups: sometimes it can be resolved with relative ease, but sometimes it fatally undermines the foundations. These are powerful and primitive forces arising from early mental mechanisms which include splitting, projection and projective identification.

Pines (1994) writes about working with borderline personalities in groups, where these high levels of primitive rage and destructiveness are routinely encountered. He suggests that such groups need understanding and containment by therapists, or other group members who are in touch with such levels of experience yet are 'organised' and able to articulate and verbalise appropriately. This is through the same process as the basic law of group dynamics – although it relies on the members of the group being in different affective states at different *times* (typically regressed or mature), rather than on just having areas of healthy functioning which they assimilate through working together. However, in a therapeutic community, most or all of the members are likely to be frequently and acutely in touch with raw and primitive feelings, and the therapists are, if anything, *less* directly active than in out-patient therapy in the expectation that members will be of most help to each other. This explains the paradox that group members with greater levels and concentrations of disturbance can come together to provide a higher level of understanding and containment: the contained can act as the container.

Pines also describes how splitting or fragmentation of the group and scapegoating of vulnerable individuals can be consequences of failure to hold adequately such turbulent emotions. Therapists on TCs need to be acutely aware of these dynamics, and retain the capacity to think about them – particularly as a staff team – when under a barrage of destructive feelings and processes.

Another important group analytic concept is the 'dynamic administration'. This is all the work the therapist does to ensure the security of the setting in which the group takes place: from laying out the chairs and making sure the group is undisturbed, to dealing with phone calls and letters from other professionals, and balancing group membership by selecting patients. In a therapeutic community, much of the dynamic administration is the responsibility of the whole community, and not just the staff. For example, most TCs involve members in the process of assessing and selecting those coming for admission, and this is crucial in establishing a community culture that is 'owned' by all the members, rather than imposed by staff or external agents. It needs to be done very openly and thoroughly, with mutually agreed processes, in order to avoid practical and dynamic problems.

Group analytic theory is also used in working with median groups (12–25) and large groups (more than 25), which have different processes, preoccupations and functions. A useful idea when working with the socialising forces of larger groups is Pat de Mare's *Koinonia* (1991); he defines it as 'impersonal citizenship and good fellowship … a form of togetherness and amity that brings a serendipity of resources' (p.2). This spirit of democratic citizenship only evolves slowly in unstructured median and large groups: it is a powerful socialising force in which individual difference becomes subordinate to collective responsibility and shared agency. In TCs, its development is deliberately nurtured and facilitated by structures such as community meetings and voting procedures, but the experience of *koinonia* comes and goes as mature and regressive functioning wax and wane.

The application of group analytic theory in therapeutic community practice has been well documented (for example, see Chapters 14, 16 and 20). This chapter concentrates on the workings of Winterbourne Therapeutic Community to help highlight some common practices and difficulties.

A GROUP ANALYTIC DAY PROGRAMME: WINTERBOURNE TC

The Winterbourne Therapeutic Community, based in Reading, is a day unit offering intensive group psychotherapy in conjunction with a socio-therapeutic programme of activity groups and community meetings for up to 18 people. It is an integrated part of a NHS district psychotherapy service. The community is for people who have experienced abuse, trauma, neglect or deprivation in childhood, resulting in persistent or recurrent mental health problems. It is staffed by trained or trainee psychotherapists with professional backgrounds in mental health. There are several group analysts and others trained in humanistic and psychodynamic fields. Large and small therapy groups, together with different daily activity groups and unstructured community time are sandwiched between a community meeting at the beginning and end of each day. This chapter will give an outline of the programme: the full information booklet about the TC, and other details about the service, are available on the website http//:www.winterbourne.demon. co.uk

Foulkes wrote that group analysis was 'psychotherapy of the group, by the group, including the conductor'. Espey (1997) comments that the therapeutic community is 'psychotherapy of the community, by the community, including the staff team'. There is no individual therapy and all is contained within the group as a whole.

With an overall group analytic framework, the therapy offered comes from an integrated approach with different elements emphasising members' past, current and future history (see Figure 4.1). The overall structure – those aspects which are common to any elements of therapy within the programme – is concerned with the practical issues of dynamic administration, as well as therapeutic ones such as the central importance of always looking at clinical material in the light of relationships.

Different theoretical approaches, such as transactional analysis groups or cognitive behavioural interventions in community meetings, easily fit together in this framework and make intuitive sense as valuable parts of the whole therapeutic experience.

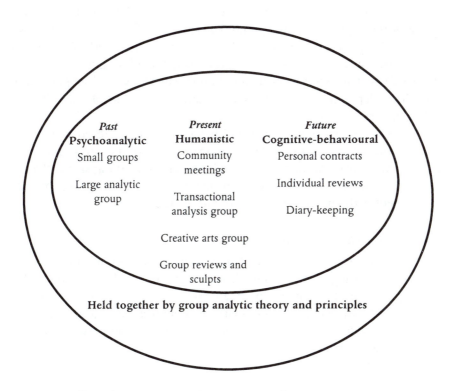

Figure 4.1 Different therapeutic approaches in a group analytic container

The programme

The groups

On joining the community members are assigned to one of the three small psychotherapy groups which meet twice a week, with six members each and two therapists. The three large groups at present are a creative arts group, an analytic group and a transactional analysis group.

The community meeting

The community meeting is the forum where the day-to-day running of the community is discussed and all the issues about boundaries are brought in. Whilst Rapoport (1960) spoke of an atmosphere of permissiveness, the community needs rules and guidelines to provide a safe and holding environment so members can see, to some extent, where the boundaries lie (see also Chapter 8). The meetings are democratic affairs where freedom of expression is encouraged, and relationships and feelings are examined in an open, non-judgemental way. Decisions are sometimes made with regard to personal contracts, suspensions, discharges. Votes are taken on a one member one vote basis, including staff.

The meeting has a structure with one of the members reading out the agenda at the beginning of the group. The agenda differs on each day of the week but always includes apologies, absences and issues to mark. The 'contact slot' is where any contacts since the previous day are brought in, including phone calls that members make to one another when they need support out of hours. The telephone support network is an important feature of a day-TC, and will be discussed below.

Members then raise any issues which they would like to address in the group. Events taking place outside the group often fill the meetings: arguments in the kitchen, incidents during the activity groups, something said at the bus stop – to name but a few. The structure and agenda of the meetings provide containment without being too rigid or bureaucratic.

Joining the community: case conferences

Prospective members are allocated a 30-minute section of the morning community meeting to talk about their backgrounds and their motives for wishing to join the community; then members and therapists have an opportunity to ask questions and discuss their application to join. Following this there is a vote to decide whether the group feel that this person is suitable for therapy at the community.

Members' responsibility

At every possible opportunity, members are encouraged to empower themselves in making decisions and carrying them out, so as to foster a greater sense of their own effectiveness, or agency. In an outpatient psychotherapy group, the dynamic administration is the responsibility of the conductor, while in a therapeutic community much of this task is handed back to members to own for themselves. It is the members' responsibility to make sure that there are enough chairs in the room and tissues on the table; members are also included in meetings to discuss the day-to-day running of the whole building. Each member has at least one job in the group which include chair, secretary, treasurer and storekeeper. Members rotate jobs every eight weeks: they have elections to decide the right person for each job at that time.

Members also have a food budget, and they shop and cook for the whole community. There are four food groups: one each for preparation, clearing, planning and a support group, and they rotate each week. Responsibility for looking after themselves is handed back to the members: ensuring that there is enough food for the week and enough money to pay for it. It appears to be of great therapeutic benefit for the member to struggle with the responsibility of these roles: it is often problems with these jobs that leads members to explore issues around sharing, being part of a team, envy and rivalry.

Staff roles

The staff team are also allocated food groups and we take part in other work groups which happen throughout the week. This means that the therapists are seen in a variety of different settings in the same way that the members are: this is quite different to normal practice in group analytic psychotherapy. In an outpatient group, there can be conflict between the three aspects of a therapist's role: dynamic administrator, conductor and group member. In a TC, there are many more facets to the therapist's role and it is much more varied and open to critical scrutiny.

Perhaps the most formidable task for the therapist working in a therapeutic community is to be able to manage his own personal and professional boundaries in an environment where these roles are so frequently interchanged. As well as being conductors in the twice-weekly small groups, therapists cook with the members, we eat dinner with them, in the activity groups we may play football or board games, in the work groups we may help organise the fund-raising or take part in building work – and in the unstructured time we sit and have a cup of tea, maybe chatting or perhaps just quietly sitting there. A much greater degree of self-disclosure is inevitable, even if this is largely non-verbal. Can the therapist cook? Is he competitive during the activity groups? To what extent does he take part in conversation round the dinner table? The role of the therapist is interchangeable between group conductor and community staff member which requires acute awareness of personal boundaries. This interchange of roles is deliberately and actively taught to staff in the Open Psychotherapy Centre's unique training programme in Athens (see Chapter 16).

Transference and reality

The members also need to adapt to different roles within the community. In such an intensive environment, the pull towards regression is immensely powerful, yet members are constantly required to maintain their 'adult selves'. They may come out of a therapy group after a painful and distressing session and then be expected to cook a meal for the community. The messages to 'grow up' and 'be little' ebb and flow throughout the day, and are accentuated by the fact that members need to go home at the end of each day, and cope with all the normal responsibilities of the rest of their lives. For many, this includes being single parents, coping with housing difficulties and external relationships or isolation.

While asking a lot from the members, I believe this moving in and out of regression helps provide containment in the community. Among the members, many of whom have an ICD-10 diagnosis of emotionally unstable personality disorder, the 'as if' quality to the transference can be experienced as very real, and become so overwhelming that there is a risk of the transference becoming psychotic. Because the therapist is also working in the whole therapeutic milieu, this allows the transference to become diluted at times by letting members experience a more reality-based relationship, by grounding them in the practicalities of day-to-day living.

> Jonathan, a man in his mid-forties was voted in following his case conference at the community. Soon after joining, Jonathan developed an intense negative transference with his female small group therapist. He spoke in the group of paranoid fantasies he had about her. Jonathan believed that she was passing on information to social services and also to his ex-wife. He believed that every time she had a file or a piece of paper in her hand, it was information about him. He would shout at her in the groups, feeling persecuted every time she spoke to him in the meetings. For several weeks the staff team were anxious that these delusional ideas were heralding the beginning of a psychotic breakdown. However, the therapist experienced Jonathan very differently outside the formal groups: where he appeared warm and engaging. While seemingly inconsistent, this different quality of contact allayed the team's anxieties.
>
> In one group, after a weekend, Jonathan spoke about how he had been preoccupied with his relationship with his female therapist. He went on to talk about how he only experienced these persecutory ideas in the

groups and not when he was chatting to her in the kitchen or pottering about in the garden. Jonathan said that it seemed ridiculous that a few steps up to the group room could so strongly affect his feelings towards her. Exploring this further he spoke of experiencing her as very powerful in the group and as having authority over him. He said that in the kitchen, doing the washing up together, chatting about the weather or a television programme, he realised that she wasn't this tyrant he had created.

Through this insight, Jonathan was able to think about the transformation between feelings in the group and feelings outside the group, understanding the 'as if' quality to his relationship with her, and starting to understand how this came to play in many of his relationships.

The group matrix

A sense of belonging to something worthwhile and important, of feeling contained and supported, and of experiencing oneself as being valued and heard, are the essential therapeutic factors which the TC culture nurtures. The process of attachment is often a painful one – as members struggle with their familiar patterns of rejection seeking behaviour, within a culture where many members are very familiar with the process themselves, and understand the complexity of it (see also Chapters 6 and 11).

The mother–infant dyad is the starting point in attachment theory, and it is translated into group analytic terms in Foulkes' concept of the Matrix (1964). The word *matrix* comes from Latin and means womb. Foulkes describes the group matrix as a network, and the individual a nodal point.

> The matrix is the hypothetical web of communication and relationship in a given group. It is the common ground which ultimately determines the meaning and significance of all events and upon which all communications, verbal and non-verbal, rest. (Foulkes 1964, p.292)

Several group analysts have contributed to our understanding of the group matrix (Ahlin 1985; Glenn 1987; Roberts 1982; Van der Kleij 1985). Ahlin comments on the difficulty in verbally expressing that which is an experience and coins the phrase 'group spirit' to describe its illusory nature. Glenn parallels the concept of the matrix with Bowlby's formulation of the 'secure base' linking attachment theory with group analysis. Glenn describes her experience of the group matrix as being about a sense of belonging. The matrix provides a secure base which allows members through their contact to experience a belonging. Figure 4.2 represents the 'hypothetical web of relationships' which exist in the group.

The telephone support network at Winterbourne could be seen as an electronic representation of this web of relationships – the matrix in wires.

Through this phone network, individuals are actually connected by electrical lines. Out of community hours (the structured day is 9 a.m. – 3.30 p.m.) members are encouraged to phone one another if they feel the need for support. For example, they may want to self harm and need some contact with someone they trust, to help them find a different way of coping. Higgins (1997) writes 'The community culture is one of empowerment and agency and the telephone support network clearly places responsibility for the individual's safety with the individual and in turn the group.' At Winterbourne it is the whole group, and not an isolated individual, or the staff team alone, which is the container.

WHAT IS A GROUP ANALYTIC THERAPEUTIC COMMUNITY?

Group analysis looks upon the group as a whole – and not as individuals in isolation. Notably, each individual's actions and responses have direct consequences for the whole group, and members of a group analytic TC are usually aware of this, in that their experience of the group (in positive and

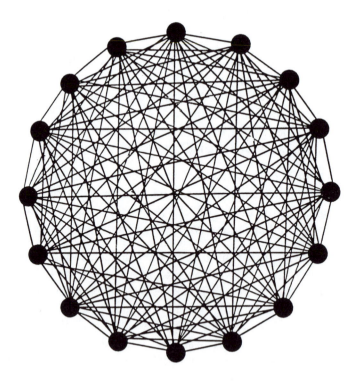

Figure 4.2 The 'hypothetical web of relationships' which exist in a group

negative ways) is the 'ground' against which the 'figure' of their individual needs and contributions is set. The absence of any individual therapy places this process unavoidably at the centre of the therapy.

Whilst members attend the community with a variety of different symptoms, each has problems which can be understood in a relationship context. Members re-enact these difficulties in the group, and therefore are encouraged to explore and alter problematic patterns. Socially unacceptable behaviours are challenged in a supportive and empathic way which, once a member has settled in, can be experienced as containing rather than persecutory. The group analytic principles of dynamic administration and experiencing relationships within the matrix provides a framework into which a variety of therapeutic elements can be incorporated.

As more disturbed patients are treated in groups, strategies and concepts need to evolve to accommodate and explain the processes involved. For example, much of the work for the staff team involves struggling to bear the unconscious destructiveness which is often present and projected. Many group analytic methods can be well adapted to work in TCs, but some unexpected paradoxes emerge: such as the way in which a high level of psychopathology in all the group members can provide a better level of containment than might happen in a more mixed group. One could make a hypothesis that this is because they are all so familiar with regression and primitive emotional defences, and soon learn as TC members to move in and out of such ways of functioning: they may therefore be much better at supporting each other through such states than a less disturbed patient, or a therapist, could be. Or it may be that in a whole group of highly disturbed people there is less opportunity for projecting away one's healthy parts, less impoverishment and less envy.

These and other clinical phenomena which are part of the daily business of a TC need to be examined: because of the intensity of the regime and the level of disorganisation in the patients, TCs have much to contribute to our understanding of handling deep and primitive mental mechanisms in groups.

REFERENCES

Ahlin, G (1985) 'On thinking about the group matrix.' *Group Analysis 18*, 111–119.

Bion, W.R. (1959) *Experiences in Groups.* London: Tavistock.

Bowlby, J. (1977) 'The making and breaking of affectional bonds.' *British Journal of Psychiatry 130*, 210.

Espey, A. (1997) Personal communication.

Foulkes,S.H (1964) *Therapeutic Group Analysis.* London: Allen and Unwin.

Glenn, L (1987) 'Attachment theory and group analysis: the group matrix as a secure base.' *Group Analysis 20*, 109–126.

Higgins, B. (1997) 'Does anyone feel they need support tonight? 24 hour care in a day unit.' *Therapeutic Communities 18*, 55–61.

Mare, P.B. de, Piper, R. and Thompson, S. (1991) *Koinonia: From Hate, Through Dialogue, to Culture in the Large Group.* London: Karnac.

Nitsun, M. (1996) *The Anti-Group: Destructive Forces in the Group and Their Creative Potential.* London: Routledge.

Pines, M. (1994) 'Borderline phenomena in analytic groups' In Victor L. Schermer and Malcolm Pines (eds) *Ring of Fire.* London: Routledge.

Rapoport, R. (1960) *Community as Doctor.* London: Tavistock.

Roberts, J. (1982) 'Foulkes' concept of the matrix.' *Group Analysis 16*, 111–126.

Schermer, V.L. (1994) 'Between theory and practice, light and heat: on the use of theory in the "Ring of Fire"' In Victor L. Schermer and Malcolm Pines (eds) *Ring of Fire.* London: Routledge.

Van der Kleij, G. (1985) 'The group and its matrix.' *Group Analysis 18*, 102–110.

CHAPTER 5

Nursing

The Importance of the Psychosocial Environment

Richard Byrt

EDITORS' INTRODUCTION

Richard Byrt has worked as an RMN in various settings, including three therapeutic communities, most recently on Cairngorm, which was a small therapeutic community at Arnold Lodge medium secure unit, Leicester. He has a PhD and BSc (Hons) in social sciences and is currently involved in quality, teaching and research, related to nursing practice and service development at Arnold Lodge.

His commitments and interests include Buddhism related to everyday life; gay and lesbian experiences and issues; users' views of, and participation in mental health services; and the uses of poetry and fiction in mental health nursing practice and education.

In NHS TCs, it is nurses who predominate in the staff team, and nurses who most influence the quality of the milieu. Moreover, it is nurses who tend to bear the brunt of the permissive regime (such as coping with a violent incident on a night shift) and share most fully in the daily grind (including the administration of the bureaucratic and anti-therapeutic processes we highlighted in the introduction).

However, as Richard points out, it is consultant psychiatrists who have held the stage and tend to be remembered, which is ironic given the emphasis on 'flattened hierarchies'.

We wanted to include this chapter in the hope that it provides something of a balance.

DEVELOPMENT OF THE NURSE'S ROLE IN TCS

Since the late eighteenth century, some keepers, attendants and later, mental health nurses, have been involved in liberalising institutional regimes, although their custodial role has often been paramount. Keepers' communication and relationships with patients were often strongly emphasised in moral management reforms in the late eighteenth and early nineteenth centuries, although some critics have seen this as a form of adverse social control (Foucault 1967; Scull 1979). At the Retreat Hospital, York and later, in some asylums in the nineteenth and early twentieth centuries, emphasis was placed on attendants and mental nurses sharing recreational, social and work activities with patients. At the Retreat, inmates were considered part of a family and ate with the staff. The Matron's 'tea parties had a valuable socialising influence on the patients' (Jones 1983, p.126, quoted in Nolan 1993, p.29).

With the growth of the large asylums, there was less apparent interest in patients' social and physical environments. However, during the 1930s, mental nurses were increasingly involved in intensive work activities with patients, and there was more awareness of the adverse effects of institutionalisation (Manning 1989).

Nursing in the First Therapeutic Communities

During the Second World War, nursing staff were involved in the first UK hospital therapeutic communities at Northfield and Mill Hill. These were started by psychiatrists to treat soldiers (see Chapter 1). Nurses at Mill Hill 'comprised many [untrained] assistant nurses from all walks of life... They did not think like most nurses, but reflected their training in art, ballet or acting' (Jones 1979, p.1). Residents, nursing staff and psychiatrists worked together closely and democratically, with a lessening of hierarchical barriers.

At both Northfield and Mill Hill, staff, including nurses, enabled patients to examine events in the life of the hospital and ways in which these related to residents' problems in both military and civilian life. Nurses participated with residents in work, leisure and social activities and, with other staff, enabled them to contribute to the solution of problems, such as poor morale and avoidance of responsibility.

Nurses' self-awareness, reflection on their practice, and beneficial communication and relationships with residents were all emphasised in these therapeutic communities, and, following the war, in Belmont (later the Henderson) and the Cassel Hospital (Barnes 1968; Rapoport 1960; Skellern 1955). Histories of these early therapeutic communities, and accounts by psychiatrists involved, suggest that the latter were mainly responsible for determining both the aims of the communities and the role of nursing staff. This is not surprising, given that the psychiatrists were senior army officers, and later, medical superintendents, at a time when this role was invested with considerable authority. Maxwell Jones described nursing staff at Belmont in the early 1950s as 'friend and sympathiser' to residents, and as offering them 'security and stability' (Jones, Baker, Freeman, Merry, Pomryn, Sandler and Tuxford 1952, p.32). Nurses were expected to deal effectively with residents' rule infringements and ensure that their own needs did not influence the meeting of residents' needs. In his classic paper, 'The Ailment', Main explored the dynamics leading to nursing staff leaving the Cassel prematurely, and referred to the dangers of a nurse taking on a crusading role and assuming that (s)he was the only person who could understand an overwhelmingly needy resident (Main 1957).

Rapoport (1960) described four components of the work of nursing and other staff at Henderson (formerly Belmont) Hospital. These included: (1) democratisation, (2) communalism (involving sharing activities with residents), (3) permissiveness (allowing expression of feelings), and (4) reality confrontation (where both residents and staff gave constructive feedback to each other). By this time, the Henderson treated people with personality disorders. Daily community meetings were established, in which nurses, with residents and other staff, enabled individuals to examine events in the life of the therapeutic community which related to their problems. Nurses were also involved, with psychiatrists, in small psychotherapy groups (Whiteley 1980).

The early therapeutic communities influenced practice elsewhere. From the 1950s to the 1970s, several small democratic analytic therapeutic communities offered structured programmes of community meetings, small psychotherapy groups and activities for residents with neuroses and personality disorders. In addition, many large psychiatric hospitals and general hospital psychiatric units had one or more wards adopting a therapeutic community approach, usually for people with mental illness. On these wards, doors were unlocked, with greater opportunities for residents to express views, and more informal relationships between the latter and staff and between staff of different grades and professions. Residents' decision-making and responsibility and the provision of meaningful, rehabilitative activity were stressed (Clark 1996).

Some innovations were started by nurses, often with the sanction of psychiatrists. Nurses reduced institutionalisation and residents' disturbed behaviours by improvements in the environment, opportunities for discussion of residents' concerns and enabling them to engage in fulfilling work, often followed by discharge and employment.

The growth of the therapeutic community approach was influenced, in part, by several studies which found that many patients led institutionalised lives and were adversely affected by all-pervasive hospital regimes. Nurses were often custodial, and made decisions for patients unnecessarily, with a failure to recognise the latter's aptitudes and abilities (Barton 1959; Goffman 1968; Nolan 1993; Wing and Brown 1970). Other research revealed that failures in communication between staff increased patients' disturbed behaviours (Caudill 1958; Stanton and Schwartz 1954) or prevented necessary change (Cumming and Cumming 1962). Such findings appear to have influenced some psychiatrists, who viewed staff communication as an essential prerequisite in facilitating therapeutic communities (Clark 1996; Jones 1968a; Martin 1962).

Later problems and developments

Liberal and permissive attitudes in the 1960s appear to have enabled therapeutic communities to flourish, but from the mid-1970s, there has been a decline in the number of wards using the therapeutic community approach, and the closure of a number of small democratic-analytic communities. This has been attributed to several factors, which impinge on the role of mental health nurses.

Increased bureaucratisation appears to have led to trusts making more demands on nurses to account for their activities and complete paperwork away from direct patient care. Despite recommendations that mental health nurses spend most of their work time in direct patient contact (DoH 1994), research has found that this accounts for about one third of their work time (Robinson 1996).

A shift in ideology within society, reflected in the NHS and psychiatry, has also affected the role of the mental health nurse and the survival of some therapeutic communities, whose values and aims have clashed with those of health authorities and trusts. In addition, nurses can be faced with conflicting demands if they are line managed by nurses outside the therapeutic community. For example, a trust manager may find 'flattened hierarchies' unacceptable.

The physical structure of present day psychiatric units also affects nurses' application of therapeutic community principles. Some appear to have been designed with little thought for the effects of the physical and social environment on patients (Barefoot 1992), with an absence of living and activities space, and of attractive grounds and other facilities. This is in contrast to moral management pioneers' emphasis on physical and social environments (Jones 1993); and time formerly spent by some therapeutic community nurses with residents in extensive grounds for communication, leisure and work projects (Clark 1996).

Recruiting nurses to therapeutic communities may be a problem in the future. Factors include difficulties in recruiting mental health nurses generally, perhaps reflecting stigmatising attitudes towards people with mental health problems (Hayward and Bright 1997). Since the introduction of Project 2000, student nurses spend less time in mental health residential settings, including therapeutic communities. Within mental health nursing practice and theory, there seems to be less emphasis on the use of the social environment and activities with patients. More apparent importance is attached to developments in assessment, including risk assessment, care planning, and (until recently) nursing models. Several recent textbooks of mental health nursing make little or no reference to therapeutic communities (Chapman 1992).

Compared with other professionals, nurses often have less power in relation to the development of therapeutic communities or prevention of their closure. This may reflect the low value our society generally places on the profession (predominantly female) and the qualities it embodies (Ritter 1997). More specifically, few nurses in higher management have been involved in therapeutic community work. There are limited promotion opportunities for nurses choosing to remain in therapeutic communities, which reflects tendencies in nursing, until recently, to separate practice from management, quality, research and teaching. Exceptions are the Cassel and Henderson Hospitals where H and I grade roles have been established and nurses have been involved in direct work with residents and in management, teaching or research.

The paucity of recognised qualifications specifically in therapeutic community work (except for the Cassel Diploma in Psychosocial Nursing) may also affect nurses' lack of power. A recent Association of Therapeutic Communities/Royal College of Nursing course is now no longer available, although the Association of Therapeutic Communities is considering the issue of training as a priority.

RECENT DEVELOPMENTS IN NURSES' ROLES

Despite these problems, there has been a number of recent developments in nursing in therapeutic communities. Some nurses have extended their skills in interventions in the wider community to enable residents to develop independence and effective coping strategies. There have also been developments in day care and crisis services: Winterbourne therapeutic community, for example, offers a telephone help line to residents in distress (Higgins 1997). There has been an increase in modified therapeutic community principles in secure units and hospitals (Reiss, Grubin and Menx 1996) and in prisons (Cullen, Jones and Woodward 1997). The ethical problems and concerns which nurses face in trying to provide a therapeutic community which is safe and secure have been described by Byrt (1993).

The nurse's role in contemporary therapeutic communities

Nurses have a key role in facilitating a social environment in which all communications and interactions, activities and events can, potentially, benefit residents. The nurse, with other participants, enables residents to:

- safely express, and eventually relieve or resolve, painful feelings and problems

- learn about themselves and their problems, including relationship difficulties

- take on responsibility and participate in decision-making. This is intended to increase residents' self-esteem and capacity to make decisions about their lives; and help them discover or develop aptitudes and abilities.

Achievement of these aims will be considered in relation to a number of aspects of the nurse's role.

Self-awareness

Self-awareness is essential for effective work in therapeutic communities. It includes the ability to recognise and acknowledge counter-transferences: positive or negative feelings about residents evoked by the latter and/or influenced by the nurse's own experiences of relationships. Self-awareness also involves the nurse's ability to recognise her/his own motivations and their influence on communications and relationships with residents. An example is a nurse realising that his need for approval made him make unhelpful 'reassuring' comments to residents.

In addition, self-awareness includes the capacity for reflective practice: the nurse's ability to honestly consider her/his communications, interventions and activities with residents and role in various groups. Keeping a journal may enable this. Nurses at the Cassel Hospital have produced several accounts of reflective practice, particularly in relation to relationships and activities with residents (Barnes 1968; Irwin 1995; Kennedy, Heymans and Tischler 1986; McCaffrey 1998).

Staff support groups can help prevent inappropriate expression of anger and other feelings towards residents, and enable staff to understand the dynamics of particular staff–resident relationships. Most therapeutic communities provide opportunities for residents to work intensively through very painful emotions. This often involves transference onto staff of positive and negative feelings towards parents and other significant people. Some residents frequently manifest immense distress, often related to childhood abuse and neglect, through acting out: the expression of feelings through behaviours involving harm to self and others. This can engender frustration, anger and therapeutic nihilism in staff. The inadequate resolution of these feelings may lead to 'therapy-interfering behaviours', for example, distant or punitive attitudes (Jones 1997). These can reinforce acting out and prevent residents from experimenting with more creative ways of dealing with conflicts. They can be helped by staff's efforts to establish trust, engage the resident in treatment and forge a 'therapeutic alliance' (Norton and Hinshelwood 1996). This involves the maintenance of consistent, caring interest in the resident and making explicit the wish to work *with* her/him in understanding the reasons for distress and finding ways to ameliorate it.

Nurse–resident communication and relationships

Effective communication between staff and residents is one of the most important aspects of the nurse's role. This is achieved, in part, by her/his approachability, non-judgemental attitude and maintenance of caring interest in residents, where possible, with empathy: felt appreciation of the resident's feelings and problems, without being overwhelmed by them. Continued, consistent concern and warmth of nurses and other community members may provide residents with a 'corrective emotional experience' (Ratigan and Aveline 1988) and a realisation that, despite earlier adverse experiences, some people do care and can be trusted.

Active and involved listening is particularly important, in both one-to-one interactions and in groups. This includes paying very close attention to what the resident says, the way it is said and her/his non-verbal communications. It also involves obvious interest, shown in the nurse's facial expression, eye contact, tone and content of speech and body posture (Stuart and Sundeen 1995). Knowing when and when not to intervene is also important. The nurse develops awareness of ways in which her/his needs, e.g. to help, may influence interventions, such as suggesting ideas, when it may be more helpful to the resident to listen and to enable her/him to express feelings and gradually find solutions to problems.

Boundaries in nurse–resident relationships

Whilst in therapeutic communities there is a flattening of hierarchies, nurses are required by the UKCC, and by their managers, to work with residents within professional boundaries, and not form friendships and close emotional relationships with residents. There is evidence that such relationships are harmful and militate against effective therapy, partly because of the power imbalance between resident and professional. Residents sometimes develop strong attractions to staff. It is necessary to be sensitive to a resident's overwhelming needs, but also clear about the boundaries and the difference between friendship and a warm, caring professional relationship.

A related boundary concerns the nurse's self-disclosure to residents. Whilst openness and honesty are encouraged in therapeutic communities, this does not usually include the sharing with residents of information about personal areas of the nurse's life. Carl Rogers emphasised the need for professionals to avoid inappropriate self-disclosure, but to be genuine and authentic: aware of how clients make them feel, and of the effects of their own feelings and needs on their relationships and therapeutic work with clients (Rogers 1967).

Decision-making and responsibility

Residents are encouraged to take on decision-making and responsibility to learn skills and effective coping strategies, and to increase self-esteem. They are also enabled to take responsibility for their behaviours and the way they express feelings. Some residents in Cairngorm therapeutic community at Arnold Lodge medium secure unit were encouraged to monitor their anger and its expression, through the use of a diary and discussion in the community meeting each morning.

Residents have specific responsibilities, often with formalised roles such as Chair and Secretary of the community meeting and those related to cooking, cleaning and other work. In some therapeutic communities, residents have responsibility for budgets for food and other items and participate in decisions about admission and discharge of residents (McGauley 1997).

The use of activities

Nurses' sharing of activities with residents can enable them to trust staff and facilitate a therapeutic alliance. This in turn may improve their use of formal psychotherapy groups. Residents' previous experience of problems in communications and relationships may be mirrored in shared activities, yielding material for examination with other community members, and helping them to find more effective ways to communicate, relate to people and resolve difficulties. Shared activities also enable residents, who often have very low self-esteem, to discover and develop talents and abilities which they can use for the benefit of themselves and other people.

Preparation for the future is stressed in many therapeutic communities, including Francis Dixon Lodge and the Henderson, which offer both pre- and post-discharge groups. At the Cassel Hospital, time as an inpatient has been reduced for some residents and replaced by considerable support by Cassel nurses working in the community (Chiesa 1997). Rehabilitation is particularly important in therapeutic communities in secure hospitals and units and prisons, where some residents have been institutionalised for many years. Part of the nurse's role is to enable residents to acquire social skills and skills related to everyday living.

Living-learning situations

The social environment can enable residents to learn about themselves and their problems by examining occurrences in the life of the therapeutic community. Any event, however apparently serious or trivial, can be used to aid residents' growth and self-understanding. This includes crises, such as aggressive or antisocial behaviours. On Cairngorm, 'Gus', a newly admitted resident, threw an armchair, narrowly missing a nurse. Another nurse quietly asked him if he could talk about what was troubling him. Gus did so in a crisis meeting, where he received support from other community members. Other residents told him that they had come to realise that they could effectively express anger without being 'macho'. Gus was given honest feedback about how his behaviour made others feel. This 'reality confrontation' enables residents to appreciate how they are perceived. Such feedback from nurses is best given in a constructive, non-confrontational way in the context of a caring professional relationship.

Facilitating the safe expression of feelings

The above example illustrates the nurse's role in facilitating the safe expression of residents' feelings and thoughts. Therapeutic communities operate according to psychodynamic principles, so that 'disorders of behaviour' are seen as expressing 'emotional conflicts and tensions in an individual's relations with others' (Kennard 1983, p.12). Formal opportunities are provided for the exploration of such difficulties in a variety of groups. Some, notably the Cassel, also offer individual sessions with nurses, as well as individual psychotherapy (Chapman 1992; McCaffrey 1998).

In some therapeutic communities, crisis meetings can be called at any time by residents or staff to examine areas of concern. For people like Gus, such meetings provide immediate opportunities to express feelings, and to learn to do so effectively and safely. The nurse's role includes observation and awareness of residents and how they are feeling. Sometimes, particularly at times of crisis, (s)he may call a crisis meeting on behalf of residents, or, in some therapeutic communities, provide individual interventions. On other occasions, it may be more appropriate to enable residents to take the initiative to support each other.

Some nurses qualify in counselling, psychotherapy and other therapies and take leading roles in these areas, whilst in a few therapeutic communities, nurses are rarely or never involved in formal psychotherapeutic activity. Most therapeutic community nurses act as co-facilitators in group psychotherapy and community meetings. Because of their close day to day contact with residents, they are particularly well placed to make observations about their interactions and involvement in activities.

Individual care planning and assessment

Chapman (1992) comments of nursing care planning at the Cassel and Henderson Hospitals:

> During... [nurse-patient] interactions... relationships are developed and the nurse gains understanding about patients' strengths and weaknesses. Nurses' observations and insights become the foundation of individual care plans which are discussed and coordinated as part of an ongoing learning and discovery process with the patient... the multi-disciplinary team, and where appropriate, with the whole community of patients... Care plans... identify patients' difficulties... strengths and capacities. The latter are used imaginatively to help resolve problems... (Chapman 1992, p.329)

In Cairngorm, initially, each resident had a keyworker who devised, implemented and evaluated nursing care plans with her/him. This sometimes resulted in over-dependence on keyworkers, so residents' ownership of the plans was agreed. These were then written by each resident, with the help of the other residents and the named nurse, on request. Residents and nurses reviewed the plans, including specific goals, in weekly 'care plan groups', at which each individual's achievements and problems were discussed. At one point, the Betty Neuman Model was used to inform this process. This model of nursing is relevant to therapeutic communities, in its emphasis on the resident's perspectives and the development of existing and new coping strategies. It also examines individuals' problems in family and social contexts (Neuman 1995).

Whilst there may be some conflict with the group approach, planned, individualised nursing care can be used to ensure that the therapeutic community is sensitive to each person's needs, related to her/his ethnic origin and culture, religion, gender, sexual orientation, physical abilities and specific physical health needs. Eliciting, and making improvements, based on residents' views, is particularly important. Nurses can learn a great deal from views expressed by mental health survivors movements and from residents' experiences of therapeutic communities.

Maintenance of safe boundaries and democratic leadership

Therapeutic communities have been criticised for 'pretending' to be democratic, but with staff 'really' in control (Chamberlin 1988). However, all therapeutic communities operate within boundaries and these need to be made clear to residents and staff. Most NHS therapeutic communities have guidelines explaining their boundaries and prohibited behaviours, usually including illicit drugs and physical violence.

Maxwell Jones made it clear that therapeutic community staff never abrogate their responsibilities. Nurses' sharing of decision-making and responsibility with residents needs to be within constraints of the law, professional accountability, agreed policies and the requirements of both senior managers and the particular needs of residents. Nurses, particularly those working in secure therapeutic communities, have to ensure that residents and other people are not put at risk and that illegal behaviour does not occur.

Nursing management in therapeutic communities requires democratic leadership, which shares with residents 'as much responsibility and authority as they are competent to manage' (Jones 1980, p.34). Often residents benefit from, and can manage, various responsibilities. At other times, particularly when many are newly admitted, or going through considerable crisis, nurses may need to provide more direction. For example, if a task needs to be completed, a nurse might make a start on it and invite residents to be involved.

Managers and staff need to be clear about taking decisive action, occasionally unilateral if necessary, if residents or other people are at risk from illegal or physically aggressive behaviours. In such circumstances, UKCC requirements that patients are not at risk of harm should be borne in mind (UKCC 1992; UKCC 1998). On the (usually rare) occasions when unilateral decisions are made, managers and staff would normally explain the reasons for their actions and listen carefully to residents' views.

CONCLUSION

Both residents and nursing staff have made vital contributions to therapeutic communities and their development. Despite the closure of some communities and the replacement of the therapeutic community approach by other treatment settings and methods, there have been developments in therapeutic community nursing practice and theory.

Democratic analytic therapeutic communities provide a specialist service for people with specific problems, but many therapeutic community principles can, and it is proposed, should, be applied in *all* residential and inpatient mental health services. Everyone has the right to treatment in a beneficial social environment; and, within the parameters of safety, to be able to express feelings and views, engage in fulfilling activities and participate in decisions affecting their lives.

REFERENCES

Barefoot, P. (1992) 'Psychiatric wards in DGHs? An architect's comments.' *Psychiatric Bulletin 16*, 99–100.

Barnes, E. (1968) *Psychosocial Nursing. Studies from the Cassel Hospital.* London: Tavistock.

Barton, R. (1959) *Institutional Neurosis.* Bristol: John Wright.

Byrt, R. (1993) 'Moral minefield.' *Nursing Times 89*, 8, 63–66.

Caudill, W. (1958) *The Psychiatric Hospital as a Small Society.* Cambridge, MA: Harvard University Press.

Chamberlin, J. (1988) *On Our Own. Patient-Controlled Alternatives to the Mental Health System.* London: MIND Publications.

Chapman, G.E. (1992) 'Nursing in therapeutic communities.' In J.I. Brooking, S.A.H. Ritter, and B.L. Thomas (eds) *A Textbook of Psychiatric and Mental Health Nursing.* Edinburgh: Churchill Livingstone.

Chiesa, M. (1997) 'A combined in-patient/out-patient programme for severe personality disorders.' *Therapeutic Communities 18*, 4, 297–309.

Clark, D.H. (1996) *The Story of a Mental Hospital. Fulbourn 1858–1983.* London: Process Press.

Cullen, E., Jones, L. and Woodward, R. (1997) *Therapeutic Communities for Offenders.* Chichester: Wiley.

Cumming, J. and Cumming, E. (1962) *Ego and Milieu: Theory and Practice of Environmental Therapy.* New York: Atherton Press.

DoH (1994) *Working in Partnership: A Collaborative Approach to Care.* Report of the Mental Health Nursing Review Team, chaired by Professor T. Butterworth. London: HMSO.

Foucault, M. (1967) *Madness and Civilisation: A History of Insanity in the Age of Reason.* London: Tavistock.

Goffman, E. (1968) *Asylums. Essays on the Social Situation of Mental Patients and Others.* Harmondsworth: Penguin.

Hayward, P. and Bright, J.A. (1997) 'Stigma and mental illness: a review and critique.' *Journal of Mental Health 6*, 4, 345–354.

Higgins, B. (1997) 'Does anyone feel they need support tonight? Twenty-four hour care on a day unit.' *Therapeutic Communities, 18*, 1, 55–61.

Irwin, F. (1995) 'The therapeutic ingredients of baking a cake.' *Therapeutic Communities 16*, 4, 263–268.

Jones, K. (1993) *Asylums and After. A Revised History of the Mental Health Services from the Early Eighteenth Century to the Nineteen Nineties.* London: The Athlone Press.

Jones, L. (1997) 'Developing models for managing treatment integrity and efficacy in a prison-based therapeutic community: the Max Glatt Centre.' In E. Cullen, L. Jones and R. Woodward, *Therapeutic Communities for Offenders.* Chichester: Wiley.

Jones, M. (1968a) *Beyond the Therapeutic Community. Social Learning and Social Psychiatry.* New Haven: Yale University Press.

Jones, M. (1968b) *Social Psychiatry in Practice. The Idea of the Therapeutic Community.* Harmondsworth: Penguin.

Jones, M. (1979) 'The therapeutic community, social learning and social change.' In R.D. Hinshelwood and N.P. Manning (eds) *Therapeutic Communities: Reflections and Progress.* London: Routledge and Kegan Paul.

Jones, M. (1980) 'Desirable features of a therapeutic community in a prison.' In H. Toch (ed) *Therapeutic Communities in Corrections.* New York: Praeger.

Jones, M., Baker, A., Freeman, T., Merry, J., Pomryn, B.A., Sandler, J., and Tuxford, J. (1952) *Social Psychiatry. A Study of Therapeutic Communities.* London: Tavistock.

Kennard, D. (1983) *An Introduction to Therapeutic Communities.* London: Routledge and Kegan Paul.

Kennedy, R., Heymans, A. and Tischler, L. (eds) (1986) *The Family as In-Patient. Working with Families and Adolescents at the Cassel Hospital.* London: Free Association Books.

McCaffrey, G. (1998) 'The use of leisure activities in a therapeutic community.' *Journal of Psychiatric and Mental Health Nursing* 5, 1, 53–58.

McGauley, G. (1997) 'A delinquent in the therapeutic community: actions speak louder than words.' In E.V. Welldon and C. Van Velsen (eds) *A Practical Guide to Forensic Psychotherapy.* London: Jessica Kingsley.

Main, T. (1957) 'The ailment.' *British Journal of Medical Psychology 30*, 3, 129–145. Reprinted in E. Barnes, (1968) *Psychosocial Nursing: Studies from The Cassel Hospital.* London: Tavistock.

Manning, N.P. (1989) *The Therapeutic Community Movement: Charisma and Routinisation.* London: Routledge.

Martin, D.V. (1962) *Adventure in Psychiatry.* Oxford: Cassirer.

Neuman, B. (1995) *The Neuman Systems Model. Third Edition.* Norwalk, CT: Appleton and Lange.

Nolan, P. (1993) *A History of Mental Health Nursing.* London: Chapman and Hall.

Norton, K. and Hinshelwood, R. (1996) 'Severe personality disorder: treatment issues and selection for inpatient psychotherapy.' *British Journal of Psychiatry 168*, 6, 723–731.

Rapoport, R.N. with Rapoport, R. and Rosow, I. (1960) *Community as Doctor. New Perspectives on a Therapeutic Community.* London: Tavistock.

Ratigan, B. and Aveline, M. (1988) 'Interpersonal group therapy.' Chapter 3 in M. Aveline and W. Dryden (eds) *Group Therapy in Britain.* Milton Keynes: Open University Press.

Reiss, D., Grubin, D. and Meux, C. (1996) 'Young 'psychopaths' in special hospital: treatment and outcome.' *British Journal of Psychiatry 168*, 1, 99–104.

Ritter, S. (1997) 'Taking stock of psychiatric nursing.' In S. Tilley (ed) *The Mental Health Nurse. Views of Practice and Education.* Oxford: Blackwell Science.

Robinson, D. (1996) 'Measuring psychiatric nursing interventions: how much care is individualised?' *Nursing Times Research 1*, 1, 13–21.

Rogers, C. (1967) *On Becoming a Person. A Therapist's View of Psychotherapy.* London: Constable.

Scull, A.T. (1979) *Museums of Madness. The Social Organisation of Insanity in Nineteenth Century England.* London: Allen Lane.

Skellern, E. (1955) 'A therapeutic community.' *Nursing Times*, April – June. Cited in Rapoport, R.N. *et al.* (1960), *Community as Doctor. New Perspectives on a Therapeutic Community*. London: Tavistock.

Stanton, A.H. and Schwartz, M.S. (1954) *The Mental Hospital*. New York: Basic Books.

Stuart, G.W. and Sundeen, S.J. (1995) *Principles and Practice of Psychiatric Nursing*. Fifth edition. St Louis: Mosby.

UKCC (1992) *Code of Professional Conduct for the Nurse, Midwife and Health Visitor*. London: UKCC.

UKCC (1998) *Guidelines for Mental Health and Learning Disability Nursing. A Guide to Working With Vulnerable Clients*. London: UKCC.

Whiteley, J.S. (1980) 'The Henderson Hospital: a community study.' *International Journal of Therapeutic Communities, 1*, 1:38–57.

Wing, J. and Brown, G. (1970) *Institutionalism and Schizophrenia. A Comparative Study of Three Mental Hospitals, 1960–1968*. London: Cambridge University Press.

ACKNOWLEDGEMENTS

My thanks to Dr Penny Campling and Heidi Carnell for their suggestions, Chris Lomas for his support, library staff at De Montfort and Leicester Universities; and particularly, to the many former residents and staff of therapeutic communities, which I have worked in or visited, and who have taught me so much.

PART II

Modern Practice

CHAPTER 6

Joining and Leaving
Processing Separation, Loss and Re-Attachment
Kingsley Norton

EDITORS' INTRODUCTION

Kingsley Norton has been Clinical Director at Henderson Hospital since 1989. Prior to this he was a consultant psychiatrist at Sutton Hospital and lecturer in the Academic Department of Psychiatry of St George's Hospital. He is an analytical psychologist (a Jungian analyst trained at the Society of Analytical Psychology in London). As a medical student, in the 1970s, he had applied to Henderson Hospital to do vacation work, but was turned down by the then Medical Director!

Despite major closure threats, Henderson Hospital has maintained its high profile under Kingsley Norton's leadership. It has produced a number of descriptive and research-based papers which have played a major role in explaining, enthusing and persuading others of the case for therapeutic communities. In fact, government funding has recently been approved for two new units in Salford and Birmingham which will be based on the Henderson model of treatment.

Issues of bonding and separation are at the heart of our therapeutic work. In this chapter, Kingsley describes how Henderson Hospital residents engage and disengage, and how TC principles can be applied to both the assessment process and continuing care.

Although the general themes apply to all TCs, specific details differ between communities. For example, both the editors feel the use of the Care Programme Approach (CPA) weakens the impetus for patients to take responsibility for themselves. At Henderson, however, a modified form of CPA is incorporated into the leaving process.

A process of separation, loss and re-attachment is involved in both joining and leaving a therapeutic community (TC). How this is experienced and expressed, however, varies from TC to TC and member to member. For example, some new members of Henderson Hospital's residential democratic TC initially appear emotionally unmoved by the change which is implied by joining, while others vividly show their ambivalence and the acute awkwardness and vulnerability of being new.

What follows in this chapter is an impressionistic account of Henderson's ongoing attempts to facilitate its resident members to join and to leave its TC. Only some of these attempts will have relevance to other TCs in terms of structures and processes. Because of this, only the elements which are likely to be generalisable are discussed in detail. The overall aim of the TCs structures and processes, concerning joining and leaving, is to facilitate the grieving process associated with separation and loss. Ideally, the people who leave are better integrated in themselves and, in being more 'joined', also better able to join with others in the future.

JOINING

Candidates for a TC are likely to be ignorant of the social reality of life inside it. How it is described to them will vary, as will the accuracy of any such account. It is truly a difficult task, however, to convey accurately the essence of a TC, since it is so complex and dynamic. Nevertheless, without preparation, in terms of inculcating realistic expectations, joining is likely to be more problematic. This may be particularly so where residential treatment and serious psychological disturbance are involved, as at Henderson. Unrealistically high or other inaccurate expectations set up the actual TC to be a disappointment and thereby jeopardise effective joining. There is a fine line, however, between preparing a candidate for what to expect and pre-empting important learning from an experience of being new.

Preparation

If adequate time is set aside, there are ways of providing a detailed picture of what prospective TC candidates can expect and what will be expected of them. Couched thus, they can be made aware of the active and collaborative nature of the TCs therapeutic endeavour. In addition, information given to candidates can usefully outline both typical and atypical, although not unexpected, happenings. It can suggest similarities to and differences from other institutions with which the candidate may be familiar. Written as well as verbal information can be provided to convey this. At Henderson, there is a brochure, containing relevant information, which is routinely supplied.

Video-taped material can be used to communicate something about the TC, by opening up a range of possibilities to improve authenticity, including interviews with staff and existing or former members. Some of their personal renditions of the social reality of the TC may strike a chord with prospective TC members or in other ways inform, illuminate and interest. However, it should be remembered that, in spite of sincere attempts to convey accurately the essence of the TC, what confronts new members, once they have actually arrived, may still not match their expectations. Thus, attempts to prepare candidates may be in vain, or at least partly so, and the member may still leave prematurely, in an unplanned and unsatisfactory manner. The latter undesirable scenario, may be more often encountered in residential TCs, owing to the fact that future members need to change their actual place of residence and also, to a certain degree, their existing set of relationships with others, even if the latter are largely maladaptive or, in other ways, unsatisfactory. The unhealthy attraction of such relationships, however, may be forceful enough to de-stabilise new attachments.

Reception into the TC

New members are admitted to Henderson Hospital, only on a non-emergency basis and at a single point in the week. In that morning's community meeting, resident members and staff will have been reminded of the new members' salient personal details. Potential problems or other concerns about the new arrivals will be aired, at least that is the intention. In this way the shock associated with 'newness' is minimised for all concerned. To a degree, therefore, joining becomes a predictable event. The more a given TC can exert an influence on the selection, and timing of arrival, of its new members, the more likely the latter are to be stably attached and truly welcomed.

The crossing of the threshold from outside to inside the TC – reception into the unit – can be marked and given importance by the setting up of a special meeting, which occurs at a regular time and place in the weekly programme. Staff and existing members who are made aware, as above, of any less savoury aspects of the new members' histories may temper their welcome. From the standpoint of the new members, who know little or nothing of those welcoming them, the meeting can feel like a one-sided transaction. It can jar with and apparently contradict ideas of co-operation and mutuality, which will have been suggested by the preparatory work. Since the overtly straightforward task of welcoming and introducing to the TC is complex and potentially problematic, the more predictable and orderly it can be made the better.

Introduction to the important rules of the TC, for example, those proscribing violence and alcohol or drug misuse, which can be literally damaging in their effect on the TC, are important to impart early as part of the reception process but they can be conveyed in many ways. Ideally, they are imparted so as to evoke respect rather than to serve as a provocation to breaking them. To minimise the risk of the latter, the various support systems (which new members may require) and social aspects within the TC can be described, even before these important house rules. However, new members are often anxious about where they stand, in terms of what they are or are not allowed to do in this new environment, particularly where rule-breaking is a presenting symptom of their emotional difficulties. New members do therefore need to be clearly informed of the TCs main rules. An inappropriately strong or early emphasising of the systems of support or 'sociotherapy', of course, runs the risk of making the TC sound like a nursing home, hotel, even a holiday camp, with few expectations of its members to try to behave responsibly. On reception, it may also be important to indicate that, in effect, therapy has already begun.

Starting therapy

New members often hold inappropriate or unrealistic expectations about what can be achieved therapeutically. They are usually unsure about how revealing they need to be about themselves, how soon they can expect to experience change and how active they need to be in their own therapy in order to produce it. Therefore, it is wise to inform them that everybody joins at a different pace, few feel at home in the first weeks or even months and most question their own decision to stay, often on a daily basis. At Henderson, a solid engagement in therapy, in terms of meaningful personal disclosure and significant interaction, is often not present until at least three months into the stay.

How soon the new member should be expected to participate in the whole daily routine of the therapeutic community is an issue. On the one hand, an expectation of immediate and full participation may be experienced as helpful and supportive, in facilitating as swift a joining as possible. On the other hand, a gradual introduction to the community may be more kindly. However, some find such a gradual introduction, despite having the aim and outward appearance of being kinder, to be in fact subtly alienating. It can maintain new members in a marginalised position with which many are all too familiar and from which they may find it difficult to progress.

It can help some new members if they take part straight away in the TC's more concrete tasks, for example, those relating to cleaning, washing up or cooking. Even then, some can feel that they are being taken advantage of. Some also feel that their psychosocial strengths and, in particular, their own capacity for providing care and support are being devalued. How soon new members in a democratic model of TC can exercise their voting rights is another issue which needs to be sensitively addressed. Spending the first week just witnessing, but not participating in, the voting system may represent a useful compromise. This is what happens at Henderson.

First groups

It can be helpful for new resident members in the TC to be told that they are unlikely to sleep much during the first night. At Henderson, even if they do go to sleep, they may well be awoken by senior members in order to attend an emergency meeting, or more than one such, in the middle of the night! For some new members, the psychological effect of withdrawal from illicit drugs, prescribed medication or alcohol will be experienced acutely during the first night and ensuing days. Many at Henderson do not heed the advice to gradually withdraw from such substances prior to admission and the joining of the TC.

For most new members at Henderson, the first scheduled therapy group they attend will be the community meeting at 9.15 a.m. on the morning after the day of arrival. This meeting may have as many as 40 people in the room and hence be an intimidating occasion for all but the most extroverted. Most new members have a fear of speaking in so public a forum and of being seen. As a result, some crave invisibility. However, others fear being ignored and find themselves participating actively or even excessively.

It may be difficult, in the first community meeting, for new members to identify and distinguish staff from the other resident members and some can find this to be particularly unsettling. At Henderson, the senior members' style of chairing this meeting can also contribute to the ease, or lack of it, with which new members settle. It varies and does not always follow the protocol of polite society. Swearing and raised voices during the meeting may further unsettle some of the new members, although be familiar to and welcomed by others. It is in this community meeting that voting (via a show of hands, counted by 'tellers') is witnessed - one important marker of the democratic nature of Henderson's therapeutic community.

New members' small group

Following this first community meeting at Henderson there is a small group for the newest resident members, which represents the first meeting of a thrice-weekly small group. This is set up primarily with an educational and supportive purpose, allowing new members to question a more senior member and also staff (who are regularly attached to the group) about any aspects of therapy or practical aspects associated with being new, including 'welfare' issues (see below). New members attend this group for the first three weeks of their stay.

Some new members appear to have grasped all of the essential workings of the TC and its overt structures by the time of their first small group, only their second formal therapy meeting! They even feel sufficiently confident to criticise what they have just witnessed in the community meeting, with an air of knowing far better than established members and staff how the community should be run.

At the other extreme are those who are too timid to ask any questions and who need to be supported or coaxed into speaking at all. Some, at Henderson, seem to gravitate early towards the in-house medical treatment for their physical or psychosomatic symptoms, thereby attempting to establish a 'patient' – staff relationship with which they are more familiar. Some experience a spontaneous remission of all symptoms and question their need for therapy. Others, believing their needs are less pressing than those of the senior TC members, do not feel entitled to any therapy for themselves. Still others are intent on pushing the limits to see whether the community's rules are enforced and, if so, how fairly and consistently.

At Henderson, those new members who test the TC's tolerance by rule-breaking are able to experience, at first hand, the sharp end of the TC's culture as well as its structure. They seem to need to encounter the whole community's focused attention via being on the receiving end of a discussion and voting system which could order their discharge from the community. Some who break rules do so within a deviant sub-culture of the community, representing superficial and brittle alliances with some of the more senior members. This seems to allow them to avoid the ignominy of being seen to struggle to join a 'therapeutic' mainstream.

Some members strive to avoid any rule-breaking, as if such a cautious strategy would inevitably yield a therapeutic result. Others, while not breaking rules, consistently ignore the community's advice, for example they form an intimate and exclusive relationship with another member. In this way, joining the whole community is avoided or, at least, delayed. At Henderson, only a few members, however, strike a balance between rule-breaking and extreme cautiousness, certainly within the first few months.

Attending the thrice-weekly new members' group helps to school members in the TC's weekly routine of therapy. By this means their entry to the small group, which meets at the same times and frequency, is facilitated. This latter small group setting will provide the main dynamic psychotherapy ingredient of the members' stay, where past and current issues are disclosed and discussed. Many of the current issues result from the extensive time for informal social interaction which the residential setting at Henderson affords its members. In this way, the sociotherapeutic and psychotherapeutic ingredients complement one another.

At Henderson, it takes most members a number of months to engage sufficiently to disclose meaningfully their relevant personal and family histories. Unfortunately some will have left the TC long before this stage is reached. Those who have stayed long enough often scare themselves by sustaining more emotional pain than they are used to. However, this provides them with an opportunity to articulate their distress and to try to ask for support from their peers, attempting tentatively to trust others.

LEAVING

Three months before a member's scheduled departure from Henderson, which itself has been negotiated with the rest of the community (up to a maximum of one year after joining), there is a determined focus on leaving. This is represented in part by attending a weekly 'leavers' group (see below). Most members bear the emotional scars of traumatic separations, for example the emergency removal into 'care' or expulsion from school. Few have had a fair chance to experience a planned leaving to a satisfactory destination, which allows for its loss to be both anticipated and also sufficiently mourned. Members thus expect that leaving the TC, to which many have become relatively securely attached, will necessarily be experienced as yet another catastrophic abandonment. Consequently, they discover or invent various means by which to avoid the attendant separation anxiety. These often mirror those deployed to minimise the pain of joining, including a regression to rule-breaking and the establishing of an intimate and exclusive relationship with another resident member. It is likely that similar or equivalent strategies are adopted by those members leaving other TCs.

Welfare group

At Henderson there are welfare groups which can be attended up to three times per week. They are primarily set up to provide members, especially those who are leaving the TC, with opportunities to sort out practical tasks related to the outside world, for example, finances, benefits, access to children, suitable accommodation or employment. Discussion in the 'after-group', immediately following the welfare group, potentially enables an integrating of relevant emotional aspects with the practical tasks.

The welfare group, like many others, frequently embodies extremes of view and, sometimes, oscillations between these. Thus members can feel totally dependent or else totally independent, either powerless or omnipotent, within a relatively short space of time. They tend to view their problems as either solely practical or simply emotional, but may veer between the two. The outside world is also viewed in terms of extremes, usually as totally negative and rejecting compared to the idealised world of the TC but sometimes vice versa.

One of the tasks for Henderson's staff in the welfare group is to facilitate members to achieve and sustain a more balanced and intermediate position between the above extremes. This is not easy to accomplish, since staff themselves are also perceived, especially by those members who are leaving, to be either completely useless or else with magical powers to effect, at will, almost anything. Staff in the welfare group thus try to 'surf the interface' (personal communication – Meg Winterbotham, social worker) between the members' polarised views, in order to help them to more accurately test reality.

During discussions in the welfare group, much remembering of past leavings and losses goes on. This enables members to make comparisons with the present and thereby also to evaluate the actual progress they have made during their period of TC residence at Henderson. It can help them to develop a more accurate and integrated sense of themselves, which includes strengths as well as weaknesses. Group discussion can serve to enrich, for example, the process of applying for 'disability' benefits, through the requirement for members realistically to evaluate and describe their weaknesses and needs. Members can then begin to avoid seeing themselves as either totally disabled or else not disabled at all and to identify what are their actual needs for after-care supports of various kinds.

The above principles are likely to apply, to some degree, to any TC. The task for staff is to facilitate an accurate appraisal of members' needs, regardless of the actual size of their needs.

Leavers' group

Henderson's leavers' group (whose staffing is designed to overlap with that of 'welfare' groups in order to maximise communication) is set up to aid the emotional processing of leaving (Parker 1989). Many senior members need the cajoling of Henderson's Community for them to join this group, which also means vacating their small group for one session per week. Such a concrete shift in their weekly routine sends an early and undeniable signal of impending separation. It warns that leaving really will take place. This can be shocking. Some resist joining 'leavers', as if to dispense magically with the actual leaving.

The discovery, at this stage, that members' presenting maladaptive behaviour, such as violence (to self or others) or drug and alcohol misuse, is still an option, can also be shocking. A number of senior members thus unconsciously 'regress' to such behaviour, as if tacitly challenging the rest of the community to focus on such an aspect and to disregard positive achievements made earlier. In most such instances, the community is not easily fooled into believing that no real progress has been made and the senior members will often receive very balanced feedback (not necessarily politely delivered), identifying their relevant strengths but also ongoing weaknesses and difficulties. Senior members, finding that their familiar maladaptive behaviour does not have its previous pay-off, in terms of personal reward or interpersonal effect on others, often view this discovery ambivalently. They are relieved to have a marker of adaptive change but anxious lest their new-found alternative ways of coping with distress will be unavailable or inadequate for them post-discharge.

Themes from the leavers' group are fed back to the rest of the community via a meeting. This is relevant since it helps the leavers to feel that they have not been overlooked, especially in favour of newer residents. It also serves to remind others of the importance and difficulty of the leaving process. Leavers often resent, however, such an open forum in which to acknowledge both their senior status and vulnerability. Those not currently leaving can observe all of this, from a relatively safe emotional distance. Having a structure and process which keeps everybody in touch with the relevant leaving issues and themes would seem to be important in any TC setting.

Leaving can feel quite traumatic for the whole TC, especially when there is regression to self-harming or other aggressive behaviour. Not uncommonly, those leaving express a strong desire to go before their scheduled time. They often have a fierce sense that they will be forgotten in any case or that the TC, and the relationships it embodies for them, will disappear from their memory without trace.

At Henderson, the amount of grieving for ex-members, at least that which is displayed and discussed in the community meeting, is surprisingly low. The reasons for this are not clear and may be largely to do with defensiveness. It may be that the grieving is very incomplete and/or that there is too much current community business to allow time to mourn openly in the more formal elements of the therapeutic programme.

Reviews

Ideally, members receive feedback from the rest of the TC members on a daily basis throughout their stay. In practice, at Henderson, the most relevant and important feedback is scattered relatively thinly. Additional focused feedback derives from 'votes', which follow infringements of the community's rules, and from scheduled reviews, at five and ten months. The latter take place within an especially convened small group of resident members and staff which is followed by a further, more 'public', feedback and discussion session, involving the whole community. The ten months' review feedback is well placed to identify unfinished emotional or practical business associated with the leaving process, as well as progress which has been made. Self-assessments and Care Programme Approach (CPA) meetings also afford this opportunity.

The last week

Members' last week of therapy at Henderson is heralded in the community meeting and there is a space for them to say something about their state of mind at this juncture. The rest of the community is thereby reminded of the impending leaving and the loss it represents, in case it had slipped the communal mind! The last day of therapy is similarly highlighted and, again, an agenda item in the community meeting relates to it. Within the final community meeting, members who are leaving are expected to say something about themselves and their stay in the TC. What and how much is actually said varies greatly. One member carried out a non-verbal enactment to music but this was unusual and the format has not been repeated. Mostly, it is a relatively sober interchange, sometimes with an exchange of presents, and often with much feeling.

Many members avoid saying goodbye to those who are leaving, in the community meeting, preferring to do this more privately, either completely away from formal groups or else in a smaller group setting. Staff therefore, need to be careful about whether and how they interpret what might appear to be a denial of real interpersonal involvement or of grieving of the impending loss. Overall, the importance of leaving Henderson's TC is strongly stressed throughout a member's stay and leaving is a sufficiently commonplace occurrence to provide the community with ample reminders of its true significance.

Aftercare

Leaving the TC involves looking forward as well as back. At Henderson there is an Outreach Service which can respond to, usually in collaboration with another service, some of the psychological treatment needs of ex-members. Geographical considerations, however, dictate that such a service is only practical for those living in the south east of England. Others need to organise aftercare with the relevant professionals in the area in which they plan to live.

Completing the CPA procedure is usually a relevant part of leaving the Henderson, which the residents themselves are encouraged to initiate, as part of the ethos of their empowerment and the exercising of their personal responsibility. This opportunity may be resisted, with the expectation that staff will take over. Such resistance often stems from members' ambivalence about leaving the TC and doubts about their capacity to survive outside in the wider community with a much lower level of peer support.

Peer pressure from both welfare and leavers' groups, together with that from other formal and informal elements of the therapy programme, usually ensure that members attend to practical post-discharge arrangements. Sometimes the relevant discussions are fraught, perhaps representing another form of 'regression' to previous irresponsible or self-defeating methods of coping and relating. Ideally, such difficulties and struggles are communicated to both the wider community meeting and to the relevant small group, where the issues can be addressed in terms of their personal meaning to the TC member concerned.

Conclusion

There is a certain symmetry to a resident TC member's completed stay in Henderson Hospital's TC, since both joining and leaving involve separation, loss and the anticipation of an uncertain future. Reflecting this, there are structural elements, for example, small group therapy meetings, welfare and leavers' groups, which are especially set up to process the emotional and practical needs of those joining and leaving. Since real practical issues involved in joining or leaving may obscure psychological distress and vice versa, staff need to be aware that only one such aspect may be presented by members, thereby masking the importance of the other. The staff's role, therefore, is to try to allow for both emotional and practical aspects to be acknowledged during the crucial phases of joining and leaving.

Some resident members deny or attempt to avoid the full emotional impact of leaving by organising, and sometimes obtaining, an inappropriately high level of therapeutic input. Fostering a full discussion in the community meeting, to decide what is an appropriate level of aftercare, may be the best course of action when there is any doubt about whether or how much aftercare is really required. In practice, it is important to avoid extremes of too much or too little. Too much aftercare may remove the potential for an adequate processing of the experience of separation from, and loss of, the TC, and too little may be traumatising and undermine future attachments and resettlement into the wider community.

REFERENCES

Parker, M. (1989) 'Managing separation: The Henderson Hospital leavers' group.' *International Journal of Therapeutic Communities 10*, 1, 5–15.

ACKNOWLEDGEMENTS

I wish to thank members of the Henderson staff team for their valuable comments and suggestions, in particular: Michele Barbour, Danka Gordon, Maggie Hilton and Meg Winterbotham.

CHAPTER 7

Boundaries
Discussion of a Difficult Transition
Penelope Campling

EDITORS' INTRODUCTION

This chapter was more of a struggle to write than I had anticipated. After many discarded pages about authority, rules, subgroups and the like, I found myself writing about death.

I am indebted to George Spaul, my predecessor and founder of Francis Dixon Lodge. He left me with many pearls of wisdom, always emphasised the importance of boundaries and talked about failings but never lost the twinkle in his eye for very long.

I am also grateful to Bob Hobson for his candour in writing about catastrophe, particularly in 'the Messianic Community' (Hobson 1979), thus contributing to a culture of openness where we can share bad times as well as achievements; a culture that will hopefully remain a feature of the therapeutic community movement.

It was Hobson's hope that sharing his painful journey might assist others in diagnosing what he called the 'therapeutic community disease', where ideology is idealised and difference cannot be tolerated.

Disturbed patients can be thought of as primarily struggling with boundary pathology. Almost all of our residents at Francis Dixon Lodge (FDL), for example, suffered violation of boundaries as children – with physical, sexual or emotional abuse. Much of their presenting symptomatology continues both to express their problem with boundaries and to violate them further – cutting or burning themselves, abusing substances, overdosing, starving, bingeing and inducing vomiting, slipping into psychosis or violently breaking the law. Feelings are experienced so intensely, that they overwhelm the individual's fragile integrity. Pathological boundaries develop that are either too permeable, leading to chaos and destructiveness, or too rigid, leading to emotional impoverishment and meaninglessness. Either can lead to suicide.

Pines (1994) described borderline patients as having difficulty managing boundaries between internal and external reality, self and other, self and group, consciousness and unconsciousness, role and person and past and present.

Much of psychiatry is aimed at direct control of the patients' boundaries, for example, with medication or by encouraging dependency on nursing staff. In therapeutic communities, we discourage unhelpful dependency on professionals, with all the problems this can entail, by focusing our attention less on individual patients and more on the community as a whole. Boundary management is thus concerned with the system, with creating and sustaining a healthy milieu, within which individuals can explore more flexible personal boundaries, and hopefully develop and internalise them.

Boundary management is thus fundamental to our work and has two intermeshed purposes. First, it is concerned with the organisational dynamic, about maintaining a healthy social system or milieu within which the primary task can be addressed and healing work can take place. Second, it is about creating a healthy, secure structure which can be psychologically internalised by individuals. In other words, the boundaries of an organisation have the power to directly effect and change the personality structure of all its members. In a therapeutic community we harness this potential, and the analysis and management of boundaries are seen as integral to therapy. In the language of systems theory, we are working in a sociotechnical system where the social system is part of the technology. Boundary management is therefore not just concerned with getting the best out of the organisation and its members, but with fundamental structural change.

This is perhaps most obvious when things go badly. Therapeutic community literature is full of examples of how major boundary changes, for example moving premises, affect the group dynamic and individual states of mind. Perhaps the most difficult event a therapeutic community has to cope with is a change of leadership. The rest of this chapter is a discussion of four tragic deaths of patients that had previously been at FDL, following George Spaul's retirement six years ago. It is a painful chapter in our history, but I think illustrates the complexities involved and the idea that boundary management is about survival itself.

None of the individuals were resident at FDL at the time of death, but they had all been residents in the few months leading up to and following the change of consultant, when George Spaul retired and I took his place, and they died within 18 months of leaving FDL. Only one death was officially categorised as suicide, but they were all young adults with histories of extreme self-destructive behaviour including serious suicide attempts. None of the four were under our care at the time of death, and two of them had received psychiatric care elsewhere in the intervening period. We were not held accountable by those outside FDL and did not have to suffer the further disrupting effects of an enquiry. Nevertheless, the deaths were mourned and caused considerable agonising in the staff team. Much of what follows is derived from staff team discussion. It is a subjective account, and any link between events is hypothetical and unprovable, and the whole subject awash with uncertainty.

The chapter examines boundaries at various levels, emphasising the links between intrapsychic, interpersonal and organisational dynamics, the exploration of which is integral to our work.

INDIVIDUAL RESPONSIBILITY

Issues of responsibility are at the heart of boundary problems, from the making and enforcing of rules to the disentangling of complex transference and counter-transference dynamics. At the heart of the therapeutic community movement is the idea that residents can take significant responsibility for themselves, and weighing up this capacity is an important part of the assessment. (Of course, this is modified depending on the client group.) At the same time however, we believe that all members of the community have responsibility for each other, and much day to day work is concerned with the conflict between individual and group responsibility. Meanwhile, psychiatric professionals are increasingly seen as responsible for their patients; not just for treating their illness and working with them to the best of their professional judgement and ability, but responsible for keeping them alive and stopping them harming other people. Even without the introduction of the Care Programme Approach (CPA) and the Supervision Register, professionals working in 'people-changing institutions' tend to be over ambitious in their objectives. The result is chronic overwork, chronic disappointment, low satisfaction and high stress (Menzies 1979). At the same time, professionals working in a therapeutic community have to manage the conflict between professional accountability and investing power in the community.

During the months following the deaths, various members of the community, particularly staff members, felt overwhelmingly responsible and burdened by guilt. There was also anger and blame. Each death had a knock-on effect, particularly amongst the network of ex-residents. Many of them started to attend our weekly out-patient group, pouring out their grief and rage at FDL for letting such awful events happen. For some, the rage and despair felt overwhelming; increasingly they made phone calls in the middle of the night leaving staff feeling both helpless and desperately anxious. Although sensible things were said about the limits of our responsibility, it was many months before we could see things objectively enough to consider referring these ex-residents on to other professionals, an action which in the short term, of course, attracted even more rage and destructiveness.

It may be that suicide is contagious, that like any form of violation, crossing the boundary between life and death, leaves other vulnerable personalities feeling it is a real possibility. One of the more frightening aspects of working in a large group with disturbed people is the way self-destructive behaviour can escalate very rapidly. At FDL, for example, we had a spate of individuals inflicting ugly cuts on their faces, people who had previously confined cutting to their wrists. More obviously, grief for the deceased may simply tip the balance for our very vulnerable residents' personalities, opening up deep losses from their insecure pasts.

For the staff team, it may be that grief over the deaths distorted our usual boundaries concerning the limits of our professional responsibility. Our acutely tuned patients would then have picked up on our rising anxiety levels. It can be deeply antitherapeutic for those tempted to self-harm, to sense that someone else holds themselves responsible for their behaviour.

In the face of high anxiety levels and the prevalent 'culture of blame', it is tempting to talk in black and white terms about the limit of our responsibility. To over-categorise the event and leave it neatly packaged and boundaried, merely pushes uncomfortable feelings into the community's unconscious. An inflated sense of failed responsibility is part of the grieving process. It can be recognised as such but cannot be short cut. Nevertheless, it is important to hang on to a balanced perspective in order to have a boundary that is meaningful enough to incorporate psychological reality. On a personal level, I have found it useful to distinguish between saying, 'I fail' and 'I am a failure'; and am indebted to Hobson's writing on the subject (Hobson 1979). As the clinical manager it was vital to remind the community of the constantly changing group dynamic, and refocus the team on the primary task – maintaining the unit as a 'therapeutic community', thus ensuring the survival of the enterprise as a whole.

THE INTEGRITY OF THE GROUP

It is notoriously difficult for any organisation to adjust to a change of leadership. Much has been written and conferences devoted to the subject. Some therapeutic communities, it must be said, have not survived such a change. Perhaps the most difficult transition is that following the departure of the first leader, the founder of the community, by definition a pioneer, charismatic enough to energise and enthuse a team to enter exciting new territory. Such a person inspires love and loyalty, and inevitably becomes idealised.

Transitions rarely run smoothly and go to plan. At FDL, George Spaul, the founder and much-loved consultant, was catapulted into retirement by ill health earlier than anticipated. I was drafted in as a locum for six months; George Spaul then returned for six months, still not well and on sick leave for much of the time, until he finally retired and I was appointed on a temporary contract. Feelings about the transition were therefore intensified by his illness, possible death and the long months of uncertainty about the future. Apart from this, there were differences about our styles of leadership, including the obvious ones such as age and gender. The community were deeply split. Many members of the community, particularly the longer-standing members of staff, experienced the sense of loss as overwhelming and found it difficult to imagine FDL surviving. They wanted things to stay the same and resented differences in my style and approach. Others were impatient for change.

'Rivalries and destructive alliances (e.g., patients versus staff or subgroups of each) can represent a relative disintegration which leads to a new differentiated and yet integrated state' (Hobson 1979, p.234). It is this process which I shall attempt to discuss: a process of boundaries collapsing under pressure, before they could be reformed, to make FDL, once again, a firmly safe and therapeutic environment.

The main focus of our work at FDL is the large group whose boundaries require constant vigilance if its integrity is to be maintained. There is no formal one to one therapy, and no system of keyworkers. Residents are discouraged from exclusively pouring their hearts out to individuals and crises are dealt with by calling a 'crisis group'. New residents and staff often find this system strange, even harsh, longing for the immediate gratification of a cosy one to one and often missing the 'special' relationship they had enjoyed with someone in a previous setting. Of course, 'special' relationships do develop with important transferential meaning, but the intensity of the transferences can be managed more easily in a group setting where there are always other voices, other perspectives and other people around to support and challenge. In a healthy community, the large group is valued and seen as providing a safe and creative place for psychological exploration. In order to sustain this dynamic, all members of the community need to be aware of rules and expectations, and feel part of the process in which these are made and enforced.

Perhaps the most important rule and the most difficult to enforce is that regarding confidentiality. All conversations within the large group must be regarded by its members as absolutely confidential, with no information passed to outsiders without the informed permission of those concerned. On the other hand, individual confidences spoken outside the groups are not respected and much work is done explaining the reason for this and encouraging such secrets to be brought into the large group, where communication should be as open and frank as possible. Confidentiality is as fundamental to the psycho-therapeutic process, as an aseptic technique is to surgery, and needs as much effort and vigilance to ensure that all members understand and respect why the boundary is drawn where it is. (Where individual or small group therapy is part of the regime, rules and expectations regarding confidentiality will be different but equally important.)

In a situation such as that described at FDL, where the community is deeply split, these boundaries can begin to break down. Individuals, feeling unheard or misunderstood, start discussing the content of meetings in other forums, most obviously within sub-groups of the community, but sometimes with partners and friends outside. Others will tell their 'secrets' to individuals, often 'favourite' staff members, rather than the group, with whom they have lost faith. Because of the splits in the staff team, the polarisation and the high levels of anxiety, staff members will be more susceptible than usual to holding such confidences, seduced by the idea of being 'special' and more understanding then others in the team. (For further discussion of this dynamic, the reader is referred to a classic paper, 'The Ailment': Main 1957). The large group is then made up of many highly anxious individuals, some holding information about others, the informers feeling guilty, confused and suspicious wondering who knows what, and the listeners, burdened and powerful. As the splits deepen, anger mounts and feels dangerous to express. The group becomes more silent and empty and the level of persecutory anxiety rises. Individuals start to 'act out', missing groups, arriving late and falling asleep; and even these signs of disturbance cannot be interpreted because the group now feels so unsafe. Rules are broken in an increasingly violent manner.

It should be said that the group is always under pressure to disintegrate in this way. Our residents arrive with deep splits within themselves and are at first only able to communicate this unconsciously, by imposing their internal reality (through projective identification) on to the new network of relationships. The majority, for example, have been sexually abused, usually within an incestuous family. Betrayal, forced secrecy, and confused roles, have been significant factors in their development and become part of their pathology. Any splits in the community, particularly the staff team, will therefore be exploited, potentially growing worse in the process and further damaging individual members.

It is useful to think in terms of the feelings and process in the staff team mirroring that in the resident community and vice versa. Important information can be gleaned from this: when one group feels completely stuck, it may be that work can be done in another setting which will move things on. Staff supervision is obviously fundamental. At FDL, this occurs at many levels, but most importantly, includes staff away days, with the whole team present and an external supervisor. It is also important, I believe, to have a clear hierarchy (flattened of course!): at FDL, I am consultant and clinical director, accountable to the chief executive of the Trust; and officially line manage the whole team. Although senior nurses collaborate in Trust nursing initiatives, they are clearly not managed by the nursing hierarchy outside FDL.

Obviously there will be splits and factions and sub-groups in any team. It is diversity of opinion and the lack of a silencing hierarchy which can make working in a therapeutic community such an enriching, creative experience. Differences should be voiced as overtly as possible. A team of staff coming from different perspectives but working together in the large group can be enormously therapeutic, challenging the residents' polarised view of the world. If this is replaced by pseudo-mutuality and stagnant ritual, residents will quickly sense the lack of genuineness. On the other hand, there must be clarity and consensus about the basic ethos. Most therapeutic communities have a small number of absolute rules, for example, which cannot be negotiated by the community. Isolated members of the team are vulnerable, particularly those who do not attend many community meetings; this can include part-timers or those working nights. Supervision needs to be comprehensive and cover all shift patterns.

I have described the disintegration and rebuilding of group boundaries from the perspective of a particularly difficult transition period, but in fact much of that described occurs on a day to day basis. There are always splits within the community, even within the staff team and the task is to keep working with differences, so that growth and healing can take place.

EXTERNAL SUPPORT AND CHANGE

It is recognised that the prognosis of a therapeutic community is much dependent on its structure being respected and supported by the higher management system within which it operates. FDL was far from secure in this way at the time George Spaul retired. A number of therapeutic communities had recently closed and resources increasingly concentrated on the chronically mentally ill. Community care was being rapidly developed and in-patient care was seen as expensive and out of fashion. The pendulum in psychiatry was moving towards more control with the introduction of Care Programme Approach (CPA) dictating a particular type of paternalistic doctor–patient relationship. George Spaul's retirement would have been an ideal time to close the unit, and indeed, this was being much discussed. I was appointed for the first nine months on a temporary contract with a big question mark hanging over the future of the unit, little appreciation of the work and much misunderstanding and concern about our practice.

It was difficult to know where to focus our energy. Resources were minimal. The building was scruffy and unattractive and staffing levels dangerously low. The external environment was changing rapidly. The NHS reforms had just been introduced, adding to the mounting levels of bureaucracy and raising anxiety about referrals being funded. With the internal market, came the 'counting the cost' culture. Everything had a price. This was a difficult ethos in which to create the accepting, permissive, affirming environment of a therapeutic community.

The mental health service was about to become a Trust and corporate values were being pushed with evangelical zeal. Protocols were being produced for every eventuality with the underlying belief that all units in the Trust should be approaching problems in the same way. There was pressure to brighten up our shop window, send in 'good news' stories, and show off to managers on their increasingly frequent visits; and little understanding that our work was to help residents face their most ugly, terrifying and tragic experiences and stick with the feelings that arise. We were increasingly required to 'play the game'; to play lip service to the latest innovation, to fill in forms with answers that would cause minimum fuss. In such a way does bureaucracy breed cynicism and corrupt attempts to build genuine relationships.

All these external changes affected both our professional boundaries and the integrity of the group. Managers in the Trust required more information about our residents. 'Critical incidents' had to be reported to them and 'missing persons' reported to the police. This left less scope for the community to manage crises and less potential for individuals within the community to discover their strengths.

Too much change can destabilise and distract from the primary task. Another emerging conflict was how much to involve the community with external changes. To involve them with all that was going on would have completely swamped the clinical agenda, but not involving them meant a loss of democracy and a restriction of the information available to them. Increasingly, I acted as a buffer in the dialogue with higher management freeing the rest of the team to practise an appropriate 'maternal preoccupation' with our residents; for it is hard to combine a state of mind delicately tuned to the unconscious needs of patients, with the rather macho world of NHS management at that time. This inevitably led to some misunderstandings between myself and the team.

Many of the changes or threatened changes have not been helpful and precious energy has been expended in our stand against them. Compromises have been made. In all this, it has been important to establish a 'bottom line'; fundamental boundaries that have to be respected if FDL is to be what it claims, both 'therapeutic' and a 'community'.

The insecurity, preoccupation with survival, together with the rapid pace of imposed change, could not help but distract from our care of residents: it may have contributed in an indirect way to the deaths, and our capacity to manage them. Perhaps the most obvious link was the pressure to fill our beds and prove ourselves economically viable. The introduction of the 'internal market' combined with our already uncertain future, and perhaps a need to prove ourselves with a new leader, may have induced us to accept residents who were too disturbed for our unit. The importance of tough selection criteria is stressed in the literature and is cited as a factor in the closure of some therapeutic communities. A wide and long-term perspective needs to be taken – with economic efficiency seen as linked with, but secondary to, clinical efficiency.

Looking back, the time of upheaval described has led to many positive changes. In particular, the boundary between FDL and the external system now incorporates a greater degree of openness. This has resulted in us being clearer about what we do and better able to communicate this to potential stakeholders. We understand more about the anxiety, both conscious and unconscious, that FDL causes those outside, and we manage it better. Staff are more outward looking, more able to foresee and prepare for potential threats to our way of working, and more willing to access a support network. Perhaps our fears are based more on reality and less suffused by fantasy. Most important, we are more confident about what we do, clearer about our objectives, and increasingly realistic in our expectations.

SUMMARY

This chapter has discussed the problem of boundaries from the perspective of a tragic series of events linked to the TC in which I work. The problem facing us is how best to help our patients without harming them in the process. I suggest the key to this work is a practice and supervisory structure constantly refocusing on the study of boundaries.

REFERENCES

Hobson R.F. (1979) 'The Messianic community.' In R.D. Hinshelwood and N. Manning (eds) *Therapeutic Communities. Reflections and Progress.* London: Routledge and Kegan Paul.

Main T.F. (1957) 'The ailment.' *British Journal of Medical Psychology 1957 30,* 129–145.

Menzies I. (1979) 'Staff support systems: task and anti-task in adolescent institutions.' In R.D. Hinshelwood and N. Manning (eds) *Therapeutic Communities. Reflections and Progress.* London: Routledge and Kegan Paul.

Pines M. (1994) 'Borderline phenomena in analytic groups.' In V.C. Schermer and M. Pines (eds) *Ring of Fire.* London: Routledge.

CHAPTER 8

Ethics and Consent
Trying to Get it Right When it is So Easy to Get it Wrong
Jane Knowles

EDITORS' INTRODUCTION

Some people are born to TCs, some achieve TCs and others have TCs thrust upon them. Jane Knowles puts herself very firmly in the last category. When first appointed as a consultant psychotherapist in Berkshire in the spring of 1985 nobody saw fit to mention the existence of a therapeutic community hiding away in a villa in the grounds of the district's mental hospital. She came across it by chance, took a brief look and decided it was not for her. Two years later a new senior nurse to the TC was appointed, sought Jane out and insisted that, as a group analyst, she should take over the consultant responsibility – with the likelihood that the unit would perish if she did not.

And so with many anxieties she became consultant to Winterbourne therapeutic community. She realised, as she handed over that consultancy to Rex Haigh in 1994, that her former anxieties had been transformed to a great love: but then that is the TC magic for you.

Jane Knowles was also Deputy Editor of the Therapeutic Communities Journal *and is the author of* Motherhood: What It Does to Your Mind; Know Your Own Mind; *and* Love: A User's Guide. *She has had several years as an NHS trust medical director, and continues to work as a consultant at Winterbourne and a group analyst at the Group Analytic Practice in London.*

In this chapter she applies her admirable 'common sense' approach to the difficult, but often neglected, problems of ethics and consent, reminding us that all therapy has the potential to harm as well as to heal. She also describes the creative approach Winterbourne TC has taken when faced with some of these difficulties.

DUTIES AND CODES, CONSEQUENCES AND MORALITY

The precise basis for ethics has been fertile ground for philosophical argument. The *deontologists* see ethics as a system of rules. (Deontology: Greek 'deon' = duty. The study of the identification and justification of duties; originates in religious moral codes; Kant developed a secular grounding for ethical duties in the eighteenth century.) The argument against such simplicity is easy however.

If, for instance, you have a rule 'do not lie', how do you account for the many situations in which lying to those who intend no good is entirely ethical? The example most often cited for when lying might be appropriate is that of knowing the whereabouts of a friend who is hiding from a potential murderer. When asked by the murderer to reveal your friend's hiding place would it be ethical to tell the truth? However, it is impossible to have an ethical stance that says that it is good to lie because then that statement may in itself be untruthful – such a stance would have inherent contradiction. In TCs we usually encourage truth and trust as a positive approach to this dilemma, as otherwise the system of rules would need to be incredibly situation specific to be truly applicable as ethical guidelines.

The teleologist or consequentialists (teleology = the doctrine of final causes; Jeremy Bentham and John Stuart Mill developed this utilitarian approach to ethics in the early nineteenth century) are more pragmatic, judging an action by its goals or consequences rather than the action itself. In a life that rarely offers an entirely right versus entirely wrong choice of actions, such pragmatism seems appropriate. But what if consequences cannot be foreseen, the decision needing to be made with only some of the facts known, for instance?

I think of ethics as a practical force of morality that springs from a desire to say and do the right things to each other. Ethics are not limited to one particular moral code, a religious one for instance, but need to span the many differences of being human. Because ethics need to be practical in order to work they must not be a yearned-for ideal. You need an active conscious mind for ethics: in order to be ethical you sometimes need to rise above not only id and ego but also an idealising super-ego.

THE CULTURAL CONTEXT

Ethics inevitably have a cultural connection. This is of importance because the dominant socio-economic group of any culture have the power to enforce ethics that serve themselves to the detriment of others. Therapeutic communities tend to develop their own ethos which I think of as ethics made into the group matrix. That the ethos is jointly made and upheld by patients/clients and staff is fundamentally important to the TC movement and holds it apart from the large arenas of psychoanalysis, psychotherapy, psychiatry, social work and the penal systems in which it is embedded. The difficulty for staff is to understand the importance of their ethical decisions on the one hand, and their limits on the other. For instance, there is sometimes a need for staff to make clinical decisions for the good of the individual patient that might fly in the face of the group's ethics.

Different TCs operate different ethical rules about sexual relationships between patients. These differences are based on reasoning: either sexual relationships during TC therapy are reasoned to be harmful or inevitable: they are deemed to be either within the remit of the group as a whole to forbid, or seen as an adult matter which is the private decision of two people able to make a reasoned judgement of their own. Both of these positions are ethically tenable as long as TCs can demonstrate the presence of ethical reasoning in the process of setting the boundaries.

ETHICAL AND CLINICAL DECISIONS

Ethics need to be able to take the universal view of an idealised observer while at the same time be practical at a particular 'coal face'. In many ways TCs are both best and worst placed to make such ethical decisions. The group as a whole can represent the universal view and the democratic vote is a way of making that view pragmatic. However, while always respecting the group and its power, staff also have a responsibility to retain the process of conscious reasoning in making ethical decisions that may be absent in individual patients and/or the group. At this point how do we differentiate between decisions made by the staff for the good of the staff and those in which reason has interrupted a pathological decision-making process: for example, scape-goating.

For example, George is very particular about the rules of the community and always picks up others if they break the rules. However, this does not make him popular, as he has a superior and annoying manner. Susan has self-harmed over the weekend and tells the community about this on Monday morning. She relates her story in a way that makes us sad for her. The whole group, including staff, find themselves wanting to be caring of her. George seems more annoying than usual in trying to make the group remember that self-harm means suspension for at least two days automatically. The group is about to vote and the outcome seems likely to fly in the face of the rules. The senior staff member then reminds the group that we have rules to be caring and that suspension is not punishment but underlines how seriously we take self-harm and how much we want Susan to learn to take care of herself. This intervention not only supports the whole group to use the rules they have developed to take care of everyone but also saves George from being the 'uncaring' scapegoat.

In order for staff members to rise above the immediate dynamics of each group we have sensitivity groups and supervision. These help. The staff group, if healthy, should be able to confront a lack of ethical reasoning in a colleague. As all staff groups have a hierarchy, however flattened, this sometimes requires courage.

GROUP PHENOMENA AND ETHICAL UNDERPINNINGS

There have been what Antonio Andreoli calls 'moments of greatness and of tribulation in the TC movement' (1997). I think the moments of greatness come when vision grows out of an ethically underpinned group phenomena. I think I witnessed such a moment at Winterbourne Community during the build up to our move from Fair Mile Hospital to our new home in a house in Reading. The move produced mixed emotions in both patients and staff. We were moving out of an old mental hospital in the countryside, 15 miles out of Reading, which had history and meaning (good and bad) for everyone. We occupied a spacious, light and airy top-floor ward in which the large group room was beautiful although we had to conduct one of the small groups in what had once been a locked bedroom. We were moving to a town house in a conservation area near the centre of Reading, and much closer to the homes of most of the patients. The house had far more pleasant small group rooms but the large group room felt much smaller than that we had been used to. The dependency culture of being in an old asylum was symbolised every lunch time when the food trolley was delivered and plugged in by a porter. Managerial discussions around whether we could have hot or cold food delivered to our new home seemed unsatisfactory and everyone had always complained about the quality of the food in the trolley anyway.

Winterbourne was lucky enough to have a new consultant just in time for these discussions who had the idea that the TC should, even though a day unit, feed and look after itself. The fact that nobody else, staff or patient, had thought, let alone voiced the idea, gives a perspective on just what a 'vision' that was – particularly as the group was at its maximum point of splitting, with its defensive position around the anxieties of the move.

However I think that the visionary quality of this idea was that it encapsulated the moral rightness I had always believed would carry us all from mental hospital to the community: it spoke of our new independence. Although the group split in opinion about the idea much as they were split heatedly over many issues surrounding the move at that time, the whole group sensed that there was an ethical underpinning of the idea of feeding and being responsible for themselves which they could not ignore. I have no doubt, in retrospect, that the 'vision' of feeding ourselves, both the reality and the symbolism, was fundamental in a move that has seen Winterbourne flourish and move forwards ever since.

Perhaps serious tribulations in TCs are experienced when charismatic leaders lose touch with the group and feel that ideas for change and improvement are thwarted by the ethical underpinning of the group's boundaries. Perhaps the reader will now be asking why such an obvious suggestion needed to be voiced by a consultant. Maybe this was due to the degree of frozen anxiety about the imminent change. Generally, it is extremely important to encourage all new members of the community, especially patients, to ask simple obvious questions if institutionalisation is to be resisted. If such questions are not actively encouraged, new members will tend to assume that there are mysterious and complex answers which only they cannot understand.

If we have learned anything this century it is that ideas cannot be enforced, however good they are. The process of enforcement is always corrupting: experience in TCs reinforces this lesson over and over again.

INFORMED CONSENT

The 'terrible twins' of TC transference phenomena, egoism and despair, both inhibit our capacity to think and act ethically.

Those coming into therapy, and perhaps most particularly TC therapy, are the most abused and potentially easily exploited, often with the least experience of exerting socio-economic power or any form of personal assertion. Their very lack of power leads to much acting out. Therapy can compound that lack of power – depending as it does on a regressive relationship. Yet in TCs we say 'regress' in some groups and 'grow up' in others. Such a dichotomy of messages requires a robust sense of what is ethical in any staff group seeking to fulfil its responsibilities and obligations. Respect for the group and respect for the autonomy of the individual may often be experienced as in conflict.

As therapists we have opinions about which patterns of behaviour are better or worse for a patient. For example we may ban self-harm and threaten suspension and/or discharge in the face of it. This is an attempt to manipulate and control an individual's behaviour because we believe it to be bad for that person. In the place of the 'bad' behaviour we attempt to insert more healthy behaviour which requires some sort of exploration of the motivation to self-harm. By invading an individual's autonomy we are seeking to make her/him more autonomous in the future. This process requires that we continually reconsider our own ethical basis and bias.

Trying to get informed consent for any form of therapy is difficult. By nature an experiential process cannot be predicted, so how do we conform to medical notions of 'informed consent' such as accurate description of the treatment, the options, the goals and the side effects. It is interesting how few patients quiz the assessing therapist about these issues or indeed the training, experience and supervision of the therapist, and yet all of the questions would need answers to begin to give the patient a chance at informed consent.

John Marzillier (1993) suggests that there are three precepts about informed consent in psychotherapy. These are that informed consent is a process, not a discrete event, that it is unrealistic to think that a therapist can provide detailed information on all aspects of therapy and that the process should be an active one between therapist and patient. Such guidelines are supported by other writers on ethics and 'informed' consent (e.g. Applebaum 1988; Pope and Vasquez 1991; Holmes and Lindley 1989; Widiger and Rorer 1984).

Handelsman and Galvin (1988) compiled a written format for informed consent for out-patient psychotherapy. They suggest a list of 28 questions under six general headings such as:

(1)   *Therapy*: A: How does your kind of therapy work?

(2)   *Alternatives*: A: What other types of therapy or help are there? etc.

At Winterbourne House we have developed a question and answer booklet covering these issues, which we send to patients when they are referred (see http://www.winterbourne.demon.co.uk/patientinfo.html).

Most TCs have booklets describing themselves, their goals, the staff, the timetable and the rules, with experiential writing, poems and drawings by previous patients or clients. This may help a prospective participant to sense the ethos both of the TC movement generally and of that TC in particular. Winterbourne sends a booklet describing itself to all those referred, the first page of which tells them 'what they are letting themselves in for' (again, see http://www.winterbourne.demon.co.uk/tc/path.html). Then they come to a Friday morning visit to see the building, meet some staff and discuss the nature of the commitment required of them: the choice to go further into the programme is explicitly theirs. For those who wish to try the next stage of engagement, there is a preparatory group meeting for an afternoon a week, which gives patients a taste of both group and milieu life. They meet more staff, including visitors and trainees, and full-time TC members rotate attendance – so there is a living connection maintained between the TC and the preparatory group. This allows the patient time to have experiential information about the process to which they will be committing themselves. Once they feel ready, patients can book a visiting week on the full TC where they are a non-talking observer to all but the small analytical groups. They are hosted by patients and staff and encouraged to debrief every day.

It is only after all this preparation that they are asked whether they would like a case conference. This event is the unique part of TC informed consent: that those who are patients already hear information about the prospective patient and have to give their consent, with the staff, as a group, for the new patient to join. The gaining of mutual consent from both new patient and the existing group, by the ritual of the case conference and the voting procedure, makes a strong working bond within which to start intensive therapy.

As part of the formal acceptance into the community the rules and guidelines are read out both to inform the new member and remind all the other members. Boundaries are marked by these rules and are important for keeping everyone involved in the process as safe as possible. In order for the rules to remain ethical Lowenstein (1991) suggests that they have to be perceived as having value for all in that the people who will have to keep the rules make them. He adds that both rules and punishments must be regularly reassessed, and that issues around the fairness of the application of the rules need to be discussed openly with staff. Rule-breakers need to be confronted directly and encouraged to seek peer group support to modify their behaviour. He recommends that the ethos of a community should make individual members aware that negative behaviour from themselves affects everyone in the community. The community needs to be aware of its responsibility to maintain the rules.

He reminds us that peer groups can influence the behaviour of individuals for better or worse and that staff have the overriding responsibility for making the community ethos one of safe and helpful behaviour to self and others. Kurtines (1986) has written about the maturational and learning process that occurs in the roles an individual can play psychosocially when they comprehend and feel safe within the rules of a community.

Therapeutic communities offer a particularly intense form of therapy to a group of patients who could be easily exploited. TCs attempt to empower their patients by giving them a real voice in the process of therapy and strong peer group support. However, by nature of the regressive force of psychotherapy patients will build a dependency on therapists. There needs to be a careful balance between the honesty of reality confrontation and the benevolence of 'the cure by love' of therapy. Patients in TCs quickly absorb psychodynamic ideas and may use them clumsily and impatiently, hurting or disempowering others in the group, often in a crude attempt to fend off awareness of their own vulnerability. It is important that staff model a reflective practice based on care and respect, balancing their frustration with patients' maladaptive behaviour and defences with an attempt to understand what causes them to cope in such a way. However careful we are to inform by verbal and written and by experiential information, therapists and patients enter a therapeutic bond together which will always be unpredictable. We need to pay close and regular attention to the ethics of our practice in order to make communities as safe as is possible.

REFERENCES

Andreoli, A. (1997) 'The quality of the human context as a factor in treatment.' *Therapeutic Communities 18*, 1, 15–26.

Applebaum, P.S. (1988) *Informed Consent. Legal Theory and Clinical Practice.* Oxford: Oxford University Press.

Handelsman, M.M. and Galvin, M.D. (1988) 'Facilitating informed consent for out patient psychotherapy: a suggested written format.' *Professional Psychology: Research and Practice 19*, 2, 223–225.

Holmes, J. and Lindley R. (1989) *The Values of Psychotherapy.* Oxford: Oxford University Press.

Kurtines, W. (1986) 'Person and situation effects on moral decision-making: a psychosocial role-theoretical approach.' *Journal of Personality and Social Psychology 50*, 784–791.

Lowenstein, L.F. (1991) 'Promoting moral behaviour in the seriously disturbed. Part 2. *Psychotherapy in Private Practice 9*, 1, 61–75.

Marzillier, J. (1993) 'Ethical issues in psychotherapy: the importance of informed consent.' *Clinical Psychology Forum,* April 33–37.

Pope, K.S. and Vasquez, M.J.J. (1991) *Ethics in Psychotherapy and Counselling.* San Francisco: Jossey Bass.

Widiger, T.A. and Rorer, L.G. (1984) 'The responsible psychotherapist.' *American Psychologist 1984,* 503–515.

CHAPTER 9

Sound and Fury
Grief and Despair in the Large Group
Teresa Black

EDITORS' INTRODUCTION

Teresa Black is a consultant psychotherapist in Wolverhampton. With her arts background and love of literature, she became fascinated by the small drama that each therapeutic community encapsulates, even though she fell into working in therapeutic communities almost by chance. Having left one community, she took the opportunity to work as consultant at Francis Dixon Lodge for a year, and suspects that this will not be her last encounter with the hurly-burly of community life, as it does tend to get under the skin. She tells us that, in her more grandiose moments, she attempts to write poetry.

In this contribution, she gives us the background to a particularly difficult community meeting at Francis Dixon Lodge, takes us into the meeting itself and follows the narrative on beyond it. She brings the characters to life, and plays the scene 'warts and all'. Honest staff reactions are described, and Teresa illustrates how she makes sense of it by using literary and poetical associations.

A DRAMATIC ENTRANCE

One of the main protagonists in this story, whom I shall call Cassie,[1] erupted into the therapeutic community in no uncertain fashion. Although when she came for assessment she had talked fluently, almost glibly, about how she loved most of all to surf the waves (I remember being in some doubt as to whether she literally meant the waves or whether she meant the Internet; either way she seemed to dip in and out of life avoiding too much pain) it also became clear that she was terrified that we might not notice her distress, so she had better make plenty of noise.

She immediately split the staff team; half thought she was a con artist who used verbal intimidation to get her own way and whom we must not take at face

---

1   Details about individual and events have been changed in order to protect the anonymity of residents.

value; others discerned beneath the facade a small child who had never been contained by any boundaries. She talked early on of feeling as though she were in a pin ball machine, banged about by the shots of her parents.

There is a graffiti board at Francis Dixon Lodge which is an old-fashioned blackboard (do such things still exist in schools, I wonder?) where views appear; it is rare to see anyone actually writing on it, but nevertheless words and pictures come and go in what often feels a very creative way; it is a large board so there is room for more besides the expected anarchic and anti-authority views. One day, I was startled by what seemed a perfect description of Cassie, although it may well not have been written either by or about her. It was the end of Macbeth's speech in Act 5, where the forces of destruction and retribution are fast closing in on him, so well known that it hardly needs quotation, but in the circumstances more apt than any clinical description for the purpose. It is the end of the speech where Macbeth has heard of the death of Lady Macbeth:

> It is a tale
> Told by an idiot, full of sound and fury
> Signifying nothing.

The beginning of the same speech comes into the story later on.

Incidentally, while musing on Cassie's dramatic yet somehow alarming arrival into the community, I heard a trailer for a programme on Radio 3 about composers who die young, and it was entitled *Brief Candles*. This is a quotation from earlier in the same speech, and it made me reflect how ubiquitous Shakespeare is in our lives, and not merely a long dead playwright, who forms the backdrop for innumerable adolescent daydreams but is rapidly discarded on getting out into the world. Moreover, Shakespeare's notion of us all being mere figures caught up in a drama – 'a poor player that struts and frets his hour upon the stage' is one of his favourite themes, and one which resonates with life in a therapeutic community. Murray Cox of course has written most eloquently and extensively on the clinical relevance of Shakespeare (1987, 1997).

Back to the above description of Cassie or those like her, who of course frequently come to therapeutic communities. Her greatest fear would be that her tale would turn out to be of no significance, and the only way she knows to get it heard is to turn up the volume. I am not specifically going to discuss diagnosis, although Cassie summed it up eloquently by saying: 'I've got a personality disorder, and they can't be cured, so I might as well behave like one.'

However, those who work in therapeutic communities would probably disagree with Freud's dictum:

Sufferers from narcissistic neuroses have no capacity for transference or only insufficient residues of it. They reject the doctor not with hostility, but with indifference... they remain as they are... they manifest no transference and for that reason are inaccessible to our efforts and cannot be cured by us. (1917, p.447)

One day Cassie came to me outside a group, which she knows she is not supposed to do, and asked for a different antidepressant and some lithium, saying that these were the only thing that could lift her out of her pit of despair. She was very angry after we decided not to give her this change of medication, saying that the medical care at Francis Dixon Lodge was 'diabolical'. A few days later she became enraged with one of the nurses because as she thought her inhaler had not come from the pharmacy, although in fact the nurse had just said he would have to check if it had arrived. In exasperation, the nurse said he was not sure if the community was the right place to help Cassie, if she were so scathing about all aspects of her care. Cassie agreed, and said perhaps she should leave, though probably the only way she would do that would be in a wooden box. The nurse came into the office, visibly shaken by the encounter. A few minutes later Cassie came up to him again and was in floods of tears, apologising for her behaviour. One minute she was full of sound and fury, raging against our inadequacies, but the next had collapsed like a deflated balloon; in the months she has been with us we never know whether to expect a crusader exposing the flaws in the system and championing the cause of the oppressed, or a terrified five-year-old uncontained by her parents' indifference. Cassie perhaps exemplifies the lack of ego strength and the volatile mood swings of the borderline patient, but often in the group emotions rage and at the time it can be difficult to see where the storms and sudden shifts come from.

Francis Dixon Lodge is unusual if not unique among therapeutic communities in that all the therapeutic work is contained within the large group, typically up to 15 residents and 4 or 5 staff. The aim of this is to reduce the inevitable splitting which occurs in a group of disturbed individuals, many of whom have formed very over-involved relationships with previous therapists or keyworkers. One resident for example has even talked about her keyworker becoming so involved with her that she moved into the same street. Paradoxically, although the violent emotions which I have been describing often seem magnified in the group, the experience is also made safer by being shared within a larger containing structure. Moreover, the pressure on individual therapists is reduced and made more bearable.

A DIFFICULT COMMUNITY MEETING

I will now describe a typical morning community meeting, although one from which the staff emerged feeling particularly beleaguered. The group started fairly quietly, but soon Tanya commented on how she had seen what she described as a cabinet full of broken glass on the landing, and how dangerous this was and how inconsiderate it was of someone to have left it there. There was no particular response to this, although it certainly conjured in my mind an acute sense of potential threat, and another resident went on to thank Tanya for 'bringing the drag queens to my room'. This referred to the previous evening where three male residents had dressed in some of Tanya's things including a black lacy mini dress. Neither of these incidents made much literal sense but both were quite disturbing, particularly as two of the three involved in the dressing up appeared to be ridiculing the other one, who was quite naive.

However, there was little time to wonder what these incidents might be about, as Jean, the resident who had said she had enjoyed the entertainment provided by the drag queens, abruptly switched to say how angry she was with a member of staff who was present in the group, saying that he had not taken an injury to her ankle seriously. Apparently Jean had fallen outside her flat and subsequently it turned out that she had destabilised a previous fracture. However, one of the residents did ask her why, if her ankle were sprained or even broken, she had joined in the disco quite so enthusiastically (this had been hired for the leaving party of a resident who left the day before). The member of staff tried to help Jean to look at her feelings about the incident, and the fact that he had asked her if she wished to go to Casualty, or whether she would prefer the duty doctor to be called to have a look at her leg. At that point Jean had stormed away, and the next day had herself gone to the fracture clinic, where she is well known, and returned to say that the X-ray had shown a definite problem, although she was a little unclear about what precisely it was. The more staff tried to get Jean to look at her part in what had happened, the more angry and defensive she became. Other residents joined in the criticism of staff. Mike said angrily: 'It seems residents don't get any help with medical problems.' Tanya joined in the theme by saying how another member of staff, who was also present in the group, had ignored her request for painkillers; and how in fact he always ignored her. Other residents joined in the attack on this member of staff even though he apologised if she had felt ignored.

The split between staff and residents was rapidly turning into a gulf, and exchanges were becoming more heated. At this point a female staff member perhaps unwittingly made things worse by querying a resident's absence from a group; residents are supposed to negotiate any absences from formal meetings with the whole community. Several residents said that this and other absences had been negotiated with the community, and that as usual it was only the staff who had a problem with it. Another resident who had been having increasing amounts of time out joined eagerly in the discussion. The member of staff who had previously been criticised for ignoring Tanya said that perhaps he had to make a choice, and decide which was more important – the work he was having done on his flat or his presence as a member of the community. The resident started shouting what choice had he got, water was pouring down into the flat below, and the council had to get access to his flat to be able to deal with it, and he couldn't trust anyone with a key. When he had finished his tirade there was a pause and then one of the female residents, who had hitherto been silent, said that it pissed her off that people were having so much time off to sort out their flats and that she had not done this; she said that she had not felt brave enough to say this before. Dick continued with his tirade, but it also emerged that he had been round the residents before the group to make sure they agreed to his requests. Cassie then came in to say that the staff's idea of negotiation was that the residents should do what the staff wanted. 'We're not going to lay down and be told what to do.' She then demonstrated rolling over and lying on her back like a dog being submissive.

The image I had in my mind at this point and through much of the group was of a terrier worrying away at something and not letting it go; after the group another staff member shared her image of a dog with a bone.

Dick, the resident who had talked about his urgent need to stay out of the community, went on to become more upset saying, 'I was dismantled and I'm getting crushed for it.' He has frequently talked of how he is terrified of losing his individuality; this makes more sense knowing that he had been sexually abused from an early age.

Later on in the group I found it a little more possible to try to understand what was happening. The residents seemed caught between the constraint of being told what to do by staff and the terrible freedom of choice; both Jean and Dick became enraged when given a choice and responsibility. I said at this point that perhaps the staff had choice whereas the residents didn't; I had just realised that both I and the senior nurse had been off the day before, and it must have felt that we did not have to justify our absences in the same way as the residents did. But I still was not in touch with the key to the disturbance in the group.

At this point, when I had begun to feel able to think, there came another attack like a broadside. A female resident, who had hitherto been silent, asked the new junior doctor about her medication, saying it was not doing her any good at all. Then Tanya suddenly said that the doctor had been smiling and could she give an explanation of this, as she obviously found something amusing. She continued to attack as the junior doctor valiantly tried to defend herself. The group ended soon after this, with a flurry of requests about dental appointments, ringing a solicitor and other such matters.

THE STAFF'S 'AFTERGROUP'

After following the group, the staff as usual went upstairs for the aftergroup, which is an opportunity to discharge feelings and to try to get some sense of what had been happening, particularly if like this one, it had been a difficult session. As soon as we had sat down, the junior doctor burst into tears and said how upset she had been by Tanya's attack, and how she felt she had retaliated. She felt that Tanya had attacked her on a sore point, which was of course why she had felt particularly vulnerable to that attack. It seemed important that the doctor shared the same name as a resident to whom Tanya had been especially attached, who left the community prematurely some months before. Although it had been evident to the staff in the group that the doctor had been upset by Tanya's remarks, she said that what surprised her most was how furious she had felt with Tanya, and how much she had wanted to retaliate, and was afraid that perhaps she had done so.

Other staff who had been attacked also talked about their anger and how they had wanted to bite back (I still had in mind the image of the terrier which holds on tenaciously and won't let go, but now I was beginning to wonder who was the biter and who was then the bitten.) Malcolm Pines, in a paper on 'Borderline phenomena in analytic groups' (1994) says; 'Don't expect the patients to care for you. By the time they are able do so they are well on the way to recovery' (p.148). This train of thought brought me back to my concern about the member of staff who had been attacked at the start of the group. I knew he had been worried about his dog, which had bitten a woman whose dog had come onto his territory. He said the group had been pretty awful, but that what had kept him going was the headline in that morning's *Sun*, which was lying on the table in front of him. The headline read 'Tiger eats arm of keeper'. At least in the group there had only been metaphorical savaging.

Nevertheless, as a staff team we were concerned about the loss of the therapeutic alliance, something notoriously hard to define but which is very evident in its absence. Later that day we talked more about why the group had been so attacking and someone commented on the fact that this group had taken place the day after Amanda had left. Amanda had been in the community for a long time and was very quiet in the groups, frequently allowing her voice to be given to her best friend; however outside groups she increasingly showed a lively and mischievous side to her personality, and also got on well with the staff. Her best friend had organised a disco for her leaving do and both staff and residents had commented that everyone had seemed to enjoy themselves, and that staff had joined in the fun, even attempting the karaoke; in particular, residents had enjoyed the spectacle of staff making fools of themselves. Nevertheless, we had had reservations about how well Amanda had actually done in the community and how well she would cope on her own. However, when she asked to speak to myself and the senior nurse the next week after she had left, attending the post-discharge group, we realised how much she had gained from her time in Francis Dixon Lodge, and how she was able to express her gratitude to us, which residents often struggle to do.

But it also made us aware of how much the morning group had been an angry and unacknowledged mourning for the loss of Amanda. I then remembered something else which had been mentioned in the group, but at the time its significance had not been appreciated. Amina, the resident who had started the attack on the junior doctor, had said she had lost her wedding ring, and thought it must have fallen off when she was giving a rather exuberant rendition of '*I will survive*' during the karaoke. The background to this was that

Amina, who is in her early thirties, had been widowed some years before, but had never got over her grief, and in fact became increasingly disturbed, culminating in making repeated hoax telephone calls to the hospital where her husband had died. It had taken a long time for her previous problems and the highly ambivalent relationship with her husband to come to light, and she still tends to revert to saying that she had a perfect marriage, even though this was clearly not the case. On Valentines Day she had talked about going to the cemetery with a bunch of red roses; but it was fascinating that several members of staff had distinctly heard her say 'A bunch of razors' rather than a bunch of red roses, which suggests they were picking up the anger beneath the surface. A few weeks before, she had remarked fairly casually at the end of a group that a gold ring had gone missing, but did not show nearly as much distress as one might have expected. This ring never turned up, and she decided not to report the incident to the police. Soon after that her wedding ring had to be cut off because she had put on a good deal of weight and her finger was becoming ulcerated; she had previously refused to have it attended to, so having the ring enlarged seemed to be a sign of progress. She had only had it back a week or two when she lost it at Amanda's leaving party, supposedly at the disco. As with the loss of her engagement ring, she appeared resigned rather than distressed, even though she had lost another link with her dead husband.

MORE THOUGHTS ON THE THERAPEUTIC ALLIANCE

It suddenly occurred to me that the therapeutic alliance with the residents had been lost at the same point as Amina's wedding ring had disappeared. In French the word *alliance* means a wedding ring; although it has lost this explicit meaning in English, the dictionary still gives 'a union between families through marriage' under alliance. And as we had seen in that morning's group, with the loss of the alliance or working together, damaging splits occur. The word *alliance* comes from the Old French word *alier*: to ally or tie together. It was as if the loss of the wedding ring symbolised the loss of the therapeutic alliance; the group as a whole could not cope with the loss of an important member and so denied it and fought terrier-like with the staff, just as Amina loses rings and damages herself rather than looking at her relationships.

This group also brings to mind the works of Edmund Burke:

And having looked to government for bread, on the very first scarcity they will turn and bite the hand that fed them.

Like the tiger in the *Sun* headline.

During that group I had wondered aloud why the residents needed to attack the staff so vociferously, thinking that perhaps part of what happened was covering up something else. In the evening group splits appeared between the residents themselves, and the group was, if anything, even more acrimonious. It had been much safer to attack the staff. The shifting nature of the co-operation between disturbed patients and the therapist is marked. A few years ago an individual patient of mine who beneath an intelligent pleasant facade was tormented by doubts about whether I could be trusted, wrote a poem which initially shocked me by revealing the gulf between the surface and the depths. The poem starts:

> As the knife went in I bit harder on the bullet,
> Determined they would witness no pain.
> They surrounded me with their sinister sincerity.
> 'We'll cut out the cancerous part and leave you cured–'
> How they reassured.

How easy it can be to enter a borderland of doubt and suspicion. When residents leave the community, the afore-mentioned graffiti board is often covered with goodwill messages for them. When Amanda left, the board was decorated with drawings of teddy bears and Teletubbies, both of which she was addicted to. All the messages were sweet and almost cloying, the obverse of what had been going on on the other side of the wall. For many days after Amanda's departure, the board remained untouched, whereas it usually changes daily. It felt as if the community remained frozen in grief for the departed Amanda, much as Amina remained locked in grief for her dead husband.

Macbeth of course has only just heard about the death of his wife when he gives his famous speech, shortly before he meets his own untimely end. A few weeks after Amanda's planned departure, the community had to cope with the premature departure of another resident, Jim, who with hindsight was embarked on a course of self-destruction similar to Macbeth's. His self-destructiveness manifested itself most clearly in his continuing to drink and drive apparently oblivious of the risks he was posing to himself and others, even though he had been given an ultimatum about this. In a community meeting where Jim had talked about his inability to give up his car and also his sense that 'things couldn't be fixed', my eyes had been drawn to a book on the table in front of him entitled *How to Keep your Car Alive*. Jim had become very angry and tearful the day before when his car had risked failing its MOT. I realised that Jim couldn't give up his car because if he did he would die; the symbolic connection had been lost and he had become his car which was falling apart and which might well prove to be his destruction. In a group a day or two before he went on a drinking binge which led to his leaving the community, Jim talked about things crowding in on him. He said he would sort out a particular problem 'Tomorrow' and then gave a rueful grin and added '...and tomorrow, and tomorrow...', echoing Macbeth's words in a speech which is much about the futility of feeling that one can make a difference.

SIGNIFYING NOTHING?

Back to the last lines of the speech, which seem particularly apt for working in a therapeutic community;

> Life's but a walking shadow, a poor player
> That struts and frets his hour upon the stage
> And then is heard no more. It is a tale
> Told by an idiot, full of sound and fury,
> Signifying nothing. (Act 5, Scene 5, lines 23–27)

These words describe Macbeth's despair and the end of his dreams, but also describe someone like Cassie or Jim, who come to the community hoping against hope that they can change – but as Cassie said defiantly in one group; 'I've got a book on personality disorders and it says they're incurable, so the staff are just conning us aren't they?'

It may be difficult to give an honest answer to such a question, which anyway feels more like a gauntlet being thrown down – I do not think Cassie wanted a statistical analysis of why therapeutic communities succeed, even if such a thing were possible. But it is important and perhaps inevitable for those who work in a therapeutic community to muse on such questions, and to wonder what is significant in effecting change.

Certainly, it often seems as if the atmosphere at Francis Dixon Lodge is filled with sound and fury, and staff often feel caught up in the same drama as the residents, so that the fear may lurk in the background that nothing of lasting significance happens.

REFERENCES

Cox, M. (1987, 1997) *Mutative Metaphors in Psychotherapy: The Aeolian Mode.* London: Tavistock Publications; London: Jessica Kingsley Publishers.

Freud, S. (1917) 'Transference.' In: *The Standard Edition of the Complete Psychological Works of Sigmund Freud. Vols 15 and 16.* London: Hogarth Press and the Institute of Psycho-Analysis.

Pines, M. (1994) 'Borderline phenomena in analytic groups.' In V. Schermer and M. Pines (eds) *Ring of Fire – Primitive Affects and Object Relations in Group Therapy.* London: Routledge.

CHAPTER 10

Creativity and Play
Reflections on a Creative Therapies Group
Bridget Higgins and Chris Newrith

EDITORS' INTRODUCTION

Bridget Higgins has ten years' experience of using the arts therapeutically in many different settings; starting off as a community artist in special education and eventually making the move to mental health and to a therapeutic community. Passionate about the arts and therapeutic communities, she has a sense of this being a very meaningful journey and enjoys the holistic sense of co-operation and community in the TC movement.

Already qualified with a BA in Education and Community Studies and an MSc in Professional and Policy Studies (Health), she is now completing a training in Integrative Arts Psychotherapy.

Chris Newrith trained at St Andrew's and Manchester Medical Schools, started training as a GP, but enjoyed a psychiatry placement so much that he changed career path. He is now a specialist registrar in psychotherapy at Winterbourne House, studying for an MSc in NHS Psychotherapy on the Four Counties training scheme, co-editing a textbook on the treatment of borderline patients who seriously offend and has a particular interest in the use of linguistics and semiotics to understand the borderline experience and psychic organisation.

He feels fortunate to have worked with the late Dr Murray Cox and to have been present at one of the last 'Shakespeare at Broadmoor' productions. This nurtured his interest in psychotherapy and the creative therapies.

Both he and Bridget believe that the creative therapies and analytic therapies have more overlap than is generally recognised. This chapter is a refreshingly open account of the creative therapy group they ran together and their reflections on it.

Winterbourne Therapeutic Community is a day unit offering intensive group psychotherapy and sociotherapy for up to 18 members. The community caters for individuals who have experienced trauma, abuse, neglect and deprivation, often in early life and resulting in recurrent mental health problems. In this chapter we hope to describe something of our experience of running a creative arts group as part of the Winterbourne TC programme.

THE CREATIVE ARTS GROUP

We began working together in this group in February 1997, with the aim of bringing together our different backgrounds in analytic and creative arts therapies and an enthusiasm for and shared belief in the healing capacity of the arts. It was a weekly therapy group lasting 90 minutes and included all community members. As staff we also had contact with the members in community meetings and the milieu.

We have worked hard in the group to develop a culture of openness of communication, empowerment and experimentation, reflecting the heart of TC principles (see Chapter 20) – agency, containment, attachment and communication. In line with this openness we were aware of our own needs for a supervision which would allow both our professional and personal relationship to develop in a way that would embody this same culture. To enable us to model a relationship that was consistently both creative and open, we remained alert and attentive in supervision to noticing our feelings and the dynamics of our relationship, thus mirroring the members' experience of change through the authenticity of developing creative relationships. We hoped to effect a creative process at both theoretical and personal levels.

This combination of the TC culture and our creative openness to possibilities has been essential to the potency of this group, and is especially valuable considering the levels of disturbance and damaging early relational experiences with which our members come to the TC. Such individuals may have internal worlds full of juxtapositions of images, sensations and affects from a primitive stage of psychic development which may not be easily compatible with the vocabulary and syntax of verbal language. Instead of the spoken word serving as a bridge between the individuals' internal world and the external world where they might experience playfulness and all its healing potential, the individual member may find him- or herself emotionally inarticulate. The opportunity in the creative group has been for members to find complementary ways of making meaning out of the chaos inside. The creation and expression of images then became the bridge for individuals between their inner and outer landscapes. The image offers both a means of expression and containment for the mass of human experience which it is hard to verbalise adequately. Indeed the image holds the possibility of far greater than 'adequate' expression; it offers form, substance, texture, sound, colour and more.

CONTAINMENT

Our clients had few childhood experiences of any positive attachment figures who could effectively contain them by providing safe ways of exploring their personal place in the world. As a direct result, they experienced difficulties in forming their own effective internal containment as adults. Indeed our clients have developed their own systems of protection which, while remarkable in circumstances of such deprivation and internal fragmentation, do not enable them to lead fulfilling lives.

This requires us as therapists, particularly in this style of group, to provide a very deliberate external containment by being open to experiencing their depth of feeling without withdrawing or retaliating – and by setting boundaries which they have learnt to trust. This offers a type of parenting which some choose to explore as a new or different experience and results in us working with transferential issues including idealisation and denigration. Containment of the group is not just a product of the setting and our own internal steadiness, but is an active process which also includes careful planning of the shape and structure of the session. It is a holding in mind of the individuals and the group and a faith in the creative and therapeutic process. Just like parents, we hold hope and anxiety, as well as thought, energy and trust which we put into the creative process in this group, and this belief in the potential for healing and growth develops in the clients.

THE SHAPE AND STRUCTURE OF A SESSION

Our planning for the session may begin with an idea for a starting point, which may be completely non-directive or a general theme which is around for the community at the time. For example, when members leave, a variety of feelings about loss will exist within the group and the individuals. Active and reflective exercises can be used to help access some personal depth to the generalised experience. In this way each art form used by the client can facilitate clarity and focus to a painful feeling which may otherwise remain vague and unformed.

We often start with a period of physical and emotional warming-up, using games and activities linked to our overall sense of the group at the time. We view this period as holistic and an integral part of the therapeutic process, where body, thought, emotion and soul can be attended to by both the individual group members and ourselves as therapists. There is a shape, structure and symmetry which exists in the group. During the warm-up we may be quite directive, modelling for them as much as is possible for each of us individually and as a therapeutic couple on any one day, something of connectedness to ourselves, our bodies and each other. A typical example of this is a verbal check-in exercise standing in a circle: ' how I feel in my body' and 'how I feel emotionally'. Each group member including ourselves responds acknowledging awareness of physical and emotional aspects of the self. Examples may be: 'In my body I feel achey and emotionally I feel frightened' or ' I have a pain in my knee and I feel full of anticipation'. Similar connectedness between self and others can be facilitated by another group circle exercise, again including therapists, of looking around the group and taking each other in visually, encouraging the possibility of seeing and being seen safely. Exercising the voice with sounds or song to physically and emotionally connect, has been for some a powerful experience of hearing their own voice and of being heard. This naturally requires a willingness and belief in the value of some self-disclosure on our part, and again we have used our supervision to explore our experiences of the personal risk and beauty of this type of practice. Our experience has been that such a willingness has produced very real connections and relationships. It obviously requires clarity and self-awareness to monitor the level of self-disclosure and personal risk involved in each group and self-support and responsibility to maintain solid boundaries.

During the session we work with the subtle interplay of directiveness and energy flow as the members' own inclination to play and experiment with their imagination develops. We have experienced an organic quality to the group as they (and we) move between different experiences of relationship as a group, as individuals and with the chosen art form. Each week there is the possibility, space and containment for the members to create, either individually or in groups, using visual or verbal images. What and how they create is up to them and is not usually linked in a deliberate way to specific therapy issues. The important thing is the experience of contact, creation and creativity. The materials for group and individual image making include using visual forms such as objects found in the room, paint, pastels, sounds or sand. Sometimes they use drama, puppetry, storymaking, poetry and movement. Much of the experience in this group involves literally embodying feelings and enacting them. This concept of actively engaging enables them to deepen the communication with their core selves and gain a more complete sense of their whole self in that moment. Actually doing something offers the members a directness of emotional contact which can be unavailable to them in groups where there may be a temptation to take a meta-position and talk about feelings as a device to avoid direct emotional contact with the self.

Using colours, shapes or actions allows the client to explore a full range of feelings and emotional states in an emotionally and physically safe space. Action involves doing, whether drama, movement or stillness. Situations can be replayed as they originally occurred or including the client's desired outcome. A drama may involve the individual describing the situation, choosing group members to play certain characters and using the 'audience' to comment after the scene about what they saw and felt. Variations include practising basic assertiveness techniques or exploring painful past scenarios which may require extra vigilance and sensitivity on the part of the therapists. Movement and deliberate stillness as a form of movement allow for energy to flow and sensation to be paramount. We have facilitated movement as a whole group, for example a sculpt using bodies to physically represent a dynamic in the group or individually with a period of reflection and image making after the experience.

Examples include the transition from moving very quickly, shaking or running, to slow motion and the full sense of every muscle playing its part, or of sitting and slowly exploring in detail one hand with another, or becoming focussed and aware of one foot and without speaking meeting other peoples feet in the room. All are examples of intra- and inter-personal connections. Shapes made by the body in response to emotion, that is, showing how something feels, adds a whole new dimension of experience and expression to a verbal statement of feeling. Using the body to show how 'small and vulnerable' feels or taking the opposite stance to the familiar can open new doors to experience. One member of the community experimented by striking a very powerful posture which enabled him to experience some of his own denied power. The body holds information which can be immediately helpful when listened to. Another took a very small position physically and discovered her feelings of frustration and anger which had not been available to her before, through her more dominant verbal articulation of feelings of smallness and vulnerability. Similarly, shape and colour can facilitate further learning through the creation of picture images or sculptures.

Emotion accessed and released through the process of creation can reveal surprising and illuminating aspects of the self and the emotion. Some clients find the materials they use, and their texture and colour, to be extremely important, whilst for others the process of making or producing is more valuable to them at their stage in therapy. A wide range of coloured papers, textured fabrics, bubble wrap, clay and sparkly bits are therefore essential therapeutic tools. The solidity of clay or frailty of gauze can clearly represent significant emotional states for some individuals, and using these materials can widen and deepen emotional experience and understanding.

The culture of possibility in this group has meant that crude x = y interpretations, for example, of the use of specific materials or colours, have far less importance than the respect the members have for each of their personal creations on that day. Again the necessity of us as therapists to feel contained and comfortable with our own range of feeling allows for a space where there is a permissiveness of expression and acceptance of, and compassion for, the members' feeling states – including the defensive structures which all human beings erect as protection. In valuing what we meet in the clients and being with what was already there, it becomes possible for real transformation to take place for some. The investment is in the here-and-now of creation and is not goal-orientated to a specific therapeutic outcome. The experience of creation is therapeutic in itself, and the act of creation is containing in itself – 'the clay's got the anger in it' as it was put of one community member whose feelings of primitive rage and rejection meant she could not accept the support of the community, but found an articulate voice in the shaping of these feelings in clay during the creative group. The art form, image and metaphor is such an effective and substantial container for unbearable and contradictory feelings that when it is balanced by the intuitive, subtle and active ability in us as therapists to be alongside, the process becomes especially potent.

A time to feed back to the group can be a useful opportunity to link the emotional and creative experience to the spoken word. An activity of closure assists the members to experience a shared sense of completion and a transition back to the everyday life of the community. The emotional experience of creation actively continues to resonate within the individual long after the end of the group. By daring to keep an alive and ongoing relationship with their emotional and creative process the member can have a profound experience of change. We have strong feelings about maintaining a culture of possibility and openness and as such the group has an organic nature and the content is not fixed. However with this client group we have found that some consistency is facilitative of creativity rather than restrictive, and generally we do keep to our sense of symmetry as a helpful containing structure by opening and closing with some sort of awareness exercise, including individuals and the whole group.

MEANING AND CONTACT

The creative arts group has provided many opportunities for the members to explore a great range of personal and universal human experience. One of the values of it being a group is the full engagement by others in the work of the individual. The group forum has the capacity to hold both the individual and the collective. This group slowly allowed for difference and similarity to be tolerated and, importantly for people who experience the world as profoundly critical, it allowed for difference not to be a terrifying threat to the core of the person. It is always a privilege and joy to witness the support and validation the members can offer each other in such a variety of forms of expression and for us to accompany them on strange and magical journeys. We have seen pure delight in the unexpected outcome of an activity – 'I don't need to say anything; it's all there, that's what being on the TC's all about', as one member proudly said in feedback as the group viewed her creation. There may also be a shared spirit, perhaps a sense of the mystery at the heart of being human – art, whatever its form, is after all an intensely human experience.

The group became a forum for the imagination, a safe transitional space where ways of being could be played with. As the trust within the group grew, some experimented with ways of being that had previously been too frightening. For example, through gentle, consistent modelling and facilitation of touch, the group became gradually more comfortable and began to make spontaneous physical contact with each other and us. Once an emotional trust had been formed it could be followed by a physical trust and these experiences of warm, safe human physical contact became particularly important for some members – both in their own right as much needed touch, and as new, different formative experiences.

THE PARALLEL PROCESS OF MAKING A CREATIVE SPACE

We actively used our own images and experiences of the sessions in supervision, which included feelings of impotence, despair and frustration – as well as awe, accomplishment and warmth. By expressing our sense of the 'treacleishness' of the group, for example, we worked in more depth with our feelings of frustration and hopelessness around their deep resistance and stuckness. Sometimes there were sensations in the group which felt to the members to be unspeakable and it was our responsibility to name them as well as facilitating the non-verbal process. Similarly, feelings which the clients found difficult to express through word or image might be expressed through behaviour. In a group where doing is recognised as important this needs to be contained in a non-critical but firmly boundaried way. The difficulties for us in working with such a fine balance between creative potential and fear meant recognising this tension within ourselves personally and professionally within the counter-transference which we clearly observed in our relationship.

Supervision was the medium through which we explored the ebb and flow of our personal and professional relationship. For us this 'raw material' of our feelings, heard by, held and discussed with our supervisor, enabled us to understand something of the nature of the dynamics between us and reflect the healthy parental function we offer the clients. As therapists we were able to safely take back our own affects and use them in this contained form to model a creative therapeutic couple in the next group. As part of this we used supervision as a space to express and explore tensions and conflicts between us, both interpersonal and transferential. We also needed to tolerate and speak of the envy we experienced being projected on to us from other members of the team about holding the creative aspects of human experience. Our own defensive feelings of hostility and envy were apparent particularly towards the end of our time together and we were able to acknowledge and work with these. Our experience of the safe exploration of our primitive feelings and the sense of being seen, heard and met in supervision continually nourished and renewed in us the capacity to truly meet the group. The containment we experienced within our supervision enabled us to make our own meaningful links between our inner and outer worlds, and to integrate our personal and professional experiences. This integration led us to provide sound containment to the group and allowed us enough flexibility and freedom to remain in touch with our own spontaneity and imaginations.

We feel that our openness to experimentation in this way, constantly learning from our mistakes and our relationship, has allowed a parallel permissive space to develop in the group. This is where internal rules can be challenged, where there is no punitive right or wrong, mess is allowed and where laughter and self-affirmation are actively encouraged. In experimenting with different ways of being as a means of exploring potentials the members can have the powerful and profound experience of being seen and witnessed 'in' their whole self. As an example, a woman discovering her power and capacity for big feelings used paper covering a whole wall, and with the support of the whole group expressed for the first time in colour and shape, her strength and size. This was hugely important for her and for the entire group as they witnessed and received her as she was in that moment.

SERIOUS PLAY

Play in its widest sense is positively encouraged and is a safe container for many complex emotions and a wonderful forum for the enactment of possibilities. The fluidity of play, particularly 'drama', as a container allows for the safe exploration of expansion. Repetition as rehearsal can be an important part of the therapeutic process. The physical embodiment of emotion through the body and the enactment of the personal drama, at the right time, offer extra momentum through action – leading to further growth and ultimately to a more solid sense of self. The individual is witnessed through all art forms, as the chaotic or fragmented images are externalised and lead inevitably to some form of integration and development of identity. Indeed rather than losing themselves in the fantasy or unreality of play the client finds a new and organically revealing experience of self. By meeting through the play and the metaphors of play, the group have had opportunities to explore the reality of their internal and external worlds. Play is serious here.

Many of our clients have not had any good childhood experiences of play and it is crucial therefore to gauge or pitch our therapeutic playfulness session by session so that it is neither 'under-' or 'over-'whelming to the group. Either an underwhelming or overwhelming of the client can lead to a shame-inducing experience, and fine tuning means the experience of play and creation can be felt to be growthful rather than persecutory. Many clients come to the TC with very fragile senses of their selves which have not been able to develop due to deep and often repeated experiences of criticism, humiliation and abuse. These are all important therapeutic issues for the individual to address and so avoiding or withdrawing from the challenge of working on the 'knife edge' of these types of therapeutic experience in the group would be irresponsible. This means that we have to be with the client as they struggle with these issues and often in the process angrily denounce the group as once again activating feelings of shame.

When using play the members can either respond to the experience as a persecutory, patronising demand to return to a frightening, often shamed younger self or from a more positive 'free child' position. There have been times when we have dealt clumsily with these issues and have needed supervision to explore our defensiveness around the verbal and emotional challenges of some of the members. Personal therapy has been essential in exploring our own individual issues of shame. Skilfully balancing our therapeutic presence when using play prevents the under or overwhelming we describe. We actively encourage the group safely into their own playfulness using our judgement, intuition, empathy and responsiveness.

THE ENDING

The completion of our group meant facing up to the realities of the ending of something fruitful. For both clients and ourselves, the conclusion of this particular relationship had many resonances. For the clients whose development has not allowed them to process early losses, the re-living of such a loss in the symbolic form of the ending of the therapeutic relationship was potentially frightening and required further containment by the therapists. It was also important that we did not diminish the equally real 'here and now' experience of losing this particular creative space and clearly allowed opportunities for this to be explored. We could only empathically be with the clients by feeling that our own ending was acknowledged and contained. As we modelled a maturing and creative relationship, the acknowledgement that this must include an ending with its inevitable feelings of loss was a crucial part of the experience. Just as we hope for the clients to have internalised something from our creative relationship, their own with us and each other, we leave with the strength of experience and fulfilment of having achieved a cycle of creation from conception and inception, through growth and fruition to a natural conclusion and close.

As we reflect on this particular ending in our lives, we remember how moved and frustrated we have felt, how impassioned we have been, and how deeply we have learnt about our own creativity and the capacity of love. Supervision was of great importance at this time, as a forum for our own issues of loss, a celebration of achievement and awareness of any possible uncontained, unconscious material being acted out. A good supervision which acknowledges, tolerates and allows us to recognise all these aspects has helped prevent our own feelings of loss spilling over into the group: another process of expression and containment. Our personal sense of commitment to working with, and not denying, these feelings has been risky, exciting and essential.

We hope we have conveyed some of the energy and enthusiasm we feel for our work in this group. We have tried to capture the essence of it and discovered in the process that once captured something of its spirit is lost. What we have found is that the extraordinary places that this group has taken us in our relationships and our sense of shared humanity exist in a wonder-full land that lies beyond words.

ACKNOWLEDGEMENTS

Warm thanks to Rex Haigh, our creative and compassionate supervisor, and to the members of the therapeutic community who took part in the creative group.

PART III

Specialist Communities

CHAPTER 11

Chaotic Personalities

Maintaining the Therapeutic Alliance

Penelope Campling

EDITORS' INTRODUCTION

This chapter is about the people with whom I work at Francis Dixon Lodge, a residential NHS therapeutic community in Leicester. The dynamics I have chosen to write about are those with which we struggle most. Theory is used in a rather hotch-potch manner, where it has felt helpful. Thus, I focus on the problems in maintaining a therapeutic alliance and explain the relevance of psychoanalytic concepts such as envy, hostile dependency, the negative therapeutic reaction and psychopathic transference.

The case is made for detailed psychodynamic formulations as an aid to risk management with a particular focus on the interpersonal triggers of suicidal behaviour. This is very different from the rather shallow actuarial type of risk assessment that is being promoted with zeal in psychiatry at the present time. It is well to remember that risk is contained through relationship and understanding — messy and unpredictable as this may be.

Most therapeutic communities within the present NHS are for those with severe personality disorder (SPD). It is not a label they appreciate and I have chosen a more descriptive and less stigmatising title of 'chaotic personalities' for this chapter. However, I will continue, apologetically, to refer to SPD as shorthand for a complex concept incorporating profound problems of living and relating; long-standing, persistent, deeply rooted emotional difficulties usually leading to dangerous levels of destructive behaviour. I use the closely related concept 'borderline personality disorder' when quoting other writers.

Much psychiatric care aims to make professionals accountable and responsible for patients' behaviour. In those with SPD, this is often not appropriate and can lead to increasingly regressed and disturbed behaviour. For this reason, psychiatry has always been ambivalent about personality disorder and it may be that the ambivalence towards therapeutic communities is in part due to their common association with this patient group.

It is to be hoped that personality disorder is no longer a diagnosis of despair and an excuse for therapeutic nihilism. Thanks to the evolving disciplines of psychoanalysis and psychotherapy, there is increasing recognition that they suffer desperate psychic pain and that their disturbed behaviour is frequently driven by the overwhelming intensity of their feelings and fragile sense of self. Importantly, there is greater awareness and understanding of child sexual abuse and an evolving link between this and borderline personality structure. On the other hand, ambivalence continues as accountability and risk management squeeze out therapeutic possibility, and poorly resourced teams struggle to provide an inappropriate type of care modelled on their work with the mentally ill. These patients are desperately in need of psychotherapy but are too mistrustful, chaotic and destructive to make this a viable option on a sessional basis in an outpatient department.

This chapter illustrates (often using Francis Dixon Lodge (FDL) as an example) the difficulties that arise when working with such individuals, and describes how a therapeutic community, with its fundamentally different structure and approach, encourages clients to take responsibility back and develop more appropriate methods of establishing and maintaining relationships.

Residents are usually referred because of their very destructive ways of expressing distress. Many of them have spent long periods of time in acute facilities, often causing havoc to other patients and staff teams and frequently getting worse in the process rather than better. Many of them have been detained in the past using the Mental Health Act, some have been in prison or secure psychiatric facilities and the vast majority have acted in a violent, high risk, life-endangering manner at some point in their history.

Programmes are highly structured, with community meetings sandwiching the day, and psychotherapy groups, activity sessions and ongoing assessments in between. If necessary, crisis meetings can be called at any hour of the day and night. The group is the main forum for psychological work and intense one-to-one contact with staff is avoided (the Cassel works with a different model, described in Chapter 3). The emphasis is on residents taking responsibility for themselves and each other. To this aim, they are involved as much as possible in decision making from the assessment stage onwards.

Much of the deliberate self-harm is more bizarre and bloody than the usual overdose that turns up in casualty, and life histories tend to be shocking and deeply disturbing. The task of therapy, put very simply, is to help the patients transfer all these 'bloody' feelings into the therapeutic forum, so that they can be contained, understood and mastered. There are two fundamental conflicts in trying to do this. The first is how to create a therapeutic relationship in which the patient feels secure enough to explore new ways of relating, and to access horrors from the past when these very horrors carry so much negative emotion that they threaten to destroy the relationship. The second is that 'acting out' has both an expressive and a defensive function. In other words, even the most bloody examples of self-destructive provocative behaviour may be an attempt to prevent some catastrophe which the patient perceives as even more destructive to his or her integrity – engulfment, psychosis, violence or complete despair.

In a therapeutic community, the very structure helps to meet these challenges: the involvement and respect for members; the strong peer group support; the cathartic Athenian stage which large group dynamics offer – enabling a tragic story to be told; the 24 hour/7 day a week crisis support; the complex network of relationships and perspectives; the focus on responsibility, appeal to healthy ego-functioning, and pressure to work, even at the bleakest moments. These factors help to engage and keep very distressed people in therapy and minimise the chance of them getting worse and destroying themselves or others in the process.

THE PROBLEM OF ENGAGEMENT

Because of their extreme low self-esteem and feelings of worthlessness, these patients find it difficult to ask for help appropriately and end up presenting with a crisis: for example, taking an overdose. This results in a crisis-response from professionals who are often forced into an authoritarian position with them, managing and often judging the behaviour rather than the underlying distress, not infrequently confirming their belief that they are 'no hopers' and that there is no value for them in the system. Resources, therefore, get sucked in, in a non-productive inefficient way, increasing the anger on both sides and making a therapeutic alliance even harder to establish. Presumably because of grossly inadequate early parenting, there is no 'basic trust' that people in caring positions have their welfare at heart.

Key figures in the past have messed things up, neglected, not understood, abandoned, abused positions of authority and power, often to the point of leaving them humiliated, helpless, raped and maimed. This then becomes the 'prototype' for future relationships, the expectation, the self-fulfilling prophecy. Looked at from this point of view, the fact that they develop any degree of trust in us becomes an extraordinary achievement, and one that has to be a constant focus of therapy.

BASIC TRUST AND ATTACHMENT FAILURE

Attachment theory confirms these observations. There is evidence accruing that the psychotherapeutic concept of 'basic trust' may have a biological basis in attachment, and recent research postulates a further link between secure attachment and reflective self-function (Higgit and Fonagy 1992). Of interest to the subject of SPD is the recently recognised pattern of infant attachment occurring in about 4 per cent of the population which is categorised as 'insecure-disorganised'. These infants 'freeze' on separation, and seem unable to sustain any organised pattern of behaviour: it is postulated that they may become the future generation of patients with borderline personality disorder. It has also been shown that these children tend to have been subjected to major parental failure such as physical abuse or gross neglect (Ainsworth 1969).

One of the main differences between working psychotherapeutically with less disturbed neurotic patients and more disturbed patients with SPD, is that one cannot take the therapeutic alliance for granted. The relationship cannot be left to develop, and mistrust analysed as it arises. Trust has to be created and the therapeutic alliance built up in a way that is tangible for, and understood by, the patient. As soon as new members become part of a therapeutic community, they are integral to the therapeutic process, part of the containing group, therapist as well as patient, on both sides of the therapeutic alliance. Holmes (1993) describes secure attachment as parental atunement and the ability to accept the child's aggression and separation-protest without retaliation. Winnicott (1971) described the secure child as saying 'Hello Object, I destroyed you'. So when we talk about a good therapeutic alliance, we do not mean something sentimental or simplistically reassuring. Warmth is certainly called for, but also a toughness, something that can be kicked against but will continue to provide consistency. It is difficult to destroy a large group.

Facing the reality and enormity of the problems in a non-judgemental way at the start of therapy can paradoxically be deeply reassuring. So, for example, we take time at the assessment to look at the patients' fears about therapy and also voice our own. We make it clear that while some people find it helpful, there is no magic cure; that change may be minimal and is a painful process which is likely to feel overwhelming at times; that far from feeling better, they are likely to feel a good deal worse throughout much of their treatment and that there will be many times when their level of fear and despair will make it tempting to leave. Putting this to them is not easy. They tend to present desperately lacking in self-esteem and motivation, so to instil them with hope becomes the first task of engagement. Or they manage those feelings by seeing the therapeutic community as the answer to everything and are deaf to uncertainties that others try to raise. In therapeutic communities, the assessment panel consists of both staff and residents. The residents constantly surprise us by their useful insights and sensitive comments and are often in a better position than staff to be both realistic about the problems and hopeful for change. Many therapeutic communities reinforce the message with written material, thus trying to convey both warmth and realism. For example, our newcomers receive a *How to Survive Francis Dixon Lodge* booklet, written by ex-residents in a chatty, humorous, informal style.

Unfortunately, referrers tend to encourage idealisation and our patients often come with the idea that no other setting can contain them and that the therapeutic community is literally their 'last chance'. Many of them arrive thinking they are going to get the 24 hour/7 day a week intravenous infusion of unconditional positive regard that they have always yearned for. They then have to manage massive disappointment and frequently drop out.

THE THERAPEUTIC CONTRACT

One of the tasks at assessment is to work on a type of psychotherapeutic contract that spells out the community's responsibilities and the new member's responsibilities. This is best conceptualised as a process and is more about attitude than hard and fast rules. At FDL, for example, we make it clear that new residents should try to talk about suicidal feelings in group, and for this reason can call a crisis meeting at any time. If self-harming behaviour does occur, it is the residents' responsibility to let staff know and we try to be as clear as possible about what the consequences will be. Residents know that they will have to talk about their self-destructive behaviour as soon as the physical danger has passed; and it is made clear that while we do not expect behaviour to change overnight, our tolerance does have limits and expectations attached. It is important to avoid secondary gain and to be clear about what the procedure will be if self-harm does occur. Pandemonium, muddle and rocketing anxiety levels will cause patients to feel dangerously omnipotent. Whilst different therapeutic communities will have different rules and boundaries (for example, with regard to deliberate self-harm or medication) the important thing at assessment is that all involved are clear about what is agreed.

It is important to be as open as possible about the possibility of suicide, and if necessary to voice the idea that this is ultimately the individual's responsibility not the community's – or, as Kernberg (1992) puts it, 'the therapist will not be more responsible than the patient himself to keep the patient alive'. There is psychotherapeutic value in this type of reality confrontation: acknowledging limits sends a powerful message to the individual concerning the psychic reality of the group members, and gradually leads to a firming-up of the individual's boundaries and a strengthening of the sense of self.

PSYCHODYNAMIC FORMULATIONS

At FDL a psychodynamic formulation is done at a staff meeting three weeks after admission. All available information is pooled and organised to provide a useful focus for the team, including predictions about transference and countertransference. It is particularly important to include a psychodynamic understanding of suicidal behaviour. Risk-assessment should always include the context and possible triggers, and as much detail as possible about relationships at the time. For example, with many borderline patients, it is perceived abandonment, or the dread of abandonment, which overwhelms them with panic, rage and despair. It is vitally important therefore that staff are sensitive to the importance of going on leave, and that they pick up generally on departures from the group. The constant comings and goings in a therapeutic community can begin to feel routine to longer-standing members of staff, whilst less experienced staff may fail to comprehend the desperation such disruptions cause to our deeply insecure residents, particularly as it is often unconscious and denied by the residents themselves.

Another common trigger for suicidal or self-harming behaviour is something that reminds a patient of the abuse he or she has suffered. So, for example, patients might harm themselves at the early stages of an intimate relationship, when otherwise things seem to be going well. A few years ago a male patient had a sebaceous cyst removed and let it be known that he would not be down to meetings for the rest of the week[1]. He had been playing a major part in testing the staff team out, constantly pushing at boundaries, and we saw this as yet another example of this process. Apparently he was up and about in the evenings when there were no groups to attend. So, after two days of this, I decided it was time to exert some authority. He eventually came crashing down the stairs, stormed through the door, screaming and cursing, then stormed out saying (and I am quoting because this is what alerted us to its being about abuse), 'I'd like to stick a Bowie knife up your fucking cunt and twizzle it around slowly so you know how much I'm hurting'. He left the room at this point, but when I came out later he'd gone into my office, left his foul-smelling, blood-drenched bandages and a message, which said 'Satisfied?' He then went off and took a serious but not fatal overdose.

It eventually transpired that the operation on his cyst brought up painful memories of very humiliating sexual abuse. It is certainly a common finding that minor medical procedures can trigger feelings of violation, shame and rage associated with pain and helplessness in those who have been abused. If we had made this association earlier, he might have felt met and understood instead of being enraged by our confrontation over authority. Unwittingly, we repeated his past: the mother who did not understand his pain and further punished him for making such a fuss. If we had understood better, things would probably have been different, and the overdose avoided.

A psychodynamic formulation of suicidal behaviour should include the patient's perception of the trigger and the meaning he or she ascribes to it. For example, two patients overdosed after their flats were burgled. Lisa, who had been severely sexually abused as a child, felt intruded upon by the experience; whereas for Dominique it was the theft of her mother's jewellery that brought back the feelings of loss and grief which were associated with the sudden death of her mother as a child. Simply identifying the burglary as the trigger would have missed vital information in both cases.

1　Names and details of residents and events have been changed in order to protect anonymity.

Of course, much of this information will not be available at a three-week review. Lacking a coherent narrative is integral to this client group's problems and diagnosis, and the three-week formulation is as valuable for drawing our attention to gaps and questions in the story as making tentative links between past history and present behaviour. The formulation is shared with the community the following day. It is then written up and forms the basis of the resident's collaboratively produced care plan. The psychodynamic formulation thus evolves as therapy progresses, and is a collaborative process involving the whole community. Many residents choose to keep their own copy of their care plan, something concrete to hold on to, when they feel lost in large group dynamics or intense feelings threaten to overwhelm the therapeutic alliance.

CONTAINING DESTRUCTIVE FEELINGS

The type of small specific holding measure described in the previous section is important in our resident group: most of them lack the capacity to hold on to their feelings and are in therapy because of their overwhelming impulse to try and rid themselves of the feelings by acting them out. Therapy involves rechannelling the angry, destructive emotions which are usually directed against themselves into the network of relationships within the community where they can be 'held' until the individuals are able to hold on to them themselves. This can lead to attempts (usually unconscious) to destroy both the therapy and the community; for example, arriving late or missing meetings, falling asleep, resistant silences and treating group members in a derogatory way. It is important to interpret these as 'here-and-now' attacks on what is being offered by the therapeutic community and to make links with the patient's self-destructive and suicidal behaviour. In other words, it is more useful to think in terms of the transference of aggression from behaviour directed against the resident's own body into the interpersonal field of therapeutic relationships, than to make links with the past. In fact, most psychotherapists would discourage forceful interpretation of the unconscious past with this client group, as it may reinforce confusion between present and past and induce transference psychosis, where the 'as if' quality in the therapeutic relationship is lost.

In a therapeutic community these attacks can be constructively dealt with within the group; for example, more experienced residents modelling new found ways of managing their distress, and the peer group confronting individuals with the effects of their action. The focus on rules and boundaries, the here-and-now, day-to-day living with 'nitty-gritty' practicalities like who is going to do the washing-up, the need to work and rub shoulders even when a few minutes earlier blue murder is being screamed, help to prevent initial treatment goals being overwhelmed by negative transference. They also go some way to control and limit dangerous pathological regression, which might otherwise be the consequence of doing in-depth psychotherapy with such vulnerable personalities.

The round-the-clock availability of the community (at FDL, residents can call a 'crisis' meeting at any time of the day or night) makes it safe enough to explore emotional material knowing that overwhelming distress can be talked about at any time. There is thus persistent pressure on our residents – who almost by definition experience feelings as so overwhelming that they cannot think and have to act – to 'give sorrow words'. Talking means thinking and sometimes even leads to listening to the other person's point of view. Thus a reflective capacity gradually develops, and with this a more consistent and elastic impulse-control and a more comfortable integration of feelings.

SURVIVING THERAPY AND WORKING AS A TEAM

However, there are times when destructiveness can take a community to its limits and beyond; it is often staff members who are on the receiving end of intense negative transference, constantly being pushed and tested. The job of the staff team as a whole in this situation is to stick to the analytic task, address rules and boundaries, and neither be destroyed nor retaliate nor succumb. Fonagy (Higgit and Fonagy 1992) has suggested that patients with borderline personality symptoms suffered the prolonged hatred of the main care-giving figure as they were growing up. To protect against the painful awareness of the violence, neglect and vacuousness in the mind of the parent, the child denies his or her capacity to think about the mental state of others. It is easy to collude with this, and vital that we should not. Our patients need us to be direct and straight with them, even when this feels really uncomfortable, and possibly dangerous. This also gives us the opportunity to model the complexity of human relationships, the fact that intense love and murderous rage can coexist very painfully towards the same person. It also challenges their simplistic, polarised map of the world made up of the very good and the very bad, with no room for a mixture of qualities in the same person.

A large staff team with different backgrounds and perspectives and the lack of a 'party line' can be very therapeutic for the same reason. There is safety in numbers, and working in a team allows different members of the group to take on different roles. Conflict between staff members can be used creatively provided it is expressed overtly and within the boundaries of the group. One member of the team may be enforcing the rules, for example, whilst another identifies more with residents and another comments on the group process. Sometimes we act as translators for each other. Thus a staff member, who is seen as being more sympathetic by the residents, tries to explain the unpopular or misunderstood stance that another is taking. It is important that individual staff members do not get stuck with a stereotype, particularly where extreme idealisation or denigration is involved. If one member is on the receiving end of persistent negative transference for example, the group dynamic within the staff team needs to be analysed. It may be that other members of the team are unable to resist the gratification involved in being idealised and are colluding with the residents' appeals to be rescued.

Many of our residents mistrust the whole staff team for the first few months of therapy, but working with a peer group of others in the same situation strengthens their sense of themselves enough to move on and explore the projections and displacements of aggression which make working with staff so frightening. It is always encouraging to see newer residents being encouraged, cajoled, soothed, challenged and confronted by those who are further on in therapy and a few months earlier were exhibiting the same sorts of destructive ambivalence.

HOSTILE DEPENDENCY, ENVY AND THE NEGATIVE THERAPEUTIC REACTION

Working conscientiously as a team is particularly important where 'hostile dependency' is a major dynamic. These residents can be extremely frustrating because whenever they feel understood and cared for, their dependency needs become overwhelming and have to be assuaged by attacking the carer in some way. This leaves them more anxious and vulnerable, more dependent; and so the cycle continues. A lot of chronic suicidal behaviour may express symbolically the attack on hated objects who at the same time are desperately needed and perceived as potentially good. For example, a patient recently responded to an interpretation by storming out, putting his arm through a pane of glass, then waving his torn flesh in front of me, screaming, 'Look what you've done!' Kleinians would talk about the same dynamic in terms of 'envy', 'biting the breast', attempting to destroy or spoil the good qualities in the person trying to care for them.

A related concept is that of the 'negative therapeutic reaction' – the attempt to sabotage everything at points of achievement or success, the patient getting clearly worse precisely at points when the therapist appears understanding and helpful. In less disturbed patients this is often due to unresolved oedipal conflicts and unconscious guilt. In our more disturbed patients, it is more useful to try to give them some conscious awareness of their envy, their profound sense of their own emptiness and impoverishment, and their consequent hatred of the good qualities in other people, particularly the capacity to love. At FDL, we have a system of internal assessments, where residents have to review their progress every three months, identifying the work they have done and setting out objectives for the next stage. I have come to be extremely wary of so-called 'good assessments' because they are so often followed by destructive acting-out. Many of these situations could probably be pre-empted by introducing a heavy dose of caution, but these patients struggle so much with feelings of hopelessness and worthlessness that it is always very tempting to sit back and stop working when they are being more positive about themselves. We are continually reminded that the cost of this neglect can be high.

LYING AND DECEPTION

Another quality that requires urgent attention in therapy is deceit: that is, conscious suppression or alteration of essential information to the therapist, outright lying or manipulative behaviour geared to disorientate or exploit the therapist in some way, carried out in clear consciousness and not as a consequence of unconscious denial or confusion. Patients who behave like this also project such tendencies on to the therapist. In other words, the more dishonest the patient, the more dishonest he or she believes the therapist to be and the less he or she can trust what the therapist says. Therapy can quickly become a farce and it is for this reason that deception has to be understood and interpreted before proceeding with other material.

Our naivety on this issue at FDL has certainly been exploited, and of course the consequences when working in a group setting are particularly damaging. One woman went into vivid detail in the group about being gang raped, getting pregnant and suffering a miscarriage. By coincidence, she had some gynaecological tests whilst under our care which revealed this to be untrue. Later, she was able to confess that much of her history was fabrication. She had suffered an empty, loveless childhood and been grossly neglected. It seemed that her lying was linked with envy and jealousy and she told how she had consciously started to fabricate at the age of eleven when she had been staying with a school friend whom she saw as having everything she wanted, particularly an 'ideal' mother. The lying was initially an attempt to obtain this woman's attention and make herself special. She had been repeating this behaviour with carers ever since.

Another case was a man who was referred to us with a concomitant diagnosis of post-traumatic stress disorder after serving with the army in Bosnia. I was nearly moved to tears in a psychotherapy group, when in-between heart-rending sobs he described the death of his best friend and fellow soldier. Descriptions of the horror of his time in the army were common, and later on in therapy he began to make links with horrors in his childhood. Six months after he had left, I had a letter from a colleague who had just discovered that far from being in active combat, this man had never been more than a cadet and had never set foot in Bosnia. He was later the subject of a court order and it was confirmed that most of his stories while in therapy were consciously fabricated. Trying to talk to him about this in retrospect was complicated. Was he lying about the lying? It seemed, however, that consciously fabricating had become a way of distracting from feelings of emptiness, shame and envy; a way of setting up an immediately gratifying, pseudo-emotional contact over which he could remain in control. Ideally, concerns over the lack of genuineness, and the capacity to lie and consciously distort information, should be shared candidly. Linking this with early corruption by a dishonest parent (often an alcoholic) can be helpful, although frequently cannot be heard until later in therapy. Kernberg (1992) talks about converting a 'psychopathic transference' into a paranoid transference, and patients who eventually confess to lying are likely to experience humiliating exposure and fears of attack and abandonment. For this reason, it is particularly important for group therapists to encourage the right balance between sternness and empathy.

The most common deceivers are those residents with concomitant alcohol or substance misuse or an eating disorder. In these conditions, deceiving others is a necessary part of the behaviour, and in some cases, central to the pathology.

EATING DISORDERS

Eating disorders are more common than they used to be, or at least they are more commonly recognised. At FDL, for example, the majority of women and a significant number of men have suffered from symptoms at some time in the past; and 25 per cent fulfil the ICD-10 criteria for ongoing anorexia nervosa, bulimia nervosa or a compulsive eating disorder. Where it is the primary condition, patients are usually seen by eating disorder specialists. This means that for the clients we see in therapeutic communities, the eating disorder is only part of the generally chaotic and destructive picture. Because the symptoms are easily kept 'secret' and do not seem as antisocial or as dangerous as other destructive behaviours, it is easy to neglect the chronic misery they can cause. It is not uncommon, for example, after a resident gives up dramatic self-burning or cutting, for the community to heave a sigh of relief and turn a blind eye to the bingeing and vomiting which have escalated to fill the gap. Male residents are particularly liable to be isolated with their symptoms and go to extreme lengths to cover their tracks and resist the profound shame and exposure which they fear feeling if their secret is discovered. The behaviour is often linked with other secret self-punishing rituals, taking showers in boiling hot water for example, or bathing in bleach; and very commonly there is a history of having been severely sexually abused.

The ideal is to create a vigilant, but non-persecutory culture where residents can talk openly about such behaviour and the underlying feelings, in a community that is prepared to listen empathetically and to give sensitive encouragement and advice, volunteering ways in which they might become helpfully involved. In practice, it is difficult to achieve a good balance: it is easy to allow things to drift in a perhaps collusive and rather directionless community, as the symptoms themselves further undermine and distort the individual's perspective. On the other hand, it can be tempting for staff members to be over directive, and then, because the symptoms are tied up with issues of control and abuse, find themselves with a full-blown and counterproductive transference on their hands.

It is important to share information and expertise with the community; so that for example, they have some understanding of the link between cognitions and physiological changes, and the self-perpetuating effect of bulimic symptoms. This type of relationship with the community, where expert knowledge is shared with all rather than possessed by the staff alone, is an important therapeutic component, increasing residents' confidence as group members, feeding into their healthy egos and building on their growing sense of responsibility. Sharing knowledge in this way has roots in the first years of the therapeutic community movement. Maxwell Jones, for example, taught groups of patients suffering from chest pain about their condition and was impressed by the potential group dynamic; whilst the Northfield pioneers taught their patients about the unconscious and about defence mechanisms, thus giving them a model to understand 'battle neurosis' and a weapon to use against it. More recently, in the treatment of borderline personality disorder, building upon and handing over knowledge about the condition are fundamental components of cognitive analytic therapy, where it is likened to erecting scaffolding to buttress a vulnerable personality (Ryle 1995, p.39).

In the case of residents with an eating disorder, strengthening the peer group dynamic in this way may enable a collaborative relationship to be maintained and challenge ingrained attitudes towards dependency and control.

SUBSTANCE MISUSE

As with eating pathology, substance misuse has increased in the young adult population and consequently within therapeutic communities. Classic teaching suggests that drug addicts should be treated in specialist units, separate from those with other diagnoses. However, an increasing number of our referrals have a concomitant problem with drugs. Often the individual is referred by the drugs service and is 'clean' at assessment and increasingly we are seeing second generation drug addicts who are 'clean' at assessment; but steeped in the drug culture, brought up in environments where a fix of heroin is as commonplace as a bowl of cereal. Most commonly, as with eating disorders, the drug misuse is part of a generally chaotic, destructive picture, not usually a big problem in the resident's mind, but significant none the less. Attempts to play down the problem are usually proved misguided; for it does seem that in vulnerable, insecure personalities, street drugs cause decompensation and deterioration, negatively affect the prognosis in therapy, and, worst of all, corrupt and distort the network of relationships within the community.

It is important to keep the staff team and community as up to date as possible with change and development in the drug culture, particularly the local scene.

Informed vigilance and 'street-wise' empathy are likely to deter residents from taking risks with illegal substances and make the community feel safer.

CONCLUSION

This chapter has attempted to give some sense of the intensity and complexity of feelings and behaviour encountered when working with severely disturbed chaotic personalities in a therapeutic community.

I have used examples from the work at Francis Dixon Lodge, which attempts to combine the traditional principles of a 'therapeutic community proper', with the increasing professional knowledge and expertise we now have about working psychotherapeutically with more disturbed personalities. Whilst these different perspectives may appear at times to conflict, focusing on the therapeutic alliance reveals that, in fact, a therapeutic community, with its practice rooted in significant power sharing, and a belief in the healing power of the group, answers many of the questions thrown up by recent advances in our understanding of severe attachment failure and child abuse, and continues to provide a challenging, humane and effective treatment.

REFERENCES

Ainsworth, M. (1969) 'Object relations, dependency and attachment: a theoretical review of the mother-infant relationship.' *Child Development 40*, 969–1025.

Higgit, A. and Fonagy, P. (1992) 'Psychotherapy in borderline and narcissistic personality disorder.' *British Journal of Psychiatry 161*, 23–43.

Holmes, J. (1993) 'Attachment theory: a biological basis for psychotherapy?' *British Journal of Psychiatry 161*, 430–38.

Kernberg, O.F. (1992) 'Psychoanalytic psychotherapy with borderline patients.', Paper presented at the conference on 'The psychoanalytical approach to borderline states', 24–25 January. Organised by the Psychoanalysis Unit, University College, London.

Ryle A. (1995) 'The practice of CAT'. In A. Ryle (ed) *Cognitive Analytical Therapy: Developments in Theory and Practice*. John Wiley & Sons, Chichester.

Winnicott, D. (1971) 'Use of an object and relating through identification.' In D. Winnicott (ed) *Playing and Reality*. Tavistock: London.

CHAPTER 12

Schizophrenia

Hospital Communities for the Severely Disturbed

Geoffrey Pullen

EDITORS' INTRODUCTION

Geoffrey Pullen's interest in the power of the psychological and social environment started when he was working as a nursing auxiliary before going on to medical school at Cambridge in 1965. He moved to the Middlesex Hospital in London for his clinical studies, where his first job after qualifying was as a neurosurgeon: a career he did not pursue any further!

He specialised in psychiatry, and was particularly influenced by group and child psychotherapy, TCs including the Shenley Villa 21 experiment, and the fringes of the anti-psychiatry movement. He moved to Fulbourn in Cambridge in 1975 as a senior registrar, and explored the use of a TC as an acute admission ward (Street) until he took up his consultant post, as a psychiatrist with a special interest in rehabilitation, in Oxford in 1980. He has developed the Eric Burden Community and Young Adult Unit there, and takes mischievous satisfaction in managing to encourage Oxford junior doctors – usually a rather serious breed – to engage in eccentric behaviour such as dressing up in fancy dress for community parties – and seeing that there is more to psychiatry than medication, custody and professional etiquette.

Geoffrey has been a member of the Association of Therapeutic Communities since its very beginning in the 1970s, and organised its conferences for many years. In this chapter, he reviews how different TC experiments in the treatment of schizophrenia happened, and describes the way in which the principles are embodied in the Oxford service he leads. He also airs some thought-provoking ideas on how therapeutic communities should be therapeutic for staff. In this regard, it is interesting that TCs generally report a low turnover of staff and low sickness rate.

In Chapter 1 of this book, Tom Harrison describes how the therapeutic community first developed through the two experiments at Northfield Hospital. At the end of the war Tom Main proposed that the therapeutic community was:

> an attempt to use a hospital not as an organisation run by doctors in the interests of their own greater technical efficiency, but as a community with the immediate aim of full participation of all its members in its daily

life and the eventual aim of re-socialisation of the neurotic individual for life in ordinary society. (Main 1946, p.67)

Maxwell Jones developed these ideas further at the Henderson Hospital (Jones 1952). Between 1953 and 1957 Rapoport, an anthropologist, and his team which included sociologists and psychologists, studied the Henderson which by then saw itself as 'treating working-class psychopaths' (Rapoport 1960). Four themes were seen to 'broadly encompass the distinctive elements of the unit's ideology', namely: 'democratisation', 'permissiveness', 'communalism' and 'reality confrontation'. It has often been suggested that an adherence to these four 'principles' could be taken as being the defining feature of a therapeutic community (Morrice 1979; Pullen 1986).

ASYLUM PSYCHIATRY AFTER THE SECOND WORLD WAR

Whilst the Second World War can be said to have directly brought about the birth of the therapeutic community it had a less direct, but still important, effect upon asylum psychiatry. The desire for a new and better society, valuing all its members, also seems have inspired a significant number of the men who were appointed asylum Medical Superintendents after the war. Bell by 1949 had unlocked all the wards at Dingleton Hospital, Melrose, Scotland (Bell 1955), starting the 'open door campaign' of the next decade. Most asylums eventually unlocked most of their doors, sometimes cautiously, and sometimes (Mandelbrote 1958) in one grand gesture. For a hundred years Physician Superintendents had been absolute rulers of their private domains. Some were enlightened despots, others petty tyrants, many it seems were as demoralised as their institutions. Finally, however, for about 20 years (c.1955–1975) a group of energetic, far-seeing, pioneers used their power and authority to transform British psychiatry.

David Clark, who described his approach as 'social therapy' (Clark 1974), writes about some of their achievements in Chapter 2. (A fuller discussion of these contributions, and of those of the antipsychiatrists, can also be found in Pullen 1999) Clark had run an acute admission ward, Friends, as a therapeutic community from 1971 until 1976 when Martin Roth was appointed as Cambridge's first Professor of Psychiatry and took over the ward. In 1975 I had the good fortune to be appointed a senior registrar at Fulbourn, at the time probably the most exciting and dynamic hospital in Britain. For the next four years I divided my time between outpatient psychotherapy and managing, with the benign support of its senior consultant Oliver Hodgson, an acute admission ward, Street. Before 1975 few acute admission units had attempted to run as therapeutic communities, the patients being seen as too ill and their length of stay too short for any effective therapy to occur. One successful ward was the Phoenix Unit at Littlemore Hospital, Oxford (Sugarman 1968). This had been opened as a male rehabilitation unit by Bertram Mandelbrote in 1961

(Mandelbrote 1965) but quickly evolved into a more comprehensive service including acute admission. It always retained a core of 'longstay' day patients in order to ensure continuity of the therapeutic culture. This well respected unit functioned as a therapeutic community until Mandelbrote retired in 1988.

STREET WARD, FULBOURN HOSPITAL, CAMBRIDGE

Street Ward (1975–1979) is probably still the most sustained and intensive British attempt that has been made to run an orthodox acute admission ward as a therapeutic community; most of its patients were in an acute phase of a psychotic illness, either schizophrenia or depression. Its 35 beds were the only psychiatric inpatient service for the adult, non-dementing population of its sector of about 150,000. Although some patients received compulsory treatment under the Mental Health Act, there was no access to 'intensive care' or other secure facilities (Pullen 1982). Street was unusual in the 1970s in claiming to be a therapeutic community whilst using both drugs and electroconvulsive therapy (ECT). A minimum desirable outcome, therefore, was to create a group living experience on Street that was not anti-therapeutic and did not interfere with other treatments. Even though the average length of admission was only 17 days there was often a powerful sense of community and shared purpose. Reality confrontation was usually vigorous and an emphasis was placed upon democratisation and permissiveness.

Residents were encouraged to share in each other's treatment as much as possible, even the use of sedation. The staff team felt it was important to acknowledge that sedation could be used legitimately both to make life more bearable for the recipient and to make him or her more bearable by others. These uses needed to be distinguished from the abuses of sedation which range from crude punishment to the more subtle feeding of the need for doctors and nurses to feel therapeutically potent. A workshop on these themes was developed and a paper published (Pullen 1980). The community was allowed to say to a physically violent resident: 'We are sorry, we feel we just cannot bear your behaviour any more.' This right of the residents, however, was matched by their duty to share in the ownership of the unpleasant task of implementing the community's decision. Obviously doctors have to prescribe medication and nurses administer it, but at least some of the residents and para-medical staff were expected to share in the procedure.

The keystone of the ward's life was the daily 'community meeting' which lasted 45 minutes (9.30–10.15 a.m.), and was attended by everyone present in the unit at that time. Street's community meeting developed its own style. There was no chairperson or agenda, little formal business was transacted and votes rarely taken. Naturally, with a constantly changing population, meetings varied a great deal, but usually they were free-floating, often emotional and confrontational, large groups drawing upon the happenings of the previous day. While within the community meeting there was strong emphasis upon the common role of community member, the staff always met immediately afterward for a 30-minute private review. The latter seemed to me one of the most important meetings on Street, in many ways taking on the role of a daily 'sensitivity' meeting. All patients attended one of two small groups held twice a week and there were also weekly sociodrama and art therapy sessions. Staff were encouraged to attend the last two in the role of community member rather than as therapist. It was recognised that the staff also had legitimate therapeutic needs and I have suggested that Street could be seen as two parallel and interrelating therapeutic communities: the short-stay patient community and the longer-stay staff community. Certainly it was demonstrated over a period of two years that nurse sickness rates were only three-quarters those of the hospital's other acute admission wards (Pullen 1982).

In purely medical and administrative terms Street was successful, with shorter stays but similar re-admission rates when compared with the other two acute admission wards at Fulbourn (see also Chapter 18). It was much harder to measure the extent to which the residents of Street gained deeper psychological insights during their brief stays. My impression was that some did, particularly perhaps the more psychologically naive who really did learn something new about themselves. In any case, I remained convinced that schizophrenia was not a contra-indication for group and therapeutic community therapy. In 1980, therefore, I accepted the post of Consultant Psychiatrist with Special Interest in Rehabilitation at Littlemore Hospital, Oxford.

ERIC BURDEN COMMUNITY AND THE YOUNG ADULT UNIT, OXFORD

Under Bertram Mandelbrote's leadership nearly all of that hospital's 'old longstay patients' had been rehabilitated, and my 'inheritance' included Ward B5 which had been 'male disturbed' until becoming a mixed sex 'medium dependency' ward in the late 1970s. In the summer of 1980 it was home to a rather ill-assorted group of 23 men and women whose ages ran from 23 to 81 years. Most suffered from a severe, chronic psychotic illness and many were actively disturbed. The hospital wing they occupied was designed by the same architects as Oxford Prison, to which it bore a close resemblance. On the first floor it had a 137-foot-long day room, ineffectually divided into three by glass partitions, with a similar space on the second floor divided into two shabby open dormitories. The windows were high and inadequate, and the only direct access to the outside was down a fire escape (Pullen 1986).

Nevertheless, as my colleague Heather Hull wrote:

My first involvement with the ward was at Christmas, 1979. At this time a group of nurses on B5 had begun to question the system, and to challenge the basic concept that the ward's inmates were a bunch of 'no-hopers'. There were attempts to change the basic running of the place; small groups of patients were encouraged to cook for themselves at weekends; staff tried to step-back a little and allow patients to join in on a few decisions; a Community Meeting was started. The changes were small in some ways but revolutionary in that they were the first heralds of what was to be a total turn around in our attitudes and practices in caring for very damaged, chronically psychotic individuals. (Hull and Pullen 1988, pp.109–110)

I introduced the staff to some of the ideas of the therapeutic community, trying to help them make their own discoveries (Pullen 1985; Pullen 1986); it was I hope, a 'living-learning experience'. The patients too embraced the changes and asserted their right to rename the ward after their recently deceased fellow, Eric Burden. Eric was a long-term patient who, when he developed an oral carcinoma, was nursed and died in his 'home', the ward. He suffered from a chronic schizophrenic illness and had a long history of delinquent and disturbed behaviour but he faced his final illness with bravery and dignity. Although at the time I had wanted to give the ward a more 'political' and upbeat name, I now believe the community was right, and that Eric's life was a powerful and appropriate symbol for our new endeavour, the Eric Burden Community (EBC).

At that time there was increasing awareness of the problem of the so-called 'new longstay' (Mann and Cree 1976). We developed, therefore, a service for the 'young adult chronically mentally ill', the Young Adult Unit (YAU). Referrals are accepted from local consultant psychiatrists of patients who meet the following criteria:

(1)   aged between 18 and 35

(2)   diagnosed as suffering from a functional psychosis (usually schizophrenia) or a borderline personality disorder

(3)   normal intelligence (i.e. IQ of 70 or above)

(4)   (a) no or partial response to conventional medical treatments (i.e. medication)

        (b) *and* breakdown of social network (usually family support)

(5)   compliance with transfer to the YAU.

These criteria were chosen to identify those young men and women who had the worst prognoses (Kolakowska, Williams, Arden, Reveley, Jambor, Gelder and Mandlebrote 1985) and who were at greatest risk of joining the 'new longstay'. Early referral is encouraged, ideally before the institutionalising effects of traditional care have taken hold, and there is no requirement regarding length of previous admission. In our experience normal intelligence is needed to be able to use our therapeutic community programme. Many of our patients are compulsorily treated under the terms of the 1983 Mental Health Act, but we still feel we can require the patient's agreement to the transfer of their care to our unit. The YAU also accepts referrals from the special hospitals (that is maximum security hospitals such as Broadmoor); for these patients we are more flexible, especially with regard to age and diagnosis (Pullen 1998). Drug use, offending behaviour, or a history of violence are not criteria but in reality most patients referred have one or more of these problems.

Once a person is accepted after referral they are first admitted to the 20 bedded mixed sex EBC for a period lasting from a few weeks to up to two years. The initial goals are, as far as possible, to assess and meet the residents' psychiatric needs and, most importantly, to form a 'therapeutic alliance'. Most patients then used to be transferred to a nine-bedded hospital hostel, Thorncliffe House, in a suburb of Oxford. Although Thorncliffe House had a small number of nurses who worked mainly at the hostel, they, like their colleagues based at the EBC, were considered as part of the wider YAU team. Medical, occupational therapy and social work input was provided by people who worked for the whole YAU.[1] The team also provides community support when the patient is discharged to either independent or sheltered housing such as a group home. There are at any one time about 25 members of the YAU community living outside the hospital. Their support includes six of the beds of the EBC which are reserved for them for 'acute admissions'. Anyone whose name is on the YAU case register has the *right* to request readmission. Part of the work of the initial admission to the EBC is to help the resident recognise, and admit to themselves, when they need the help and support of the ward. This extended partnership between hospital staff and patient is unusual, but I believe very valuable (Pullen 1987; Pullen 1988). By the time patients reach the age of about 45 most have settled in the wider community and can be discharged from the YAU. A few people need a supported or containing environment for longer and Littlemore Hospital has three continuing care wards, one a hospital-hostel, 18 Morrell Crescent, is associated with the YAU. The others are a low secure and a medium secure ward.

The YAU team tries to work with the patient to achieve optimum control of their illness. Medication is only used to attempt to help with symptoms to the extent that the patient finds them distressing, or of course, to reduce any risks posed to the lives of the patient or others. It is not the staff's role to eliminate 'delusions'. Many patients associate their experience of schizophrenia with positive feelings of vigour and creativity, and some 'titrate' these against more

1   Unfortunately Thorncliffe House was closed in 1998 as one of the measures to meet overspending elsewhere by the Oxfordshire Mental Healthcare NMS Trust.

distressing consequences by their own management of their medication. We have a very limited ability to rectify the social disadvantages of the mentally ill, but we do have social workers as integral members of the staff team. The most important work of the EBC is psychotherapeutic/sociotherapeutic. Bloch and Crouch identified ten therapeutic factors in group psychotherapy: acceptance, universality, altruism, instillation of hope, guidance, vicarious learning, self-understanding, learning from interpersonal action, self-disclosure, and catharsis. Whitely and Collis (1987) demonstrated their relevance to the Henderson Hospital. I can find no better summary of the therapeutic factors operating in the EBC.

The EBC in many ways is a 'pure' form of the therapeutic community with the community life being the primary therapeutic agent – the 'living-learning' experience. The EBC undoubtedly values 'communalism', with a strong culture of mutual responsibilities and opportunities for altruism. The formal expression of communalism is the daily 30-minute community meeting. Attendance for residents is publicly valued but not compulsory. Occasionally when the numbers attending have dropped, suggestions have been made to reduce the meetings' frequency. Every time, however, this has been vigorously vetoed by the residents. It seems important to know that the meeting reliably exists and is available, whilst having the freedom not always to attend. As in Street, the meeting is followed by a compulsory 30-minute staff feedback meeting. A verbal 'process recording' is there made jointly by the staff members who then attempt to analyse the group's dynamics. The six community meeting 'themes' described by Clark and Myers (1970) often seem relevant:

(1)   rejection

(2)   violence

(3)   sexuality

(4)   staff divisions

(5)   dependence – independence

(6)   relationships with outside bodies.

What mainly distinguishes the EBC from other therapeutic communities is not the fact that the residents are mentally ill but, rather, the intrusiveness of the legal and managerial systems. To my eyes at least, our residents seem to make use of the therapeutic community in much the same way as their personality disordered contemporaries elsewhere. (One of the striking findings from our individual psychotherapy work is how our 'mad' patients use 'normal' neurotic defences during a session.) Many patients are treated, against their will, under the terms of the Mental Health Act. For those detained under Section 41 their fate is largely determined by the Home Secretary; it has been a good few years since that post has had a liberal occupant. As David Clark points out in his chapter, staff nowadays have to cope with management which has little understanding, and less sympathy, with their aspirations. These persecutions may in fact have strengthened the EBC; an external enemy is always a useful uniting force. On a more subtle level, the rigid imposed boundaries probably make it easier and safer to be permissive and democratic within the community, the structurally destructured space of the group analytic group (Ruel 1980).

ANTI-PSYCHIATRY AND SCHIZOPHRENIA

I have so far discussed the contribution of both the therapeutic community and social psychiatry movements in the development of my own work with people suffering from schizophrenia. There was, however, a third factor which played a part in the evolution of my own ideas: anti-psychiatry (Pullen 1985). For my generation it was Laing who put schizophrenia on the intellectual and political agenda. The fact that his contribution is now largely forgotten is probably due to two main reasons. First, as Kotowicz (1997) points out, there never was a 'Laingian' theory, his ideas changing from book to book. Second, Laing and many of his colleagues seem to have become disillusioned with their own clinical work. Cooper dismissed his account of Villa 21 (Cooper, Esterson and Laing 1965) as an 'ironic addendum' (Cooper 1967). Unfortunately this assessment of Villa 21 as a 'failed experiment' (Kennard 1983) seems to have become the received wisdom. When Cooper opened Villa 21 in 1962 at Shenley he was, as far as I know, the first to explicitly use milieu therapy for people suffering from active, acute schizophrenia. The Villa had 19 beds to which were admitted men aged between fifteen and the late twenties, over two-thirds of whom had been independently diagnosed as suffering from schizophrenia. Cooper described the original programme of the unit as 'not unlike that of the 'classical' therapeutic community'. There was a daily thirty minute community meeting, formal therapeutic small groups, work groups and a significant number of staff group meetings. In addition, Cooper draws attention to 'spontaneous' groups which would form at any time around some particular issue.

On re-reading Cooper's account of his time at Villa 21, I was struck by the apparent quality of the work carried out in that unit and by the important lessons which were learnt, and then, alas, largely forgotten. The 'staying in bed problem'; the 'ludicrously trivial' nature of much hospital work; role blurring; and of course authorities' horror of 'disorder'. Cooper asks, 'a number of disturbing and apparently paradoxical questions; for example, can patients "treat" other patients, and can they even treat staff!' (Cooper 1967), but he did not stay to answer them. It is not clear why Cooper felt he had to leave Villa 21, although he makes a great deal of the larger institution's hostility. He describes the hospital's negative response to the 'reality confrontation' experiment of making the patients experience the consequence of not washing up the pots and pans, namely no more food could be cooked! When I came to Shenley some six or seven years later, however, I was told the tale with some pride; I would say there was then still widespread tolerance and respect for Villa 21. What was going on in the Villa was of course provocative, devaluing by implication the 'life's work' of other staff and challenging all the defences they relied on to survive. In such circumstances envy, hostility, and, yes, persecution will be aroused. It is not easy to deal with these forces: Cooper quit.

THE HEALTH OF THE STAFF

There seems to me to be a constant tension between on the one hand the idea that the therapeutic community is a containing environment in which to deliver psychotherapy and on the other that it is the community itself that is therapeutic. The former model obviously has attractions for the staff, retaining for them a specialist, technician role. It can also permit the continuing use of the traditional defences whereby doctors and nurses project all their 'sickness' into the patients who in turn project away all their 'health and sanity'. Projective identification, however, is a dangerous game. A spectacular casualty was the Paddington Day Centre, despite the use of very sophisticated psychotherapy (Baron 1987). I am impressed by the therapeutic power of the community itself and within the EBC this has always been acknowledged, Bloch and Crouch's therapeutic factors being evident in the day-to-day interactions. A measure of humility seems in order for the staff: most of us have not had to cope with anything like the internal and external experiences of the residents. In a very real sense the wisdom about living with schizophrenia is something shared by the residents. As one of the EBC's senior clinicians I do not see myself as a 'top' psychotherapist, but rather my responsibilities are to monitor the health of the community, intervening when necessary. Therapeutic communities that survive all seem to have a leadership whose concerns include the dynamics of the organisation and its relationships with the wider world.

In theory, the staff of the EBC would seem to be particularly vulnerable to 'burn-out'. Not only are they required to open themselves to psychosis without using the normal staff defences (Evans, Huk, Hull and Pullen 1990; Hull and Pullen 1988), but they are also sometimes subjected to physical as well as emotional assaults. It might be thought surprising, therefore, that the EBC has perhaps the least problems in recruiting and retaining staff in the hospital (cf. Street's low sickness rates). I think the answer lies in the fact that we would say 'yes, on both counts' to Cooper's question 'can patients "treat" other patients, and can they even treat staff?' I am surprised that he asked the question because for me the enduring contribution of Laing and the antipsychiatrists was their pointing out that differences between staff and patients are trivial compared to what we have in common.

The EBC, therefore, accepts that staff also have therapeutic rights and that residents have therapeutic duties. Psychotherapy can be seen as the process of helping the subject to develop explanations of themselves which they feel are meaningful and which enable them to lead a life which they find more satisfying. As defined, everyone could obviously benefit from therapy, an idea formalised in the concept of a 'training analysis'. That concept also implies that the more insightful a therapist is, the better therapist they are. If we create a milieu (the therapeutic community) which promotes self-discovery, it seems perverse to deny that it will affect the 'staff' members. Obviously the therapeutic needs of staff tend to be different from those of the residents, a reality which I intended to acknowledge by my concept from Street of the two parallel communities. The staff have different boundaries of behaviour from the patients (who nevertheless also have psychotherapeutic boundaries, we would not collude with a total regression), and they have specific duties. Within these limits, however, the community will tolerate staff exploring behaviours ('permissiveness') which are related to their own needs. For example, I would tolerate (but not enjoy!) rude, aggressive behaviour which I might guess has to do with attitudes towards authority (and father), but a refusal to comply with a professional instruction would not be accepted. In return I would assert my right to robust response ('reality confrontation').

The big bonus from taking the concept of a therapeutic community literally is that it increases the patients' opportunities to experience their potency. All of the EBC residents have been defined as 'failures' by their previous carers, and usually by themselves. The projective mechanisms I have described above leave people feeling depleted and worthless. Supporting or comforting someone else, or even helping them to understand themselves better, is probably the most therapeutic experience we can offer. For me time spent with the members of the EBC often feels like a pleasurable respite from the unpleasantness of my duties in the wider managerial world, but not always. Stuart Whitely wrote 'when a Therapeutic Community becomes settled, comfortable and static, free of anxieties, rivalries, guilt, anger, depression, love and hate, it has lost its purpose' (Whiteley 1972, p.52). The EBC would seem, therefore, still to have a purpose for the young men and women who end up under its roof!

REFERENCES

Baron, C. (1987) *Asylum to Anarchy*. London: Free Association Books.

Bell, G.M. (1955) 'A mental hospital with open doors.' *International Journal of Social Psychiatry 1*, 42.

Bloch, S. and Crouch, E. (1985) *Therapeutic Factors in Group Psychotherapy*. Oxford: Oxford University Press.

Clark, D.H. (1974) *Social Therapy in Psychiatry*. Harmondsworth: Penguin Books.

Clark, D.H. (1996) *The Story of a Mental Hospital, Fulbourn 1858–1983*. London: Process Press.

Clark, D.H. and Myers, K. (1970) 'Themes in a therapeutic community.' *British Journal of Psychiatry 117*, 389–395.

Cooper, D. (1967) *Psychiatry and Anti-Psychiatry*. London: Tavistock.

Cooper, D., Esterson, A., and Laing, R.D. (1965) 'Results of family-orientated therapy with hospitalised schizophrenics.' *British Medical Journal 2,* 1462–5.

Evans, V.M., Huk, M., Hull, H. and Pullen, G.P. (1990) 'Stultitiae laus.' *International Journal of Therapeutic Communities 11,* 157–177.

Hull, H. and Pullen, G.P. (1988) 'The EBC-madness and community.' *International Journal of Therapeutic Communities 9,* 109–114.

Jones, M. (1952) *Social Psychiatry*. London: Tavistock.

Kennard, D. (1983) *An Introduction to Therapeutic Communities*. London: Routledge and Kegan Paul.

Kolakowska, T., Williams, A.D., Arden, M., Reveley, M.A., Jambor, K., Gelder, M.G. and Mandlebrote, B.M. (1985) 'Schizophrenia with good and poor outcome: 1 – early clinical features, responses to neuroleptics and signs of organic dysfunction.' *British Journal of Psychiatry 146,* 229–239.

Kotowicz, Z. (1997) *R.D. Laing and the Paths of Anti-Psychiatry*. London: Routledge.

Main, T.F. (1946) 'The hospital as a therapeutic institution.' *Bulletin of the Menniger Clinic 10,* 66–70.

Mandelbrote, B.M. (1958) 'An experiment in the rapid conversion of a closed mental hospital into an open-door hospital.' *Mental Hygiene 42,* 3–16.

Mandlebrote, B.M. (1965) 'The use of psychodynamic and sociodynamic principles in the treatment of psychotics. A change from ward unit concepts to grouped communities.' *Comprehensive Psychiatry 6,* 381–387.

Mann, S.A. and Cree, W. (1976) 'New long-stay psychiatric patients: a national sample survey of fifteen mental hospitals in England and Wales 1972–3.' *Psychological Medicine 6,* 603–616.

Morrice, J.K.W. (1979) 'Basic concepts: a critical review.' In R.D.Hinshelwood and N.P. Manning (eds) *Therapeutic Communities: Reflections and Progress*. London: Routledge and Kegan Paul.

Pullen, G.P. (1980) 'Communal medication.' *International Journal of Therapeutic Communities 1,* 125–127.

Pullen, G.P. (1982) 'Street: The seventeen day community.' *International Journal of Therapeutic Communities 2,* 115–126.

Pullen, G.P. (1985) 'Conflicts in starting therapeutic communities.' *International Journal of Therapeutic Communities 6,* 165–169.

Pullen, G.P. (1986) 'The Eric Burden Community.' *International Journal of Therapeutic Communities 7,* 191–200.

Pullen, G.P. (1987) 'The Oxford service for the young adult chronically mentally ill: Part 1.' *Bulletin of the Royal College of Psychiatrists 11,* 377–379.

Pullen, G.P. (1988) 'The Oxford service for the young adult chronically mentally ill: Part 2.' *Bulletin of the Royal College of Psychiatrists 12,* 64.

Pullen, G.P. (1998) 'Special hospital transfers'. *Journal of Forensic Psychiatry 9,* 241–244.

Pullen, G.P. (1999) 'The therapeutic community and schizophrenia.' In M. Pines and V. Schermer (eds) *Group Therapy of the Psychoses*. London: Jessica Kingsley Publishers.

Rapoport, R.N. (1960) *Community as Doctor*. London: Tavistock.

Ruel, M. (1980) 'Process without structure. Some anthropological observations on the large group.' *Group Analysis 13,* 99–109.

Sugarman, B. (1968) 'The Phoenix unit: Alliance against illness'. *New Society 11,* 830–3.

Whiteley, J.S. (1972) 'Henderson.' In J.S.Whiteley, D. Briggs and M.Turner (eds) *Dealing with Deviants*. London: Hogarth Press.

Whiteley, J.S. and Collis, M. (1987) 'The therapeutic factors in group psychotherapy applied to the therapeutic community.' *International Journal of Therapeutic Communities 8,* 21–32.

CHAPTER 13

Community Care

The Therapeutic Approach and Learning to Care

Sarah Tucker

EDITOR'S INTRODUCTION

Sarah Tucker combines her role as project manager at one of Community Housing and Therapy's (CHT) communities with the role of training co-ordinator for the organisation. She is secretary of ATC, has co-edited the ATC newsletter and convened a working group to look at the development of training programmes for TC staff. Previously she worked for some years with CRUSE, and she came to CHT via a career as a university lecturer. She has Cambridge University postgraduate degrees in the philosophy of language and in psychology.

Sarah's first interest in TCs emerged while training in psychotherapy with the Philadelphia Association (PA). She was drawn to the PA's philosophical and deeply questioning approach to psychotherapeutic work. She is currently interested in TCs as educational places where both staff and clients spend time learning and re-learning ways of engaging with themselves, each other and the world at a fundamental level – by learning to ask questions which give their perception of these things a new articulation and focus.

In this chapter, she discusses the concept of 'care', drawing on her philosophical background and her day to day work with CHT. The breadth of her philosophical and theological ideas remind us that what David Kennard has called 'the therapeutic community impulse' is inherent in the human race.

I set out two concerns about the notion of 'care'. First, the notion of 'care' does not seem to sit easily with the therapeutic community (TC) approach. Second, 'care in the community' is apparently failing those diagnosed with mental health problems and this is partly because the community does not 'care' about these people. With these problems in mind I describe, first, a way of understanding the notion of 'care' which Community Housing and Therapy (CHT) has developed from the ideas of the philosopher Martin Heidegger, which is not only integral to the TC approach but is also at the heart of what is needed if 'care in the community' is to succeed. I describe how the approach to care developed by CHT provides the basis of a way of rectifying the current problems with 'care in the community'.

CHT is an independent voluntary organisation which runs five residential community projects for severely mentally ill people, four in south-west London and one in Eastbourne. Each project has between nine and fifteen clients who have a variety of diagnoses including schizophrenia, manic depression, personality disorder and depression. CHT's approach has grown out of TC theory and is grounded in an educative framework. The work carried out by staff in CHT projects is fundamentally the work of verbal education. Dialogue with clients, whether in groups, one to one sessions or informally, forms the core of contact between staff and clients.

In the second section I describe the central features of the way in which CHT puts care into practice inside our projects by outlining our underlying approach of educating clients via dialogue to become active citizens developed from the ideas of the philosopher and theologian Martin Buber, the philosopher Emanuel Levinas and the psychoanalyst and philosopher Jacques Lacan. I describe how, by learning to use language and dialogue, staff teach clients to care and to become fully involved.

CARE IN THEORY
'Care' and the TC approach

One of the things that new staff learn when they join one of our projects is that they are not there to 'care' for our clients in the sense of making them cups of tea on demand, tidying their rooms for them, making telephone calls for them, making decisions about what to do for them or constantly attempting to alleviate their emotional pain by *always* responding with soothing words.

For example, a new member of staff may be given the task of working with a client on cleaning the sitting room. The client is diagnosed with schizophrenia and has what he calls 'panic attacks' where he becomes paranoid and believes he is being chased by insects. On this occasion he stops hoovering after about three minutes and sits down on the sofa reporting to the new member of staff that he is having a 'panic attack'. The member of staff feels anxious and worried at this and at the fear of witnessing some 'symptoms'. She also feels that the client must be in such pain at this moment that she should not disturb him but rather comfort him and then do his cleaning chore for him.

This kind of care which results in doing the job for the client, whatever it may be, promotes the client's dependency, passivity and sense of him- or herself as ill and in need of being looked after. This kind of care leaves the client stuck where he is, unable to engage with the world or other people, for the carer does it all for him. It is the kind of care which promotes a hierarchy between clients and staff, for the clients give up their personal and integral power by letting the staff act and make decisions for them.

As such, it is a kind of 'care' that is not part of CHT's approach, an approach which has grown out of TC theory. It is at odds with each of Rapoport's four principles (1960): it is undemocratic in that it promotes hierarchy, it is prone to non-permissiveness in that the staff take control, it is prone to smooth over and avoid reality rather than confront it and it keeps a sharp barrier between staff and clients, thereby preventing significant communalism. It is incompatible with CHT's approach which precisely focuses on what this kind of 'care' hinders: namely, educating clients via dialogue actively to participate in, engage with and become involved with their lives and the world, including other people.

However, while staff learn that they are not there to 'care' for clients in this sense, it does not mean that they learn that they are not there to care in another, more fundamental, sense which I believe lies at the heart of the our approach.

'Care in the community'

With respect to people diagnosed with mental health problems 'care in the community' is failing partly because the community does not care about them. Patients discharged from hospital into the community frequently remain quite isolated from other people. There is a lack of real integration into the community. Often these individuals live on their own in bed-sits or bed and breakfast accommodation, their primary contacts being with mental health professionals, who may not be part of the actual local community, and other people diagnosed with mental health problems whom they meet at the community mental health support facilities. Perhaps the only contact they have with the community of non-users is a weekly visit to the post office to cash in their benefit cheques and a daily visit to the shops to buy a newspaper or cigarettes. These occasions often occur without any meaningful communication (see Al-Khudhairy 1997; Ross 1996).

So often the result of this isolation and implicit exclusion from the community is the recurrence of the old problems and readmission into hospital only for the whole process to begin again. Those seeking care in the community have their troubles exacerbated because they are catapulted into the community with very little advice, education or support on how to be part of it. The community does not 'care' in the sense that it ignores and fails to engage with those seeking care in it.

One response to this concern is to educate the community to care: to educate local shopkeepers, employers, members of the church, members of local schools, neighbours and so forth about the reality of the lives of those living alongside them, albeit diagnosed with mental health problems. Further, to educate those seeking care in the community in how to avoid isolation and in how to take an active part in their lives.

However, in the endeavour to educate the community to care it is important to be clear about what is being requested of the community. It is necessary to be clear about what is meant by care. It may seem idealistic to expect every shopkeeper, schoolteacher and student, employer and neighbour to 'care' in a highly prescriptive, moral sense of becoming worthily altruistic and doing helpful things for these people. It may seem too much to expect them to feel deeply moved by the plight of those who are less well off, materially and emotionally, than they are. However, it is not primarily in this sense that CHT aims to educate the community to 'care', but in a more fundamental sense which, I believe, not only lies at the heart of resolving the problems of 'care in the community' but also is integral to the TC approach.

Care as the craft of involvement

For Heidegger 'care' constitutes the essence of what it is to exist as a human being and part of what this means for him is being along side people and things in the world in such a way that one can fully engage with them (see Heidegger 1962, especially 'Care as the being of dasein' pp.225–273). Care is primarily a craft. Part of this is the craft of being alongside and being involved with the world. By being involved with the world in the present we are able to both anticipate and realise our full future potential as human beings.

There is a mode of practical care where one is involved and engaged with material objects. Thus a carpenter cares for the raw wood as he is able to become involved in his craft with his chisel in creating a particular object out of the wood. There is also a mode of personal care where one is engaged with other people. Thus we care for other people as we are able to become involved in the craft of engaging in dialogue and conversation, common activities and so forth.

By looking at the nature of a particular kind of *practical* care, namely crafts such as carpentry, we find the basis for the nature of personal care and the essence of care in general. The starting point of the carpenters craft is creating a use for a piece of wood. For example making a piece of wood into a table is creating a use for it. In so doing the carpenter is *involving* himself with the piece of wood and forming a certain kind of *relationship* with it. It is a relationship in which the carpenter opens himself out to the piece of wood and takes enough care in the sense of *precision* to find or perceive the piece of wood as articulated in a way in which he can *do something with it*. This *creative relationship* is implemented with certain tools. The carpenter uses a chisel, a saw, some sandpaper and so forth and as he uses these tools he becomes *submerged* in his active relationship with the wood; he becomes submerged in his craft. Carpentry, being a craft, is learned by apprenticeship to others. The student learns to become involved in caring for the wood in all the ways just described by being alongside an experienced carpenter and by assimilating the subtle ways in which the carpenter forms this fully involved relationship with the wood.

These features not only characterise the craft of carpentry which is a kind of practical care. They also characterise the various forms of personal care. Thus the starting point for the craft of personal care, that is, engaging with other people, is finding a 'use' for another person. For example, in finding a common topic of conversation or a common activity to join in, one creates a 'use' for another person. Finding this 'use' starts in language, in a dialogical relationship with another person. In so doing, one is *involving* oneself with the other person and forming a certain kind of *relationship* with them. It is a relationship in which one opens oneself out to the other person and takes enough care in the sense of *precision* to find or perceive the other person as articulated in a way in which one can *do something with them*. This *creative* relationship is implemented with the use of certain tools. One uses perception, thought, and especially language and dialogue to enter into this involvement with the other person and as one uses these things one becomes *submerged* in an active conversation or activity with the other person; one becomes submerged in the craft of personal care. Just as with practical care, the student learns this craft of caring for another person by apprenticeship to others. The student can only learn this craft by being alongside another person and by assimilating as if effortlessly the subtle ways in which this person forms a fully involved relationship with another person. That is, the craft of care is learnt experientially.

Thus care means being in a relation to other people and things that enables one to take part in something with them, be it making a table or a friendship or a conversation. Someone who cannot care is someone who does not see a way of making a piece of wood into a table, either because he does not pay attention to the potential of the wood or because he cannot create a way of using himself or another object to do so. He is someone who cannot invent a way of using language to engage with the other people in the room with him, either because he does not perceive the qualities in those others with which he can make contact or because he cannot design a way of using himself to make that meeting with them. He is someone who does not pay attention to the qualities of the things or people in the world in order to act in conjunction with them.

It is this involved, engaged, participative sense of care that CHT staff learn to practise themselves and in which they also educate clients. Rather than 'care' for the client who is having a panic attack in the sitting room by doing the hoovering for him and soothing over his anxiety, the new member of staff will learn to care for this client by using dialogue to engage with him. The member of staff will open out a dialogue with the client about how he is feeling and why he thinks this might be so. Perhaps the client does not want to clean the sitting room, or perhaps he feels extremely stuck inside himself and expresses this by becoming anxious when he begins to change his environment. The member of staff and client will enter into a dialogue which has no fixed answer as its aim, as to why the client feels as he does, but, rather, engages the client in an ongoing questioning of himself and of the bases upon which he has previously acted and spoken. In this dialogue the member of staff may frustrate the client but because the client engages in this active enquiry he becomes open to change. In order to involve themselves with the client using dialogue in this way the member of staff must take enough care of a precise kind to find the point of contact with the client.

The member of staff will help the client to focus back on the task at hand, perhaps reminding him that the rest of the community are relying on him to do it. She will offer to do the cleaning *with* him, emphasising that they will do it together. Further, she will show the client how to use the hoover and cloth to engage in the task of cleaning so that the client learns as an apprentice what it is to care about the sitting room, allowing himself to see the room as something with which he can do something, becoming submerged in what becomes a craft. Rather than leave the client isolated with his 'ill' symptoms by doing the cleaning for him the member of staff is involving herself by using dialogue, with the client and further, importantly, by cleaning the room with the client, showing him how to become involved in the detail of the job, she is helping the client to care himself: she is opening him to be moved to be involved with his environment and the other people with whom he lives. This kind of care requires mutual active participation by both staff and client.

It is this sense of care that is necessary for the community to exercise if 'care in the community' is to succeed. Manning stressed that the TC movement has implications beyond the specific therapeutic communities for people suffering from mental health problems. He believed the TC movement to be 'resonating with other emergent social groups and values in wider society' (Manning 1976). It is the practice of care as the craft of involvement which I believe still needs to resonate more profoundly into local communities if 'care in the community' is to work. The community needs to be able to become involved and engaged with those seeking care in it as people with whom they are living side by side in an everyday way.

For example, it means local shopkeepers and post office counter assistants having conversations with their customers, including the ones who are diagnosed with mental health problems. It means finding out who those people are, taking an interest in them as fellow human beings. It means local employers extending their work experience placements already available to school leavers to other sections of the unemployed community including those diagnosed with mental health problems. For this they need to learn about the issues surrounding mental health and in particular those on their placements. It means teachers in schools educating their students about mental health issues so that when they leave they will be able to engage with those seeking care in the community in an ordinary way and attend to their own potential mental health problems without enormous fear and ignorance. The ethos of care as involvement and participation that CHT staff practise in their projects and in which they educate clients needs to be extended to the wider community. Via our project action committees we are involved in a number of such community initiatives, creating a mutual dialogue between users and employers, schools, churches and other members of the community. In this way we educate the community to care.

CARE IN PRACTICE

Peter Hawkins notes that 'the whole of the therapeutic community process, not just staff training, is essentially educational' (Hawkins 1979, p.220). Education via dialogue essentially involves active participation on the part of the client or student and the staff member or tutor. Every interaction between staff and clients at CHT is built on the belief that clients can be educated or re-educated to be active citizens by means of dialogue. By using dialogue we empower clients to have their own say and to use their 'vocal power'. Following Levinas, CHT believes that 'the relation between self and other ... is language' (Levinas 1961, p.39). Dialogue requires responsive hearers and listeners. 'There is no word without reply, even if it meets with silence, provided it has an auditor.' (Lacan 1968, p.9). In our projects we create a vocal milieu, a community of the word in which clients learn to speak in a way in which others will listen to them and in which clients regain a sense of themselves through verbal exchange and involvement. Three aspects of this are *dialogue as active participation, education via dialogue* and *interpretation as translation*.

Dialogue as active participation

Plato's conception of philosophy itself was of an active pursuit and so it is not an accident that he uses dialogues as a form in which to write his philosophy. The Socratic dialogues reflect his view that philosophy is an active ongoing enquiry which raises questions and never ends with a final fixed answer (see, for example Plato's *Phaedrus* (275d–276a)). Dialogue essentially involves active participation in two ways. First, because dialogue takes place in the spoken word, it involves spoken engagement. Second, because dialogues come in the form of questions and provisional answers, one who engages in dialogue, be it focused on questions about himself, other people, activities or ideas, is involved in active enquiry. He is engaged in the pursuit of further understanding and an opening out of the bases upon which he has previously acted and lived his life. Thus one who is able to enter into dialogue becomes an agent in the world who takes responsibility for his own degree of understanding, his own questions and responses to others.

The idea that education is aimed at reaching a final fixed answer presupposes a passive student who takes in and regurgitates ready made answers without digesting them. Such learning requires that the teacher tells the student the answers. By contrast, in dialogical learning the teacher does not tell his students the answers. Rather, he frustrates them, asks them difficult questions and, above all, makes them think deeply about what they are doing and why. In this way the student actively engages in the pursuit of understanding. Education aimed at reaching a fixed answer takes place without understanding, without touching, affecting or changing the student. Dialogical learning draws the student into a dynamic process of reflection which affects the student and can result in change: a manifestation of his active engagement.

In groups, individual sessions and informal interactions we use dialogue to educate clients to take part in every aspect of their lives and thereby to care. This means actively engaging in practical things such as cooking, cleaning, shopping, changing plugs, gardening, doing the laundry, mending a car engine, opening a bank account or taking a bus to a new place. As well it means engaging in dialogues about themselves, about their inner lives and about how they relate to other people. Finally it means engaging in finding employment, move-on accommodation, entering into dialogue with neighbours, local shopkeepers and other members of the local community.

Education via dialogue

Education is inextricably tied to dialogue (see especially Buber 1937, 1965). Dialogue not only involves active participation but furthers the development of a *relation* between student and tutor and it is the development of this relation which is primarily educational. No education can take place when the student is in effect by himself in isolation. It is through a dialogical relation between staff and clients that staff involve themselves with clients and teach them to engage with themselves, other people and their environment. It is through this relation that clients and staff develop mutual care.

The dialogical model of education can be distinguished from two other models, the 'free' model and the 'compulsory' model (see Buber 1965, pp.83–92). The free and the compulsory models have positive features but they can essentially leave the student or client in isolation out of relation to their tutor or staff member. Thus, they can leave the client uninvolved with the world and with themselves, they leave the client uncared for and unable to care himself.

The free model takes as fundamental to education the nurturing of innate creative instincts of the student. In this model the role of the tutor is to stimulate the development of these instincts and potentialities in the student in a non-directive way so as to leave the student room to realise the full extent of his individual, unique creativity. One example of a practical way of doing this is encouraging clients to express and create a sense of themselves by making their room their own. By encouraging them to choose how to arrange it, how to decorate it and to choose their own furniture and objects.

A negative consequence, however, of the free model of education concerns the problems of a non-directive approach which takes the word 'free' to stand rigidly for 'freedom from intrusion' in order to allow self-growth. For example, by suggesting that a client make their room their own we are providing them with a space to take responsibility and make their own choices which will reflect their internal sense of self. If however, the client responds by leaving the room exactly how it is with clothes strewn about and without any personal objects and when we confront him about this he says, 'This is how I want my room', we will not be educating the client to make his own free choices or nurturing his creative potential by leaving him at this point, without making an intervention. We will be leaving the client stuck with his difficulty with finding his inner self. We will be leaving the client unable to 'grope out over the outlines of self' caught in a 'life of monologue' (Buber 1965, p.20).

By contrast the compulsory model takes as fundamental to education a directive and authoritarian approach in which the tutor as master tells the students how things are and what to do. Like the free model the compulsory model of education has negative consequences if taken to extreme and used exclusively. Taken to its extreme this model results in an unreasonable exercise of authority and power by the tutor towards the client. Extreme and rigid direction results in the tutor imposing upon and interfering with the clients. This in turn results in the client rebelling and becoming angry to the degree that they become alienated. In this alienation the client is again left in isolation unable to learn from the tutor. It is not that rebelling or becoming angry is negative. Nor is the exercise of a certain degree of authority on the staff necessarily negative. While many things are permitted we set a minimal but clear set of limits. For example, violence is not acceptable. Rather, it is the alienation that results in cut off isolation which is negative.

A real dialogical relationship involves 'inclusion' which is a particular way of being with another person (Buber 1965, p.96). Inclusion is to be distinguished from empathy which involves trying to understand and feel what it is like for the other person. For empathy involves giving up oneself, one's own concreteness and attempting, as it were, to become the other person. In this way it destroys the basis upon which a dialogical relationship can exist. For it destroys one of the participants in that relationship. A dialogical relationship requires two concrete people. If we only ever empathise with the client he will lose the sense of being he gains from being in relation to someone else. Rather, inclusion involves extending ourselves to the other by making an activity in which we and the client take part come alive for the client.

For example, when we find a client's room untidy and dirty we may first of all empathise with the client, trying to understand how they must feel as this is reflected in their external environment. However, it will only be when we practise inclusion that the educative process will take place. By a joint activity of tidying with the client we actively engage the client. At a deep level by our active participation with the client in tidying the room we form a relationship with the client. This provides the beginning of a sense of meaning and achievement out of which the client learns to engage in his own life. This dialogical relationship engenders a sense in the client that he exists, 'that meaninglessness, however hard pressed you are by it, cannot be the real truth' (Buber 1965, p.98). The client may then go on to find the world around him meaningful and *this* is the essence of the educational process – being able to find meaning in the world.

Interpretation as translation

The unconscious is structured like a language and is in some sense a language, albeit one which is foreign to us (see, for example, Lacan 1968). In the process of learning to take part in their lives staff teach clients to translate their unconscious language to conscious language. This process essentially takes place in language, in dialogue with others. This involves learning to pay attention to the underlying vertical layer of meaning of the client's speech and language, like learning to read the different lines of an orchestral score. Staff will not be helping a client to translate his unconscious language if they only concentrate on the information of what is said. For example, when he says day after day, 'There is no milk in the fridge' and we reply 'Why don't you go and buy some.' In order to translate the client's unconscious language staff help clients to look deeper beneath the content of what he says repeatedly. We learn to read the question the client is asking and the response they are unconsciously trying to evoke.

It might be that the client is speaking, in his unconscious language, to his mother and asking why she repeatedly failed to look after him properly. Having identified both to whom the client is posing his question and the nature of the question we are in a better position to help translate these words with the client. We might say instead, ' You always come and tell me there is no milk in the fridge. Maybe you want me to make sure there is milk. Maybe you need to check that I am looking after you properly.'

CONCLUSION

By means of the vocal milieu, including dialogue as active participation, education via dialogue and interpretation as translation, clients learn to care in practice. By learning to speak, learning to have dialogues, learning to use language to find a point of contact between themselves and others and using language to translate their own inner chaotic dialogues into a text which makes more sense, clients learn to care. That is, they learn to perceive and find the world a place in which they can submerge themselves, a place in which they can be involved. Not only do clients learn to care but further, staff learn to care for clients by teaching them through dialogue to do these things. Finally, both staff and clients invite the community into their projects in order to educate them to care by taking part and involving themselves in ordinary ways.

Through dialogue with clients, staff teach clients to become involved and thus they teach clients to care in a way that is consistent with and can make a considerable contribution to the TC approach. Through dialogue staff and clients teach the community to become involved. It is this that is needed if 'care in the community' is to work.

REFERENCES

Al-Khudhairy, N. (1997) 'Are users of mental health services in the community living in a social ghetto?' (CHT Campaigning Group) Forthcoming.

Buber, M. (1937) *I and Thou.* Edinburgh: T and T Clark.

Buber, M. (1965) *Between Man and Man.* New York: MacMillan.

Hawkins, P. (1979) 'Staff learning in therapeutic communities: the relationship of staff supervision to self-learning.' In R.D. Hinshelwood and N. Manning (eds) *Therapeutic Communities: Reflections and Progress.* London: Routledge and Kegan Paul.

Heidegger, M. (1962) *Being and Time.* Translated by J. Macquarrie and E. Robinson. Oxford: Basil Blackwell.

Lacan, J. (1968) *Speech and Language it? Psychoanalysis.* Translated by A. Wilden. Baltimore and London: The Johns Hopkins University Press. Originally 'Fonction et champ de parole et du language en psychanalyse.' *La Psychanalyse 1,* Paris 1956.

Levinas, E. (1961) *Totality and Infinity.* Translated by A. Lingis Duquesne. Pittsburgh University Press. Originally *Totaite et Infini.* The Hague: Martinus Nijhoff, 1961.

Manning, N. (1976) 'Innovation of social policy – the case of the therapeutic community.' *Journal of Social Policy 5,* 3.

Plato (1982) 'Phaedrus.' In E. Hamilton and H. Cairns (eds) *Collected Dialogues* pp.520–522, translated by R. Hackforth. Princeton, NJ: Princeton University Press.

Rapoport, R.N. (1960) *Community as Doctor.* London: Tavistock.

Ross, R. (1996) *Living in the Community.* The Sainsbury Centre for Mental Health.

CHAPTER 14

The Prison Communities
Therapy within a Custodial Setting
Roland Woodward

EDITORS' INTRODUCTION

Roland Woodward is somewhat bemused as to how he has changed from being a 14-year-old dyslexic who could read but barely write into a principal psychologist who, as well as writing this chapter, recently co-edited a book on Therapeutic Communities for Offenders *(Cullen, Jones and Woodward 1997).*

Perhaps it was this personal metamorphosis that gives him the faith and motivation to work with serious offenders, first at Glen Parva, later at Grendon and then at Gartree, where in 1992 he opened a therapeutic community for prisoners serving life sentences .

This chapter covers the development and structure of TCs within the British prison service, including the three new concept TCs for drug abusers. This type of hierarchical TC is much commoner in America, where it is a mainstream treatment for drugs and alcohol. In this volume, it is also mentioned in the contribution on research (Chapter 17). A further book in the series about this very different model of therapeutic community practice is planned.

Roland's particular interest is grief work with people who have murdered relatives, friends or partners. He believes that the therapeutic community setting gives the opportunity to explore fundamental existential issues and allows people to engage with each other at a level of intimacy which transcends their scars and damage.

INTRODUCTION

Since the opening of HM Prison Grendon Underwood in 1962, therapeutic communities (TCs) within the British Prison Service have passed through cycles of popularity. The current prison TCs reflect renewed interest in this form of therapy, spurred by a growing body of research demonstrating that TCs can be successful in the prison setting. The modern prison service now recognises that TCs offer an effective way to challenge criminal behaviour and that different models can be applied to specific sub-populations.

Until recently the only TC model that had been used within the British prison system was the *democratic* (or *non-hierarchical*) model. This situation has changed with the opening of three *concept* (or *hierarchical*) TCs, as a result of the prison service responding to the need to provide an extended service for drug and alcohol dependent prisoners.

The creation of a TC in the prison setting has to contend with several factors that TCs in other environments do not. It might appear paradoxical to set up a therapy-based unit in a situation that is primarily seen as one of punishment and retribution. Although prison service practitioners have always maintained that the role of prison must be rehabilitative as well as punitive this has not always been the message sent by politicians or received by the general public. Currently, the emphasis being given to the service by its Director General, Richard Tilt, is one of balance. There is a clear recognition of the public's expectation that offenders should be secured from the public, but this is balanced by work specifically aimed at reducing reconviction rates. The conflicts of purpose created by this are most greatly felt within a prison that contains a TC. Genders and Player (1995) put it thus:

> The major task of the prison is to contain a population of conscripts under conditions which are conducive to the maintenance of good order and control, defined in this instance as the avoidance of any kind of disruption to routines and regulations. Within the therapeutic community, attendance is voluntary and the primary objective is treatment, which may be designated as the alleviation of pain and suffering. The very enactment of treatment, however, may require, and even demand, the expression of symptomatic attitudes and behaviour, which could well threaten order and question discipline. (p.121)

Coupled with this is the difficulty of creating – within a hierarchical institution – an island of non-hierarchical and democratic practices. Prisons have set rules and a strong expectation that they will be adhered to by prisoner and staff. There is in prison a strong set of 'external' rules. Within the TC setting the aim is to reduce social divisions and to enfranchise the community members. This means involving them in the exercise of power through choice and engagement in the process of rule-making. Ultimately people in a TC comply with the rules that the community makes because they internalise the rules through engagement in the process of creating them.

The result of placing a TC in a prison or, a TC prison in the prison system, is to create a tension, which often leads to conflict. They are often viewed with suspicion by both staff and prisoners. When established practices are modified or abandoned in the name of therapy, some managers have problems understanding what part they have to play: TCs have an uncontrollable sense about them which makes staff feel challenged in their various roles. This needs to be met by an active effort to build bridges of understanding between the 'prison model' and the 'TC model'. An examination of all the surviving TCs in British prisons shows that they have invested a lot in this collaborative activity.

DEMOCRATIC (NON-HIERARCHICAL) THERAPEUTIC COMMUNITIES IN PRISONS

HMP Grendon Underwood

The oldest penal therapeutic community in England and Wales, possibly the world, is that at HM Prison Grendon Underwood. First conceived by Dr Norbert East and Dr W. H. Hubert in a report published by them in 1939, the prison opened in 1962.

In its original conception Grendon was to be a place where it would be possible:

> to investigate and treat mental disorders, generally recognised as responsive to treatment, to investigate offenders whose offences in themselves suggest mental morbidity, and to explore the problems dealing with the psychopath. (Commissioners of Prisoners 1963, in Genders and Player 1995, p.6)

From then until 1986, the role of Grendon gradually changed until a report on its future suggested development in four main ways:

o to continue in the treatment of sociopaths

o to develop work with sex offenders

o assessment of long term prisoners for sentence planning and parole board reviews

o set up a rescue unit for short-term treatment of prisoners' acute breakdown or a severe prison crisis.

All of these recommendations were implemented, although the rescue unit did not survive for long.

Grendon is still the only prison in the country that is run as a therapy based institution: it comprises five TCs in separate wings. It is a medium secure prison that holds approximately 250 adult male prisoners with at least 18 months left to serve, providing a national resource to the British prison service. Approximately 40 per cent of the population are life sentence prisoners who are working their way through the stages of the life sentences structure.

Each of the therapeutic community wings has a population of 35 to 42 residents and a multi-disciplinary staff team consisting of a wing therapist, a principal prison officer, who has responsibility for two wings, two senior prison officers and ten prison officers. Each team also has a psychologist, probation officer and a part time wing tutor from the education department (Cullen 1997; Genders and Player 1995).

Referral and assessment

The major route into Grendon is via referral through Prison Healthcare services, which is a contact point throughout the prison system. As a medical transfer procedure, this also allows Grendon to return prisoners to referring prisons. A 'Discretionary Lifer Panel' or the Parole Board may recommend a prisoner for Grendon, or psychologists, chaplains and prison governors may advise referral.

Between 160 and 220 prisoners are referred to Grendon each year. Each of these will have been screened to ensure that they have at least 18 months to serve, are motivated to change, accept the basic restrictions of no drugs, sex or violence, and are free of psychotropic drugs at the time of transfer to Grendon.

On arrival at Grendon the referred prisoner joins the assessment unit where he undergoes a very detailed appraisal. Psychology, probation, chaplain, education and wing staff conduct interviews in the first weeks of being in the unit. This information, together with extensive psychometric and observational data of the staff on the adaptation behaviour of the prisoner is placed before a case conference held at the end of the initial assessment period. If this process finds no contraindications to therapy, he moves on into the process. Once an inmate has been accepted, he enters a phase of therapy preparation: he learns what is expected in therapy and then outlines major themes that he will need to work on. The prisoner then moves onto a therapeutic community wing.

The therapeutic community wings

The routine of the prison allows all the communities to hold their community events at the same time. Each morning the entire establishment enters into community based therapy. All the communities hold two full community meetings and three small group sessions per week. Every resident is expected to attend all of these events as part of their commitment to therapy and the community. Around this core is fitted a range of activities including other forms of therapy such as psychodrama, art therapy, life skills and cognitive skills courses.

The small groups tend to focus on the offence-related behaviour of the individuals either directly or through the developmental histories of the members. The wing staff teams facilitate the small groups. They last for an hour but may extend if it is thought that either the content of the material or the emotional state of the individual warrants extra time. The normal process at the conclusion of the group time is that the community comes together for 'feedback'. A representative of each group feeds back to the whole community a brief resumé of the content of the group that has just occurred. This whole process informs the community of the relevant information required so that all know what work is being done and are aware of current sensitivities.

The community meetings generally fulfil three functions as follows:

○ exercise of the powers of the community members to organise themselves: work places are allocated, and elections held for community offices

○ discussion and formulation of community policy on specific issues

○ discussion of therapeutic issues that arise within the community including individuals' behaviour, intergroup conflict and resident/staff issues.

Each community elects its own officers such as chairman to conduct the business. There are a wide range of roles that are taken by residents: some may represent the community within the wider prison setting, for example food representative; others may service the community by taking up the 'reps' jobs, for example tv/video rep.

Grendon has provided the basic template for the other non-hierarchical TCs in the Prison Service. The descriptions of the other TCs will concentrate on the factors that make them different from Grendon.

The Max Glatt Centre (MGC), HMP Wormwood Scrubs

The MGC was originally set up in 1975 to provide a service for prisoners displaying addictive and compulsive behaviours (Glatt 1985; Jones 1997a, 1997b). The MGC was originally known as the Annexe, Wormwood Scrubs, and has been sited in various areas of that prison. Wormwood Scrubs is a large local prison that contains a wide variety of prisoners, from short-term remand prisoners to a life sentence population. Given the transient nature of many of its population the MGC has proved extremely adept at surviving the many changes in prison policy that have affected the host establishment.

Originally the MGC dealt only in the addictive behaviours, but soon started dealing with other compulsive behaviours, including gambling problems and sexual offending. Recently, the centre has begun to work with 'personality disorders' and prisoners with violent offending patterns.

The MGC combines community meetings and small groups with cognitive-behavioural programmes, for example offence focused role play groups, relapse prevention modules, thinking skills courses and an 'emotions' group. It also provides time for sub-groups of the community such as sex offenders and substance abusers to work together. An extension of practice is the inclusion of agencies from outside the prison system. Both Alcoholics Anonymous and Narcotics Anonymous visit and run groups for those who wish to join them.

Being part of a larger institution has always been problematic for the MGC. It is difficult for the MGC to maintain its programme with the level of integrity that it would wish due to the way the general staffing problems impinge on it. It is not uncommon for the members of the staff team to be allocated other work within the prison, disrupting their participation in the MGCs programme and at times curtailing it.

Gartree Therapeutic Community (GTC), HMP Gartree

The GTC opened in 1993; it is the only TC devoted entirely to life sentence prisoners (Woodward and Hodkin 1996). It is part of a larger institution, Gartree Prison, which is the only prison in the country that is occupied solely by life sentence prisoners. It houses 364 inmates, about 10 per cent of the life sentence population of the country.

Unlike the MGC, Gartree therapeutic community is housed in a separate wing. For the 21 residents, the GTC provides a physical location which they can call their own and know that they are not going to be intruded upon. The staff team work exclusively on the GTC, making them a cohesive flexible and creative group with input into wider staff training and committees.

All the GTC residents voluntarily come from the population of Gartree. Both the entry process and the therapeutic programme mirror that at Grendon. The community always meets in the mornings, which allows the residents to participate in the normal prison regime in the afternoon – ensuring the integration of residents and community into the overall establishment. It is important that the community residents are seen to be working and participating in as many aspects of prison life as possible, in order to allay the myths that they are either mad or in need of protection due to the nature of their crime.

The residents of the GTC are reviewed every four months: they are each given the responsibility of asking people to write their assessments and co-ordinating the replies. Residents also write a self-assessment and hand all the assessments collected to the staff team in time for the review meeting, at which feedback is given. This includes issues to work on, along with appropriate praise, criticism and recognition for the work that has been done in the previous four months. The staff also consider whether or not the resident should stay in the community, and whether he should be asked to consider other options about his future.

Unlike other TCs in the prison system, the GTC expects residents to take longer than 18–24 months to complete therapy, and this is supported by research evidence (see below). Also, life sentence prisoners appear to need longer because of the specific issues of killing which need to be addressed. Very often residents have killed people that they loved or who were friends and, being the cause of the death themselves, they deny their own feelings of loss – which inhibits the grieving process. Once a resident has been able to acknowledge that their guilt has inhibited their grieving, a period of appropriate mourning often takes place. Then, aspects of the positive relationship that the person experienced with the victim prior to killing them can be retrieved. This exploration of grief and loss may take several months and extends the time needed for therapy to be fully effective (Woodward and Hodkin 1997).

One further reason why therapy may be extended is due to the technique of working thorough the offence via the documentation and the scene of crime photographs. This powerful technique requires a resident to recommit the offence using the photographs as stimuli whilst being guided through the full range of sensory experiences. Because of the intensity of the experience this process has to be taken slowly and therefore extends the therapy period.

The Chiltern Unit, HM Young Offender Institution Aylesbury

This unit is the newest TC in the prison system at the time of writing. It was opened in February 1997 as part of the new Healthcare centre at RM Young Offender Institution Aylesbury.

There are 14 places and, like the Max Glatt Centre, it aims to provide a cognitive behavioural input in addition to group work. Music and art therapy and the opportunity to work with families of the residents have been built into the programme. The expectation is that residents will stay for a minimum of twelve months and a maximum of two years.

The unit is to move to a larger area in the main body of the establishment, which will mean that it can expand and offer up to eighteen places and a wider range of activities.

Research on democratic therapeutic communities in prisons

The late 1980s and after have proved to be a watershed for prison TC research, especially in terms of reconviction. Early work by Gunn *et al.* (1978) had shown that there were significant changes in relevant personality characteristics including levels of reduced anxiety and depression, and positive changes in the attitude of TC members to authority figures. Genders and Player (1995) confirmed some of these findings in their latter study of Grendon. More recently Newton (1997) showed that the longer residents were in therapy, the more likely they were to show decreases in 'tough mindedness', extra-punitive hostility and external locus of control. Additionally, they were also likely to show less guilt and self-criticism. Newton suggested that there was a progressive treatment effect, although Jones (1989) showed a non-linear progression. He demonstrated that at an early point in therapy self-esteem may become lowered and levels of anger may increase. He postulated a link with attrition rates; it would appear that the point at which he found the changes was when residents were at greatest risk of leaving a community. If this stage could be passed then positive gains could be made.

More recently a sharper outcome focus has been brought to bear, examining reconviction rates. Gunn (1978) had found no significant improvement when looking at Grendon graduates after two years of release. There was some indication in the earlier work of Newton (1973) and George (1971) that there was a drop in reconviction rates if the samples had stayed in therapy over one year. Cullen (1993) and Newton and Thornton (1994) both found that there was a reduction in reconviction when time in therapy and the manner of leaving therapy were taken into account. An independent study by Marshall (1997) confirmed the findings of Cullen (1994) having expanded the Grendon sample size to over 700 subjects. Jones (1998) confirmed this for a sample of ex-prisoners from the Max Glatt TC at Wormwood scrubs.

The research demonstrates that the democratic TCs in prison have a significant effect on recidivism rates, that there is a non-linear treatment progression and that time in therapy and the manner of leaving therapy are crucial factors (Rawlings 1998).

CONCEPT (HIERARCHICAL) THERAPEUTIC COMMUNITIES IN PRISONS

Three further British prison TCs started in December 1996 as part of a prison service initiative to reduce the levels of drug use. In the examination of how best to accomplish this, research suggested that the concept TC model was an effective treatment. The Prison Service therefore contracted the Phoenix House Foundation in New York to develop a generic therapeutic community programme specification. The result of this was that three concept TC programmes were established: Channings Wood, Portland Young Offender Institution and Holme House (Clark 1997).

This uses a very different model of TCs from the democratic ones, and there is considerable emphasis on the role of staff as individual counsellors and guides. The notion that the 'doctor knows best' is strong within this form of TC. Status, privileges, and other rewards provide residents with motivation for upward mobility; downward mobility with its loss of status and privileges serves as a sanction and deterrent to negative behaviour.

In common with democratic TCs, the primary mechanism by which these units aim to alter behaviour is by inculcating in residents the ability to take responsibility for themselves and for others.

The generic programme specification

The programme specification has objectives for both residents and the TC programme. Its aim is to take the residents through the three phases of treatment: *orientation, primary treatment* and *re-entry.*

Objectives for residents

○ achievement of a drug-free lifestyle which includes stable employment, positive relationships, and no further criminal involvement

○ development of individual treatment and sentence plans with realistic and pro-social goals

○ recognition of self-worth through work and therapeutic experiences

○ achievement of academic skills and certification necessary to maintain stable employment and self-sufficiency

○ achievement of skills towards National Vocational Qualifications certification to increase employability and self-esteem

○ learning communication skills and coping strategies to foster positive relationships in the future and to repair relationships harmed in the past, especially those with family members.

Objectives for therapeutic community programme

○ provision of highly structured programme based on self-help and group therapeutic tools that also offers individual, group, and family counselling; job functions, education about substance misuse, relapse prevention, family dynamics; and training that includes life management skills, vocational training, job readiness, and parenting

○ reduction of positive urinalysis for drug misuse among participants

○ make available resources to assist programme participants upon their release

○ meet treatment and security needs of the establishment

○ foster concepts of 'right living' in participants, in particular those of reciprocity and responsibility as members of society as a whole

○ the development of a therapeutic community that is culturally responsive and geared to meet the needs of its residents.

The drug users in these TCs are a difficult section of the prison population: they are targeted by other prisoners who see them as a source of income. There are also likely to be attempts by prisoners outside the TCs to sabotage the projects either by providing drugs to the residents or by infiltrating the units. Some prisoners see such units as a challenge to their power within the institution and will therefore attempt to undermine it for no other reason than it represents what is deemed to be good by the authorities.

Research on concept therapeutic communities in prisons

The research available on the concept TCs is dominated by the work from America where the use of this form of intervention has been increasing in the custodial services. Wexler's review (1997) shows that there is clear evidence that the application of this form of intervention with drug abusers is significantly effective, and this effectiveness is increased when appropriate TC aftercare is provided. Rawlings' review (1998) notes that there are high dropout rates from this form of TC, particularly in the first few weeks of treatment. Results from the three new British units is awaited.

CONCLUSION: GLANCES BACK AND A LOOK TO THE FUTURE

It should not be forgotten that some prison based TCs have come and gone. The renowned Barlinnie Special Unit (BSU) was established in 1973 as a regime to deal with some of Scotland's most difficult prisoners. It closed in 1995 and has been written about frequently, in an attempt to understand its fall into decline (Cooke 1997). It generated intense interest both at home and internationally as it initially coped with some extremely violent prisoners in a community setting. Over time the nature of the unit changed until residents and staff failed to maintain the boundaries and the commitments of the community. Eventually it closed at the recommendation of an HM Inspector of Prisons working party report.

MacKensie (1997) wrote an obituary for the HM Young Offenders Institute (HMYOI) Glen Parva TC that closed just before Christmas 1996, after 17 years of operation. It provided much needed support for some very disturbed young men during its operating time, and there are plans to open the TC again if the right circumstances can be generated. The Albatross unit at HMYOI Feltham was facing severe difficulties in May 1997 (Fowler 1997). Attempts are being made to find a way forward and return to a therapeutic structure.

The future for TCs in the prison service is currently looking hopeful. At the time of writing the prison service is in the process of contracting out HMP Marchington. This is to be a large category B training prison, which is to encompass a separate 200-place TC complex. It is expected to open in the year 2000.

HMP Askem Grange, a womens' open prison, is investigating the possibility of opening a TC for its inmates; it could be the first TC for women in British prisons. HMP Foston Hall, a closed women's prison, is also exploring the possibility of starting a TC programme.

Currently, it would seem that the time is right for development of TCs in the prison service. There has, for example, been tentative discussion of a further large new TC prison in the future (beyond Marchington) and several prisons have spontaneously considered setting up TCs. This has been spurred on by research that shows that TCs affect people in a positive manner, and can reduce reoffending. This, coupled with a new found political will to express the view that prison has to be a balance between incarceration and constructive rehabilitation, provides fertile ground from which new TCs may grow.

As the prison service has become more aware of the positive role good TCs can play in the rehabilitation of offenders, it has begun to restructure itself to support TCs, and a policy group has been convened to oversee the policy relating to TCs and to advise the Prisons Board accordingly.

It would seem that the prison service has finally emerged from the 'nothing works' era of the 1980s. It has also survived the period of intense political scrutiny resulting from the escapes from HMP Whitmore and HMP Parkhurst which produced enormous anxiety regarding security aspects of imprisonment. With its population and pace of growth higher than ever before, the British Prison system has had to re-examine how it can best serve the public. The British Prison system is finding for itself a renewed positive role with its population through the pragmatic use of proven rehabilitative programmes, and at the forefront of this move forward are the therapeutic communities.

REFERENCES

Clark, D. (1997) 'Therapeutic communities for drug misusers.' *Prison Service Journal, 111*, 14–19.

Commissioners of Prisons (1963) *Report for 1962*. London: HMSO.

Cooke, D.J. (1997) 'The Barlinnie Special Unit: Rise and fall of a therapeutic experiment.' In J. E. Cullen, L. Jones and R. Woodward (eds) *Therapeutic Communities for Offenders*. Chichester: John Wiley and Sons.

Cullen, J.E. (1993) 'The Grendon reconviction study, part 1'. *Prison Service Journal 90*, 35–37.

Cullen, J.E. (1994). 'Grendon: The therapeutic prison that works.' *Therapeutic Communities 15*, 4, 301–311.

Cullen, J.E. (1997) 'Can a prison be a therapeutic community? The Grendon template.' In J.E. Cullen, L. Jones and R. Woodward (eds) *Therapeutic Communities for Offenders*. Chichester: John Wiley and Sons.

Cullen, J.E. (1998). *Grendon and Future Therapeutic Communities in Prison*. London: Prison Reform Trust.

Cullen, J.E., Jones, L. and Woodward, R. (eds) (1997) *Therapeutic Communities for Offenders*. Chichester: John Wiley and Sons.

Fowler, A (1997) 'Felthams' Albatross Unit.' *Prison Service Journal 111*, 12–13.

Genders, E. and Player, E. (1995) *Grendon: A Study of a Therapeutic Prison*. Oxford: Clarendon Press.

George, R. (1971) *Grendon Follow-Up 1967–68*. Grendon Psychology Unit. Series A Report No. 47.

Gunn, J. Robertson, G. and Dell, S. (1978) *Psychiatric Aspects of Imprisonment*. London: Academic Press.

Glatt, M.M. (1985) 'The Wormwood Scrubs annexe: reflections on the working and functioning of an addict's therapeutic community within a prison.' *Prison Care*, November.

Jones, L. (1988) *The Hospital Annexe: A Preliminary Evaluation.* Directorate of Psychological Services. Series II Report. Prison Service, Home Office.

Jones, L. (1997a) 'Developing models for managing treatment integrity and efficacy in a prison-based TC: Max Glatt Centre.' In J.E. Cullen, L. Jones and R. Woodward (eds) *Therapeutic Communities for Offenders.* Chichester: John Wiley and Sons.

Jones, L. (1997b) 'The Max Glatt Centre.' *Prison Inservice Journal* May 111, 19–21.

Losel, F and Egg, R. 'Social-therapeutic institutions in Germany: Description and evaluation.' In J.E. Cullen, L. Jones and R. Woodward (eds) *Therapeutic Communities for Offenders.* Chichester: John Wiley and Sons.

MacKensie, J. (1997) 'Glen Parva therapeutic community – An obituary.' *Prison Service Journal* *111*, 26.

Marshall, P. (1997) *A Reconviction Study of HMP Grendon Therapeutic Community.* Home Office Research and Statistics Research Findings No. 53.

Newton, M. (1973) *Reconviction After Treatment at Grendon.* CP Report Series B No. 1. Prison Service, Home Office.

Newton, M. (1997) 'Changes in test scores during treatment at Grendon.' Unpublished research paper. Research and Development Unit Report, HM Prison Grendon Underwood, Aylesbury, Bucks.

Newton, M. and Thornton, D. (1994) 'Grendon re-conviction study, Part 1 update.' Unpublished internal communication.

Rawlings, B.(1998) *Research on Therapeutic Communities in Prisons. A Review of the Literature.* Produced for the Prison Service. Department of Sociology, University of Manchester.

Wexler, H (1997). 'Therapeutic communities in American prisons.' In J. E. Cullen, L. Jones and R. Woodward (eds) *Therapeutic Communities for Offenders.* Chichester: John Wiley and Sons.

Woodward, R. and Hodkin, G. (1996) 'Another British first – Gartree therapeutic community for lifers.' *Prison Service Journal January 103*, 47–50.

Woodward, R. and Hodkin, G. (1997) 'Surviving violent death.' *Prison Service Journal 111, May.*

CHAPTER 15

Children and Adolescents
The Renaissance of Heart and Mind
Melvyn Rose

EDITORS' INTRODUCTION

Some forty years ago Melvyn Rose moved from normal teaching to work in approved schools. He was shocked by the effects of their institutionalising processes and so set out to provide a more therapeutic environment for disturbed young people. Eventually, he went on to set up Peper Harow and the Peper Harow Foundation. Although Peper Harow has now closed, a recent BBC 'fly on the wall' television documentary, using old footage from the 1970s and following up some of the boys into their adulthood (and parenthood), was widely acclaimed as a tribute to both the quality of care provided and the capacity for psychosocial rebirth.

Melvyn did a stint as chairperson of the ATC and has published a number of books and papers. He also acts as a consultant to various organisations including the Ministry of Education in Moscow.

In this chapter, he writes wisely about potential pitfalls in our work as well as the potential for growth and healing. The consensus at present seems to be that these troubled children and adolescents need individual therapy to nurture their development, as well as the group and therapeutic milieu. Other themes and conflicts are common to all TCs, for example the internal and external pull towards institutionalisation, the balance between permissiveness and safety, and the advantages and disadvantages of charismatic leadership. He also talks about the need for 'stern love' which seems to encapsulate a quality which other chapter authors have struggled to describe.

We hope that the history and principles of the therapeutic schools movement – including such well-known institutions as Summerhill, Caldecott Community and the Mulberry Bush – will feature in a future book in this series.

INTRODUCTION: EMOTIONALLY IMPOVERISHED ADOLESCENTS

Most adolescents are able to function in social groups with little effort. They can enjoy learning and can increasingly anticipate the social milestones towards their adulthood positively, albeit with some realistic apprehension and sadness at the ending of childhood. For others, such a tolerable transition is impossible.

These are the adolescents at the extreme end of a spectrum of disturbed functioning. Their presence in a classroom, or in any other normal social group is noticeably exceptional. They are often inattentive, hyperactive, disruptive, and confrontational. There has been enough negative experience in their previous lives to have inhibited their psychosocial development, leading to a serious lack in their psychological capacity to function age-appropriately. How can their inner world even be contacted in order to help them begin to understand exactly what has impeded or perverted their psychosocial development? The simplistic adjurations of politicians and other 'experts' in bar-room psychosocial development, telling such youngsters to 'pull their socks up' cannot work, for these youngsters lack the internal resources to do so. They already believe the worst of themselves. Nor are the inherent benefits of the psychodynamic psychotherapies generally effective for them, because adolescents – even more than adults – are extremely fearful of acknowledging how desperately different from their peers they really see themselves as being.

SOCIETY'S FAILURE TO PROVIDE TREATMENT

Yet in her classic paper, 'Communicating with Children', Clare Winnicott (1964) showed that it is possible to communicate with such children, and help them to make sense of their self-destructive behaviour. Ten years earlier Fritz Redl and David Wineman had shown by experiment and publication in the USA, by what means such children might be helped (1951, 1952). Teachers and other members of the statutory helping professions are rarely able to offer the level of commitment to such children that they need, even if greater awareness of the seriousness of adolescent problems is increasingly being recognised as an important aspect of what schools should provide.

Recognising the limitations of formal school situations for such children and adolescents at the extreme of emotionally disturbed functioning, many educationists, such as A.S. Makarenko (1951) in the USSR of the 1930s, or George Lyward (Burn 1956) for nearly fifty years in Britain, have been able to provide the time and the context in which the psychological change, which disturbed adolescents need to make, could take place.

Yet the general influence of such progressive educationists has not been effective. Indeed, despite all the best intentions of Children's Acts of parliament and government-led child protection protocols, adolescents and young adults who have been in care, are still many times more likely to breakdown as they struggle with the transition to adulthood (Morgan 1998). Attention has been fixed upon their behaviour rather than upon the causes of that behaviour. The professional failure to develop effective treatment – whether by educationalists, or by the medical profession – and the lack of government encouragement for them to do so, contrasts with what the therapeutic community movement has been able to develop predominantly for disturbed adults since the 1950s.

ADDRESSING PSYCHOSOCIAL DEPRIVATION – THE INHERENT POTENTIAL OF TCS

Therapeutic community practice has influenced many other psychosocial methods of treatment. Sometimes its process has formed the significant context for an eclectic therapeutic package of group-based therapies, perhaps including group analysis, or addiction rehabilitative programmes, or music, or art and drama therapies. Yet what will have mattered most to patients, especially in a residential context, is not so much the particular therapy, or even the staff's hard-won professional status, so much as their feeling that their daily experience was consistently being made relevant to their real psychosocial needs. Such patients share the staff's perspective that within the overall residential environment lies an auspicious opportunity for those deprived of the emotional building blocks of self, whether this has existed since their emotionally deprived infancy, or as a consequence of specific unresolved psychological trauma.

Spending time in therapeutic communities with socio-psychoanalytically based programmes, has made it easier for individuals with life-corroding emotional problems to recognise themselves and to be recognised, not as categories of medico-psychosocial sickness, but as whole individuals, whose overall functioning has been impeded by their emotional problems. There has also been an increasing recognition that, despite the inadequacies of its individual members, the group as a totality can produce a powerful psychotherapeutic experience. Where the group can 'hold' each individual and create a sense of common group identity, individuals find that they can play an important role within the community – irrespective of their own severe problems. The group provides a positive alternative to personal disintegration and madness. Instead of all self-esteem being dispersed, the individual's worth becomes part of the group's responsibility for its members. A continuous focus on the psychotherapeutic process counterbalances the emotional corrosiveness of lifelong problems and allows alternative, group-promoted experiences, such as hope and self-respect, to become individually nurturing. On many occasions the discussions and other interactions between residents illustrate interpersonal generosity and interpersonal sensitivity of the highest human order. The evidence of dramatically changed psychological functioning is sometimes so incontrovertible as to compel enthusiasm for this form of treatment.

MANAGING THE THERAPEUTIC PROCESS

However, despite the positive potential of the therapeutic community, its organic process, especially one that carries so much psychopathology within it, can rapidly become counterproductive . Thus, although staff are absolutely required to engage in the emotional issues of everyday life, they have another commensurate task, which is to step back from the regressive treatment process and clarify what is actually occurring within the sea of community activity. As Ponce reminds us in his paper, 'Erotic countertransference issues in a residential treatment center' (1993), there are many ways by which the residents – perhaps especially when they are adolescents – can defensively avoid the demands that positive relationships with staff and peers make. There are also many ways by which staff members' countertransference can be unrecognised, rather than be appropriately acknowledged and managed. However, the existence of positive relationships between staff and residents are essential to the task. *Transforming Hate to Love* (Rose 1997) cites ex-therapeutic community residents' recognition of this.

> I felt there was something about Celia [member of staff], something really comforting. Not like a mother... She would understand. After a while, I felt really close to her. She was always important to me.
>
> *(Albert)*

This from someone whose actual mother had compulsively starved him of emotion from birth onwards. Or:

> There was a lot of support from the staff. For the first time, here were adults who were on your level. They got pissed off with you and had a laugh and everything. You could see, even in the most delinquent moments that you weren't in a playground. This was something serious. You knew that there was a chance of sorting something out, instead of winding up in some bog in Piccadilly ... there was always hope around.
>
> *(Rupert)*

In my experience at Peper Harow therapeutic community for adolescents (Rose 1990), it was clear that such a relationship does not arise by chance. Ensuring that the staff's many personal qualities develop into specifically therapeutic skills is part of the primary organisational task of the community. In the same way, ensuring that the right symbolic physical and material ingredients are present and effective should also be a clear management objective.

At Peper Harow, the therapeutic process itself intendedly aroused the staff's commitment to their task, but managing what transpired in their one-to-one and in their group relationships required considerable supervisory and evaluatory resources from outside consultants, who were independent of the structural hierarchy. Much of a member of staff's discussion with consultant psychotherapeutic and psychological consultants took place in front of other staff, either in the whole group, or in small groups of colleagues, though staff also had the opportunity for individual and confidential discussion with external consultants. This, unsurprisingly, sometimes aroused tension between external consultants and the senior internal managers and this in turn needed to be anticipated and managed.

GEORGE LYWARD: MANAGING THE COMMUNITY AND MANAGING CHARISMA

As one examines the multi-levelled complexity of interactive issues and relationships that make up the entity called a therapeutic community, so it becomes clear that each potentially positive element also carries the seeds of contradictory problems. The question this poses to management is where one should draw the evaluatory line between them. An argument concerning what kind of leadership is most appropriate is especially likely to arouse contradictory views.

George Lyward, of Finchden Manor in Kent, was certainly capable of exemplifying such conflict. Sadly he published very little before he died in the 1980s despite his fifty years of work with adolescents in the residential situation, so that we can now only catch the echoes of Finchden Manor's astoundingly creative and psychotherapeutic environment. The way he could clarify the meaning of psychological and behavioural functioning in his community is frequently illustrated by pictorial memories of incidents that arose out of daily community life and which Lyward turned into psychotherapeutic high drama.

Indeed, those fortunate enough to remember George Lyward sometimes describe him as though he had been a kind of magician. However, inspiring though he was, he also brooked no contradiction. Onlookers were sometimes stunned by his sudden transformation from benign genius into a 'bullying monster'. Catching sight of the observer's shocked face, he would re-direct his fury, 'And don't you stand there looking so superior! If you ever want to really help these people, you'd better learn an unpopular lesson. "No" means "no". And obligations are not matters of choice or personal convenience!' How easily he could have been hated at that moment, yet time persuades that fudging issues with disturbed adolescents demonstrates not respect for the youngster, but collusion and the further undermining of the adolescent's ability to trust.

Too much of what passes for 'democratic rights' , in institutions whose ostensible task is a therapeutic one, simply gives rein to destructive self-expression. When youngsters' capacity to manage their own behaviour is beyond their own capability, staff and the rest of the group should be required to lend their surrogate control without their authority being undermined. While we cannot deny how easily power over the vulnerable can be exploitative, it does not follow that authority and power are of themselves to blame. Power and authority undoubtedly need to be managed effectively, so as to ensure that their application is indeed to 'stand-in' for the youngsters' own current deficiency. But without such authority, the structure necessary to help people and especially adolescents, to reconstruct their lives cannot exist. Pretending otherwise, for whatever reason, is to allow self-destructive people to throw away the very lifebelt that might save them.

Lyward's endless reference was to 'stern love', because it was clear to him that the boundaries which define self and others, upon which all relationships are based, had never properly been established in the infancy of the adolescents that lived in his house. Whether the physical separation of birth has become internally acceptable, derives from a mother's ability to empathise with her baby and to reassure him or her that her love can still nourish, even if what connects them is no longer physical. When she can communicate that, the infant can quickly recognise that his or her autonomy has desirable benefits that are even more satisfying than symbiotic dependency. But if that early lesson is not learned, then the ongoing insecurity can undermine the infant's sense of autonomy. It is not surprising that Lyward often said that his teenagers were really like emotional one year olds. 'If they begin to develop to the level of three year olds, then they begin to have a real future!' he would declare. The 'stern' element of his phrase, 'stern love', underlined the absolute therapeutic requirement for the community's emotional nourishment to be recognised and accepted. Loving disturbed adolescents is not an easy task in the face of their endless self-destructiveness and their compulsion to reject one's care. However, the kind of love that has a therapeutic effect is neither mawkish nor self-gratificatory.

It is also not easy to restore normal psychological functioning, once it has come to a standstill, or once its operation has become perverse. Simply gathering a group of disturbed people together, even if their accompanying staff are intelligent and highly-qualified, will not by itself fire an organic, psycho-social therapeutic process into life. The emotionally frozen personality can hardly relate with others, irrespective of how positive the staff's ability to communicate might be. The adolescent group's initial resistance to the very nourishment it needs for recovery and growth often seems unremitting.

A variety of strategies are required to circumvent the adolescents' self-defeating, defensive shell. Each individual's psychological injury pervades their life and its effects are visible, whether they are functioning as an individual or as a member of a peer group. Bettleheim was right when he said that 'Love Is Not Enough' (1950). The manifold and psychosocially damaging effect of an individual's psychopathology requires specifically containing measures as well as love. Something like Lyward's 'stern love' is really essential if the youngster is to become capable of recognising the symbolic significance of the environment. Its consistent message may well be that the youngster is potentially loveable, but the individual has to be continuously re-inspired and challenged in order to stay in touch with the environments' message, or the illumination of initial insight will fade. Despite the controversy surrounding so-called charismatic leaders, perhaps their potential importance is to arouse the whole group's motivation.

STAFF IN THE 'ONE-TO-ONE' RELATIONSHIP

It can be seen that if psychological maturity can be gauged against someone's capacity to love and to work in the widest sense of these activities – then one source of therapy should derive appropriately from the transferential relationship with the therapist. Symbolically, the relationship is full of surrogate-parental, ego-nurturing exchange. It is the essential foundation of an individual's renaissance, equal to, and complementing, the contribution of the whole group and environment.

An individual's refusal to acknowledge love or nourishment may mask a state of unconscious terror. As his or her frostbitten emotions begin to unfreeze in the consistent warmth of the therapeutic relationship, pain rather than absence of feeling is bound to make itself felt. The response may well be an increase in extremely destructive behaviour. The journey from a frozen childhood and adolescence to a creative and loving adulthood, will inevitably be a passage of fear and grief. Thus the staff, with their complementary therapeutic task, cannot avoid daunting emotions either.

A recent study looks at the use of a psychodynamic assessment method for staff selection and development at the Cotswold Community (Khaheelee and Tomlinson 1997) – a residential therapeutic community providing care, treatment and education for emotionally deprived boys. This technique uses the Defence Mechanisms Test and an in-depth interview, and it produces a personality profile for each staff applicant. Accurate predictions can then be made about the probable length of stay for individual staff, and also some of the difficulties they are likely to have in various professional roles. It shows how a detailed understanding of personal and emotional factors can greatly aid the process of staff selection, development and turnover.

Sophisticated understanding of the psychological process of normal and pathological growth provides precious insight as well as support to the therapist in the unsteady world of adolescent treatment. However, perhaps it is the managed emotionality of the therapist that will enable understanding and insight to be applied most effectively. At the heart of therapeutic change is the re-establishment of the emotionally nourishing link between one person and another – a quality that germinates the seeds of what hitherto has been dormant and buried. This has many implications for therapeutic communities, as well as for the individual therapist.

THE THERAPEUTIC ENVIRONMENT AND
ANTI-THERAPEUTIC PROCESSES

While the core of psychological change may derive from transferential phenomena, the community context for that relationship is essential. The environment in all its forms and especially in the form of the peer group, provides an essential nurturing context for psychological change. The individual member of staff also needs sustenance. He or she needs the affirmation of the staff peer group, in recognition of the worth of his or her loving, professional skills – perhaps just as much as the resident needs affirmative interaction with his or her peer group. The resident also needs some respite from transferential intensity without 'switching it off'. Thus the social community fulfils the function of a container, yet at the same time it offers the chance of experiencing the personal enrichment that derives from seemingly ordinary 'play' – as it were – with peers, to which is added unusual significance because of their mutual therapeutic objectives. The richer the environment in terms of its culture and its ego-affirming entitlement to laughter, the more it will be able to encourage, augment and reinforce the actual experience of psychological change.

For this reason, recognising the significance of the environment for either promoting or undermining growth and change should be a central responsibility of the therapeutic community. Yet it is too often overlooked, allowing a creeping institutionalisation to invade the process. If this happens, then the community's process becomes reduced to a masquerade. Supposedly therapeutic discourse, such as community meetings, operates like jargon, pretending to meaning rather than actually promoting it. When the residents begin to sense the bureaucratisation of the ostensibly psychotherapeutic process, their anxiety and their habitual consequential behaviour can become horrifying.

Perhaps the residents are more likely to recognise such deterioration before the staff. In reaction, the staff's ability to 'play' with the residents becomes undermined and they tend instead to find good reasons why the community's formal activities should be prioritised. 'Therapy' can so easily become punitive. The youngsters' perverse ways of expressing their needs and the emotionally drained staff's resistance to their demands, leads to polarisation. Both Goffman's (1968) and Morris's (1963) classic texts demonstrate the unrelenting power of institutions to drain hope and identity from the individuals resident within them. But to the extent that insidious institutionalisation exists, so will the process of change tend towards standstill. The battle against anti-therapeutic institutionalisation can never finally be won, because the tendency towards it arises whenever the staff's buoyancy is reduced. Thus, the institutionalising tendency and the staff's capacity to cope with the relentless demands on them, are essential issues that should be at the forefront of the community's awareness.

The comparatively recent recognition of the extent to which children and young people with disabilities are liable to exploitation, of course, demands an overdue and an effective concern for their safety (Utting 1997). But, as both Butler-Sloss (1988) and Clyde (1992) have shown, serious damage can be unintentionally inflicted upon the very children the authorities set out to protect. Similarly, mechanistic procedures are a worrying feature of many children's homes, special schools, juvenile penal institutions, and adolescent hospital units. Such procedures are intended to be in the ostensible service of child protection, or children's 'rights'. Unfortunately, those responsible for the really critical task of making those children's psychological needs the institution's absolute priority, often lose this focus and implement procedures at the expense of therapeutic relationships. The same purblind reversal of the priorities of need is true of health and safety regulations as applied to institutions. Inspectorial concern with germs can reduce homely buildings into hygienic aridity. They become littered with notices indicating which room has which title, as though those who live there need to be told this any more than each of us needs a label on our own kitchen door to help us to find the heart of our homes! Fire notices, public payphones and bulk-bought furniture and food all remind children not that they are valued but that they are less than the priority of regulatory objectives. It is obviously inappropriate to apply the same regulatory approach to a therapeutic home for children as a factory, or the regional hospital!

Of course, any group, whether a family or an institutional one, must develop some bureaucratic procedures for the sake of common comfort, even if this limits the freedom of the individual. However, whether any member of that group feels such restrictions to be oppressive or dehumanising, depends on the extent to which they also feel respected as individuals and as acknowledged members of the group as a whole. The affirmation of the individual is a continuously changing variable within a well-functioning family, or in a therapeutic community. Interpreting the significance of the continually shifting balance between the individual and the group is as important a task for staff as it is for parents in a family.

Fortunately, within the web of complex balances that manage and motivate individuals and groups in a therapeutic community, there is always an inherent and psychodynamic capacity for healing and for re-ordering emotional injury and dysfunction. If the psychopathological problems of the group shift their balance towards destructive behaviour, then the dynamic process of hope and the urge towards growth can re-orientate that balance back towards its appropriate and healing functioning. Compared with this natural sophisticated group adjustment process, mechanistically imposed legislation instructing how life should be lived in a community – what relationships should exist between staff and youngsters – often seems carping and simplistic, rather than helpful. A therapeutic community's particular psychotherapeutic objective requires a continual judgement as to where the balance should lie between artificial structures designed to guarantee child protection, quality assurance and basic standards of hygiene and the organic flow of a psychodynamic environment. Incidentally, 'protection' should include psychological protection as well as protection of the youngsters' physical and social needs. However, if all these issues are in good order, a therapeutic community is the most effective situation for ensuring that the conditions intended by regulatory structures will actually be achieved.

MANAGING THE BALANCE

A therapeutic process requires the roots of disturbed behaviour to be examinable and that can only happen when behavioural expression is not too constrained. When behaviour is likely to become exceptionally anti-social and even dangerous, at which point should staff oppose it and how might they do so? It should be remembered that for young people who may never have been appropriately helped to recognise boundaries in infancy, their own loss of control can also be an emotionally debilitating experience, so that for psychotherapeutic reasons alone staff will need to help contain behaviour in a way that would be inappropriately controlling for ordinary adolescents. Equally, if the peer group is entrusted with enough room for social manoeuvre, its capacity for enforcing positive values is recognised as a major resource in the containment process.

So far, we have considered three broad areas that require careful ascertainment of the appropriate balance between their inappropriate extremes. The first was the design of the environment which needs continual evaluation if it is to enhance the self-image of residents, and not tend towards institutionalisation. Second, we have acknowledged the need for a balance between ensuring that young persons are not exploited, while also ensuring that the youngsters' adolescent autonomous identity can develop by not misguidedly over-regulating their relationships with staff. (High quality clinical supervision would offer a much greater guarantee of the essential, non-exploitative, psycho-social therapeutic process.) The third area concerns the need for a very careful balance between accepting the expression of destructive compulsive behaviour as a precursor to insight, and self-control and the repression of such behaviour – especially when repression is not so much for the benefit of the individual's psyche, but rather in the interests of adult comfort.

While all of these issues are a fundamental part of the staff's task, whoever leads such a community has the particular responsibility for ensuring that a balanced process exists. The evaluative process that underpins this kind of managerial judgement is perhaps different from the weighing up of considerations such as value for money.

Once more, 'getting it right', resisting the desire for a compliant community, encouraging staff to take that one tolerant step further, are all exemplified by good leadership. Clay's recent biography of R.D. Laing (1996) reminds us that for all his personal problems Laing was an inspirational figure, who in his capacity as leader of the famous Kingsley Hall community in London's East End, offered vision and hope to patients personally. While thus demonstrating his belief in the capacity of the most despairing to become motivated to turn their lives' direction around, he simultaneously both taught and encouraged his staff to have confidence in their own resources as people. He thus used his charisma to maximise the resources available for the community's primary objective. However, did his charismatic centrality undermine the significance of other staff, or did it offer a model that taught by example?

No single style of management is likely to be ideal for all. Hopper (1997) refers to various kinds of personal psychopathology illustrated by some charismatic leadership which must arouse anxiety as to the consequences for those who are dependent and vulnerable. However, Hopper does not argue that leadership itself is inherently either positive or negative. If one argues that it takes a great deal of inspiration to initiate a changed attitude to self in psychologically injured people and especially in resistant adolescents, then the real issue to be addressed is that of how the charismatic leader's intuitive skills, for instance, can be managed rather than undermined. It is a truism that those who have themselves suffered psychologically are especially likely to care about those with similar experiences. Like all psychotherapists, there is a great danger in the leader's misinterpreting his or her own counter-transference, unless self-awareness and insight are being continuously resourced by sophisticated and organisationally structured supervision.

SUMMARY: THE ENVIRONMENT THAT HEALS

The therapeutic community, whether engendered in mental health or in educational settings, recognises the capacity of the residential setting to generate healing and growth despite its residents' severe emotional problems. All effective therapeutic communities establish conditions in which residents experience respect for their potential, and which, whilst recognising their need to learn how to be dependent in safety, still emphasises their equal need to take responsibility for their own growth and change. In so many instances, what triggers the resident's new sense of responsibility is the certainty of the staff's own commitment. The staff's example represents the quality at the heart of the process – a quality which could be described without sentimentality as love. The emotional balance that is to be restored in each individual is the integration of the capacity to strive and achieve and the capacity to love and to be loved. If that objective informs the context for the overall relationships within the therapeutic community, it is likely that whatever its human limitations it will still be a place of hope and healing.

REFERENCES

Baron, C. (1987) *Asylum to Anarchy*. London: Free Association Books.

Bettleheim, B. (1950) *Love Is Not Enough*. New York: The Free Press.

Burn, N. (1956) *Mr Lyward's Answer – A Successful Experiment in Education*. London: Hamish Hamilton.

Butler-Sloss, E. (1988) *Report of the Enquiry into Child Abuse in Cleveland*. London: Department of Health and Social Security.

Clay, J. (1996) *R.D. Laing – A Divided Self*. London: Hodder and Stoughton.

Clyde, J. (1992) *The Report of the Enquiry into the Removal of Children from Orkney*. Edinburgh: The Scottish Office.

Goffman, E. (1968) *Asylums*. Harmondsworth: Penguin.

Hopper E. (1997) 'Traumatic experience in the unconscious life of groups: A fourth basic assumption.' S.H. Foulkes Annual Lecture. In M. Pines (ed) *Group Analysis 30*, 4. London: Sage Publications.

Khaheelee, O., Tomlinson, P. (1997) 'Intrapsychic factors in staff selection at the Cotswold community.' *Therapeutic Communities 18*, 4.

Makarenko, A.S. (1951) *The Road to Life*. Moscow: Progress Publishers.

Morgan, P. (1998) 'Children condemned by political correctness.' London: *The Sunday Times*, 8 March.

Morris, T., Morris, P. (1963) *Pentonville*. London: Routledge and Kegan Paul.

Ponce, D.E. (1993) 'Erotic countertransference issues in a residential treatment center.' In G. Northrup (ed) *The Management of Sexuality in Residential Treatment*. New York: Haworth.

Redl, F. and Wineman, D. (1951) *Children who Hate*. New York: The Free Press.

Redl, F. and Wineman, D. (1952) *Controls from Within: Techniques for the Treatment of the Aggressive Child*. New York: The Free Press.

Rose, M. (1990) *Healing Hurt Minds: The Peper Harow Experience*. London and New York: Tavistock/Routledge.

Rose, M. (1997) *Transforming Hate to Love*. London and New York: Routledge.

Utting, W. (1997) 'People like us.' The Report of the Review of Safeguards for Children Living Away from Home. London: Department of Health – Welsh Office.

Winnicott, C. (1964) 'Communicating with children.' In R.J.N. Tod (ed) *Papers on Residential Work: Children in Care*. London: Longman, Green and Co.

PART IV

The Future

CHAPTER 16

Training

Establishing a Professional Identity

Ioannis K. Tsegos

EDITORS' INTRODUCTION

Ioannis Tsegos is a psychiatrist and group analyst who trained in London, but returned to his native Greece to establish the Open Psychotherapy Centre (OPC). He is also founder of the IGA (Athens) and the European Group Analytic Training Institutions Network (EGATIN). In this chapter he describes a training therapeutic community which was set up in 1982. It is one of four at the OPC. Ioannis is a strong advocate of the combined group analytic and therapeutic community approach and he considers the communal way of carrying out work in therapy as much more interesting, eventful, enjoyable, productive and less expensive.

As he himself concludes, the training scheme should be taken not as a model, but as a paradigm. Nevertheless, his detailed description of its workings provide a platform for some very interesting ideas which he develops in the text. For readers who want to study the detail of the OPC's community training, we have included some complex tables which contain a great deal of information. However, for those wanting to gain a basic understanding of the training's philosophy the tables do not need to be studied in detail.

As editors, we do take issue with one of his starting premises: that TCs still reject the idea of formal training. Most of us now think that staff in TCs are increasingly well trained, although sometimes in rather a haphazard and idiosyncratic manner. Indeed the ATC in the UK is planning a basic TC training at the present time (building on the success of regular experiential weekends) and is intending to collaborate in the co-ordination of European training standards. Holland, Finland and Norway all have recognised TC trainings. However, the OPC training is well worth focusing on as it is particularly rigorous and radical in how it has incorporated the TC philosophy into its whole identity.

We hope the readers will find the Greek cultural perspective and radicalism exciting and thought-provoking, and a stimulus to think hard about what sort of training is needed for this sort of work.

INTRODUCTION

Training staff for working in therapeutic communities has usually been rather haphazard and very variable, with the practitioners emerging having no clear professional identity. This chapter will argue the case for rigorous training to produce staff better able to tolerate the demands of such work, with a more recognisable and definable field of professional expertise. For this purpose, a training scheme which has been operating since 1982 is described. It is based on the cornerstones of group analysis and the theory and practice of therapeutic communities. Foulkes, who founded group analysis, commented on this association in 1946: 'The relationship and mutual penetration of these two fields of observation artificially separated as psychotherapy and social therapy is a fascinating study as well as of great practical importance.'

Training has a paradoxical history in the fifty years or so since the appearance of therapeutic communities. Although the approach has enjoyed a worldwide appreciation, the training of staff has been either neglected or actively rejected. The main pretext has been that formal training is incompatible with the basic idea of the communal approach! Indeed this issue has often been met in TC circles with discouragement (expressed openly or silently) or with shallow and insubstantial arguments against rigorous training. As a result of this it is not surprising that the two most important results of any training (skill and efficiency, and a professional identity) are often lacking in TCs and their staff. Furthermore, confusion, job dissatisfaction and loss of morale are not at all uncommon (Tsegos 1996c; Tsegos and Athitakis 1997).

The following training scheme is a result of the communal and group analytic approaches which are promoted in theory and practice at the Open Psychotherapeutic Centre (OPC) in Athens. This is a private non-profit-making organisation where four therapeutic communities and four training communities are operating. There is a non-residential daily TC, two fortnightly weekend TCs and a seven week summer TC. There are also four Institutes: the Athens Institute of Group Analysis (founded in 1982), the Institute of Psychological Assessment (founded in 1984), the Institute of Psychodrama–Sociotherapy (founded in 1985) and the Institute of Family Therapy (founded in 1989). These four function as the training communities (TrCs). The theoretical basis of this extensive use of the communal way of training follows from Foulkes' exhortation that 'psychotherapy can best be taught in the ongoing process of a therapeutic situation' (1975). In practice, it follows Jane Abercrombie's application of communal procedures with medical and architecture university students (1983). This was done experimentally then, but important elements of it are now being used in mainstream medical education.

THE OPEN PSYCHOTHERAPEUTIC CENTRE (OPC)

The rapid development of the centre, and particularly the broad use of the communal approach, is owed mostly to its independence and the vigour of the training activities. The centre is financially autonomous: it is not included in the state budget and therefore not liable to the state bureaucracy. Some of the training activities, such as the group analytic programme, have been in existence for some time and began before the inauguration of the OPC itself.

The training for the TC workers is based on the experience of the group-analytic training, where for reasons of staff shortage communal training was successfully instituted. We were sufficiently convinced about the merits of the communal approach for training to decide to face the vicissitudes of forming a new training for TC workers, using again, of course, the communal methods. This was despite such a training having no precedents to guide it, and our acute awareness that most TC practice seemed to abhor training and professionalism. Besides these discouraging preconditions, we were also aware of the negative preconceptions which we were going to meet amongst the prospective students to whom we would advertise such an innovation. Also, because of novelty of this training model, there was an absence of a recognised professional identity. Last and not least, there was the poor prospect for graduates of finding employment – apart from working in a TC setting. This important issue was settled quite successfully by incorporating the training of psychodrama into the training for TC specialists, as this is a socio-psychotherapeutic method, which has an established professional identity.

The training constitutes a self-contained postgraduate course open to individuals already trained into one of the fields of therapy, prevention, rehabililitlion or education, and who are interested to work either as staff in TCs, or to use TC principles in commercial organisations or schools. It also equips those who wish to practise psychodrama privately. The main feature of the training is that it functions as a TrC, which we define exactly as we define a TC:

> A TC or a TrC is a method of psychotherapy or training which with clarity, responsibility and flexibilty mobilises and utilises the healthy and real part of the ego of clients, therapists, students and trainers for their improvement and for the function of the place by pursuing to derive maximum knowledge and experience in relating and leadership. (Tsegos 1988, p.2)

The 'real and healthy part of ego' is crucial: Brian Haddon (1979) writes that 'the concentration on a person's sick part to the exclusion of healthy attributes was in itself unhealthy'. The programme is thus based on 'ego-training in action' (Foulkes 1964, p.82 and p.129) and has as its objectives:

o the acquisition of relevant skills

o the acquisition of a clear professional identity

o the consolidation of TC theory

o the learning of the role, by differentiating it from status and quality

o the familiarisation in the art of leadership, by differentiating power
from strength.

Most of these objectives have been achieved quite successfully with the happy
marriage of sociotherapy and psychodrama – and so far about 40 qualified
practitioners, including psychiatrists, nurses, social workers, teachers and
others, are working in different settings – including several organisations and
private practice.

THE SOCIO THERAPY – PSYCHODRAMA
TRAINING COMMUNITY

As it is difficult for an intensive and rather complicated training programme to
be described in words, I will try to do this with the help of several schematic
representations. Table 16.1 represents an outline of the whole training. The
introductory course comprises of 28 lectures and an equal number of sessions in
small experiential groups, plus three or four sessions in a large experiential
group. There is no selection procedure for the participants.

During the introductory course, candidates may apply for the full training, for
which they are interviewed initially by one trainer and then by a panel of three.
If they are successful in this, candidates are recommended to start their personal
therapy in a mixed (i.e. with patients) group. After a few months, or more, and
with the agreement of the conductor of the group, they can participate in the
preliminary course. This consists of weekly theoretical seminars for clarification
of the objectives and understanding the communal culture of the training.

Table 16.1 An outline of the training programme	
Courses or Phases	*Duration*
I. Introductory course in group psychotherapy	9 months
II. Preliminary course (1st year). Formation of the year's (class) group	6–9 months
III. Qualifying course (2nd–4th year). Formation of the community group (training community)	3 years

During this period a group has already been formed: that of the students and
the two trainers. It is required that this group is conducted by the students in
rotation. It includes an evaluation of students and they enter the proper

qualifying course in October at the beginning of the academic year. The start of the training activities, and particularly the entrance of new members, is considered a very important event and it is marked with the first Symposium (which is a formal dinner) offered to the whole TrC by the trainers (at their own expense!). The symposium underlines the communal spirit of the training.

Perhaps further clarification is needed here, because there is a prevailing view that a TC must be residential, and a day facility cannot be a true 'community'. My view is that this confuses the meaning of *collectivism* with that of *communalism*. The first implies a central political control (kolkhoz, Kibbutz, military camps, residential schools, hierarchical TC, etc.), and the second implies exactly the opposite: a group of people functioning through decentralisation of control and respect of privacy. Collectivism is characterised, among other things, by a controlled common living and working environment, and also by communal sleeping and eating activities (dormitory and dinning room). In contrast, a community is characterised by everyone participating in decisions concerning function, preservation and culture, but with segregation of living and sleeping arrangements (family, housing, etc.) and only dining together for specific meals. In a residential TC, the staff operate as in a community, but the residents as in a collective.

THE 'GROUP ACTIVITY'

In the last few years there has been gradually increasing recognition of the importance of group activity in therapeutic communities, and particularly the small group which is regarded as 'the symbolic heart of the modern Therapeutic Community' (Manning 1989, p.69). This general acknowledgement needs clarification, as psychoanalytically oriented groups are rather unsuitable for the communal approach, while group-analytic ones are more kindred in terms of theory and practice.

The students' participation in a mixed group for their personal therapy is required. This is to make them lose a part of their 'medical' attitude and way of thinking, and so to understand and acquire that of the patients. Through this experience, they are going to become acquainted or 'contaminated' with the powerful role of the weak, by adopting it themselves for a while (Tsegos 1996b).

It is important to clarify that the entire training programme comes into being not merely through their active participation in a number of groups, but with the sense that they themselves are members of a community – which entails several responsibilities in order to accomplish all its objectives. These responsibilities are carried out with others in a number of different size groups. The size depends on the purpose, and this overall 'group activity' is characterised by a continual alternation between different membership

Table 16.2 Enumeration and short description of the activities of the training community of sociotherapists-psychodramatists

Activities	No.	Description	Size of group	Developmental level	Hours per session	Frequency	Duration	Real hours required (minimum)
PERSONAL THERAPY IN A GROUP AND IN A PSYCHODRAMA GROUP	1	Proper group-analytic group (mixed: patients and trainees)	S	R	1.30	Once or twice a week	4 years	400 hrs
	2	Proper group-analytic psychodrama group (mixed)	S	R	1.30	Once a week	2 years	200 hrs
SUPERVISION OF THE PSYCHOTHERAPEUTIC ACTIVITY	3	A group of fellow students with an experienced observer	S	R	2.00–2.30	Once a week	3 years	200–250 hrs
THEORY	4	Participation in TC and GA theory	S	R	1.30–2.00	Once a week	3 years	240 hrs
	5	Participation in Lectures with external speakers	L	R	1.30	Once every 3 months	3 years	36 hrs
	6	Participation in the politics of sociotherapy	L	R	1.00–1.30	Once a week	3 years	200 hrs
SENSITIVITY COMMUNITY MEETINGS	7	Trainees and trainers	L	P	1.30	Once a month	3 years	30 sessions
STUDENTS SELF-EVALUATION GROUPS	8	Trainees only	M	P	1.30	Once a month	3 years	12 sessions–16 hrs (approx.)
INTERTRAINING COMMUNITY MEETINGS	9	Trainees and trainers of the four training communities	L	P	1.30	Once a month	3 years	30 sessions
SYMPOSIA (FORMAL COMMUNAL DINNERS)	10	Trainees and trainers	L	P	Varies	Once every 3 months	3 years	15 meetings
PARTICIPATION IN WORKSHOPS AND CONGRESSES	11	Participation in workshops organised by foreign organisations (e.g. GAS London, the ATC, etc.)	L	R	Varies	Varies	Two workshops in 3 years	
CLINICAL EXPERIENCE								

No.	Activity	Size	Level	Ratio	Frequency	Duration	Hours
	co-conductor b) Psychodynamic groups and sociodynamic groups of the psychotherapeutic community	The quick open group – analytic groups and the sociodynamic groups of the TC				once every 15 days		
14	c) Psychodrama groups	The psychodrama groups	S	R → A	1.30	Once a week	2 years	100–200 hrs
15	d) Experiential groups	Small closed groups (members of the introductory course)	S	A	1.30	Once a week	9 months a year for 1–2 years	108 hrs
16	e) Large groups	The large groups of the introductory course, of the TC and of the TrC	L	R → A	1.30	Once a week	1 year	65 hrs
17	TEACHING EXPERIENCE	Participation in the introductory course as: *lecturer or chairperson*	L	A	1.15	1–2 times a years as: *lecturer or chairperson*	3 years	16–20 hrs
18		Conducting the supervision and theoretical seminars of the 3rd year students	S	A	4.00	Once a week	3 months	48 hrs
19	TRAIN. COMMUNITY'S POLICY MEETINGS	Trainees and trainers	L	A	1.30	2 for each academic year	3 years	8 sessions roughly
20	ADMINISTRATIVE ACTIVITIES *(according to the year study)*	a) Arranging various practical matters for the seminars	S	A	Varies	Varies	For the 2nd year	Varies according to each activity
21		b) Co-ordinating the introductory course	M	A			3rd year	
22		c) Secretariat	S	A			4th year	
23		d) Students' co-ordinating committee (the 4th year students and the conductors of the younger group)	M	A			4th year	
24	TRAINERS' COMMITTEE	Trainers only	S	A	1.00	Once a month	4 years	Varies
25	WRITING EXPERIENCE	Submission of short theoretical papers		A		One per year	2nd and 3rd year	5000–13,000 words
26		Qualifying thesis		A			4th year	Over 50,000 words

Notes: A = Adult level; P = Peer level; R = Regressed level; S = Small (<7 persons); M = Medium (<15); L = Large (>15)

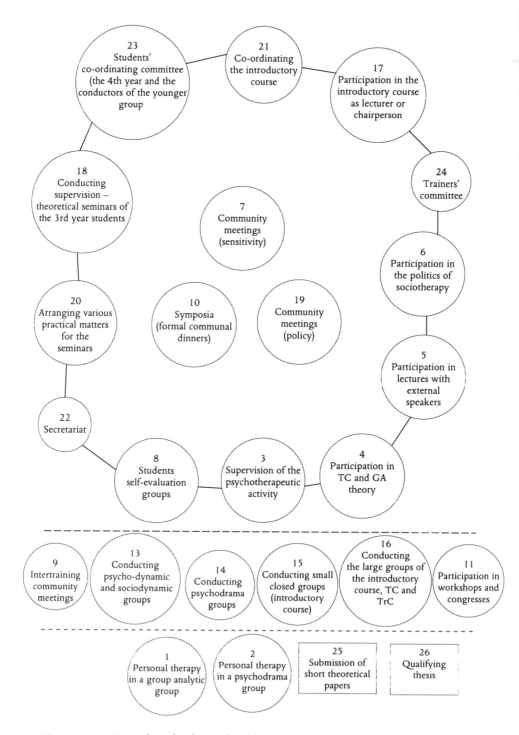

Figure 16.1 Activities that take place within (above the 1st dotted line), some outside (below the 1st dotted line) the training and the therapeutic community and a few outside the premises of the OPC (below the 2nd dotted line)

activities and roles. Table 16.2 shows some of the characteristics of the many constituent groups, and Figure 16.1 shows where they take place.

The content and purpose of the group activity

During the four years in the TrC, together with the requirement of clinical practice in a TC (usually a TC of the OPC), students form a large number of relationships by participating in different activities. These can be divided into two main orientations, sociodynamic and psychodynamic, which are traditionally, but somewhat artificially, distinguished (see Table 16.3). They occur in various combinations and provide the opportunity to communicate in different ways (K, L, M) as well as to use and familiarize students with different means of expression (H, I, J).

In this 'laboratory' of relationships, we can observe the interweaving of these two kinds or relating. The *psychodynamic* aims to reinforce the process of *relating to self,* and it is acquired mainly through personal therapy (group analysis and psychodrama), in mixed groups (D and E), and through their contact with patients (initially as co-conductors, and later as conductors of several patients' groups). The vehicle of expression for this process is internal dialogue, and occurs mostly without words (J); the main way for communication is the imagination-fantasy one (M).

The *sociodynamically* orientated relationship which promotes the dialogue with the outer world and cultivates *relating to others,* is pursued by participating in group activity of C and G (C for trainers and students, and G for students alone). Here the main vehicle of expression is language, and the main functions are thinking, pretending and performing (I), while the prevailing means of communication is the symbolic (L).

The other kind of sociodynamically orientated relationship is the one which mainly aims to cultivate *relating to reality.* This is assumed to take place in the trainers' committee for trainers alone (A), in several activities for students and trainers (B) and students alone (F). Relating to reality is mainly characterised by action (H) where participating, deciding and creating are the prevailing characteristics, with reality as the main way of communication (K).

The dynamics of the facts of relating

With this extensive use of group analytic and community groups, it is assumed that trainees' personality traits (PTs) can be modified through participation in this experience. This can also increase learning ability in certain areas of knowledge (learning faculties, LFs). The factors shown in Table 16.4 indicate the aspirations pursued by this training, and constitute a summary of its theory.

Table 16.3 Correlating relationship orientation of trainers, students and patients with participation, means of expression and ways of communication in a therapeutic community and training community

Relationship's orientation	Participation					Communication and expression	
	A Trainers only	**B** Students and trainers	**C / D** Students and trainers	**E** Students and patients	**F / G** Students alone	**H / I / J** Means of expression	**K / L / M** Ways of communication
Relating to reality — Sociodynamic (dialogue with outer world)	Trainers' committee 24	Participation in TC and GA theory 4; Participation in lectures with external speakers 5; Participation in the politics of sociotherapy 6; Sensitivity community meetings 7; Intertraining community meetings 9; Participation in workshops and congresses 11; Training community's policy meetings 19			**F** Conducting the supervision and theoretical seminars of the 3rd year students 18; Arranging various practical matters for the seminars 20; Co-ordinating the introductory course 21; Secretariat 22	**H** Action (mainly) DECIDING PARTICIPATING CREATING Feeling Thinking	**K** Reality (mainly)
Relating to others — Sociodynamic (dialogue with outer world)		**C** Supervision of the psychotherapeutic activity 3; Symposia (formal communal dinners) 10; Participation in the introductory course as lecturer, chairperson 17			**G** Students' self-evaluation groups 8; Students' co-ordinating committee (4th year and the conductors of the younger group) 23	**I** Language (mainly) THINKING PRETENDING PERFORMING Creating Deciding	**L** Symbolic (mainly)
Relating to self — Psychodynamic (dialogue with inner-world)		**D** Personal therapy in a group 1; Personal therapy in a psychodrama group 2		**E** Personal therapy in a group 1; Personal therapy in a psychodrama group2		**J** Silence (mainly) FEELING THINKING Participating	**M** Imagination – Fantasy levels (mainly)

as co-therapist

Initial interview (out-patient department of the OPC) 12
Conducting psychodynamic and sociodynamic groups of the TC 13
Conducting psychodrama groups 14
Conducting small closed groups (introductory course) 15
Conducting large groups of the introductory course, of the TC and of the TrC 16

as therapist

The training's basic philosophy: insight through relationships

There is no doubt that the prevailing 'philosophy' or ethos of the Institute providing the training is of considerable importance. 'Philosophy' here refers to a broad concept which is characterised by professed elements such as the institute's ideas, principles, objectives and aspirations. However, a philosophy is also constituted by hidden and unexpressed (even unconscious) components which are as decisive as the declared ones. This second group, the 'hidden' ones, are matters related to tradition, habits, immediate objectives and anxieties of survival. They are coloured mainly by the teachers' personalities and aspirations, and by the institute's state at any one time.

Whether hidden or declared, the prevailing targets of any training institute will differ: for example, in a state-supported institution compared to an independent one; or between a well established one and a beginner. Also, within any given institute, the objectives of the teachers are not the same as those preoccupying the students: for example teachers may be mainly worried about the survival, prosperity and the glory of the institute, while students are concerned to gain their qualification within the shortest time and with the minimum effort! The fact that they both constitute a community does not imply that they must relinquish their different objectives: indeed they should not.

Although the two existing objectives differ considerably, these differences are not usually discussed. When they are, they are frequently dealt with by 'interpreting' them. This is so particularly as one of the professed ideas of all psychotherapeutic institutes is achieving insight, which, as I shall try to show, should not be the only objective. Nevertheless, there is a way to 'throw a bridge across' if both sides (trainers and students in this case) are reminded that their basic job is to learn, to teach, and especially to enjoy the richness of emotions in the art of relating. After all, if 'insight without emotional experience is of limited value' (Foulkes 1969), then this is particularly true for real relationships – and much less for the reductionistic ones ('as if') of psychoanalysis (Tsegos 1996a). Therefore, insight can be best acquired by exercising the art of relating as taught and learned by forming these real relationships through participation in many groups of different sizes and purpose, and of dissimilar population. The students learn most while relating in activities with fellow students and with their teachers and clients: the issue of abstinence can then be examined in the light of the reality of the socialising procedure, and not under the ideological shadow of psychoanalysis.

Personality traits pursued by the group analytic and the communal approach

In Table 16.3, we have seen how several kinds of relationships, means of expression, and principal ways of communication are pursued by participation in various activities. Let us now see if we can define some of the necessary ingredients that are required for satisfactory working relationships (see Table 16.4).

Columns 1 and 2 enumerate some basic characteristics of the two approaches for the sake of differentiation. I would name the first one as 'individuocratic' or 'personalitic' or 'psychoanalytic', and the other as 'personocratic' or 'prosopocratic' or 'group analytic'. The former is of the persona, and the latter is of the *prosopon*.

The word '*prosopon*' is a neologism that is needed to indicate a difference between the meaning from the word *person*, which etymologically stems from the Latin word *persona*. This means a mask for the actor by which he changes the prosody – so it has a phonetic-vocal origin; the etymology of the Greek word *prosopon* (Πρόσωπον) indicates a face turned to someone (πρός: to ὤψ, ὠπός – face). It means 'I see' or 'I look' to someone or something, and this has a meaning more appropriate to our hypothesis – for the importance of the relationship, and the eye.

The individuocratic approach (of the person) has the advantage of being the better known, the more prevalent, and, as an ideology, the most popular among the majority of the psychotherapists. This is probably because it goes along with the pathology of rationalism and meets the appetite for power which is not uncommon in helping professionals! The second, that of the prosopon, though more difficult to comprehend, is richer and particularly more harmonious to group analytic and TC approaches.

Therefore, an important condition for the student is to be able to differentiate between the role and the person. This is pursued first by participating as patient in a mixed (patients and trainees) group analytic and psychodrama group, and also in several other groups with different and continually alternating roles (Tsegos, Terlidou and Yerasi 1997).

The juxtaposition of some of these concepts (in columns 1 and 2 of Table 16.4) is intended to differentiate their similar and often confusing meaning. For example *insight* is placed opposite to *relationship*, and *self-disclosure* opposite to the importance of *visibleness and presence*. It goes without saying that there is no intention to do away with the central concepts of psychoanalysis such as transference: the purpose is to point out the not-infrequent abuse of the transference material, while often disregarding the importance of trust.

Another example is again the issue of abstinence: although a useful (and to some extent preventative) measure, its effect is often in the service of producing 'role'-type personality traits instead of cultivating the qualities of the prosopon, which is what is needed in this work. Furthermore, I fear that the extensive use and abuse of abstinence in psychoanalysis has been embraced unaltered by some group analytic practitioners (Tsegos and Karaolidou 1993) and we should define our prime duty as protecting the procedures and objectives of therapy or training (i.e. the boundaries) and not further reinforcing the already powerful role of the trainer or therapist.

Table 16.4 Therapeutic and training factors of a communal training programme

Personality traits (PT)				Learning faculties (LF)
Differentiating personality traits		Communal factors	Structural-maturational factors	Learning factors
1. Of persona (mask) – role	2. From person– authenticity (approaching self)	3. For differentiating power from strength	4. For the 'ego training in action'	5. For some learning faculties
Individual	Prosopon personhood Freedom in responsibility	Citizen Citizenship	Continuous crossing of boundaries with: Constant interchange between:	• Cognitiveexperiential (associative) interplay
Regression	Progression		• developmental levels	• Creation
Insight	Relationship's interpersonal experience	Exposure and concern Relationships on a:	• intrapsychicinterpersonal	• Familiarisation with the learning-unlearning procedure
Unilateral selfdisclosure	Bilateral visibleness and presence	• seniors level • peers level • juniors level	• socialcommunal • transpersonal-imaginary	
Reductionistic (as if)				• Give examples rather than provide models
Analytical approach	Re-creational approach	Familiarisation with authority and subordination	Points of reference: • roles • groups (type, size) • conductors • patients • community-society	Learning through: • Interpersonal action and the synthetic procedure (supervision) versus guidance and vicarious learning
Mystification of the transferential elements	Unification of the self through the incorporation of the group and the community			
Intellectualistic family re-enactment	Imaginary family's and subsequent group's re-enactment	Communal re-enactment	The multiplication of the procedure of the:	• Creativity vs passive copying and repetition
Individual neutrality	Personal Alterity		• presence-absence (between whiles) • participating non-participating interplay	• Paradigm vs model
Mystification of weakness and omnipotence	Demystification of weakness and omnipotence	Differentiating: Leading–coordinating, status from role, authoritative from authoritarian		• Taking into account the importance of the between whiles (in Greek: 'meson', 'metaxi') in order to reinforce the discerning faculty than that of the criticism
Power	Strength		Strengthening of the self through incorporation of	
Mystification of guilt	De-incrimination of shame and joy	Realistic reciprocal participation into practical activities for 'the inevitable and the expedient'	• levels • points of reference • and the between whiles 'absences' ('meson', mean) of boundaries	
Mystification of sorrow	Legitimisation of humour and wit			• Cultivation of the common sense ('sensus communis'), beyond a simple acquirement of knowledge, skills and rationalism leading to ideology
Cultivation of fear: • religious sects • totalitarian parties • psychoanalysis	A genuine mutual respect and suppression of any kind of an oppressive instrument	Participation in festivities Following rituals		
Abstinence: (domination and submission via intimidation)	Protection of the therapy and not of the therapist	Relating orientation		

I will not expand upon guilt, shame, fear, sorrow, joy and humour: I hope that the juxtaposition in the first two columns is sufficient. I would only like to add that regardless of the role students undertake in different groups, my strong suspicion is that the experience of the large number of eyes meeting him or her with their own gazes is crucial; whatever this gazing influence may mean, I suspect that it is of primary and not secondary importance (Tsegos 1996a).

Communal factors: differentiating power from strength

The numerous activities of the four TCs give opportunity for several personal 'workshops' for trainees which provide the chance to experience the responsibility of being conductors, the dependence of being conducted, or of functioning on an equal level.

Through this 'up and down' or 'elevator' kind of process, students are involved in relationships on several levels (senior, peers and juniors) corresponding to the three main developmental faces (see Table 16.5, and Figure 16.2). This makes the procedure colourful, rich and particularly strengthening: it also acts dramatically in demystifying power by differentiating it from strength.

Table 16.5 The three main levels of functioning in the training community	
Level of functioning: *Role of the:*	*The trainee in the training community:*
REGRESSED (R)	• Relates to self • Is put in the position of the unlearned, the child • Accepts, obeys • Functions from a hierarchically lower level; is led
PEER (P)	• Relates to others and to reality • Discusses, questions, participates on equal terms with the other members of the TrC (trainers and trainees) • Functions on a horizontal level
ADULT (A)	• Relates to reality and to others • Makes decisions, takes responsibilities, administrates, teaches, manages • Functions from a hierarchically higher level; is leading

Power is a feeling which lasts as long as we maintain a powerful role, while strength is the feeling we keep after losing or moving on from a powerful role, but nevertheless surviving emotionally. Another strengthening procedure is the ability to differentiate between *leading* and *co-ordinating*, as well as between *status* and *role*, and between concepts such as *authoritative* and *authoritarian*. There is no doubt that all these concepts and roles can also be taught by the internalization process, by means of observing seniors; however, the experience of enacting or playing these roles by oneself or by frequently observing peers carrying them out, adds a memorable experience (Tsegos 1993).

The adoption of a communal method for training and treatment does not aim to provide a pseudodemocratic veneer. It flows from a conviction that an important element for future therapists is to make them able to act as responsible citizens: the ability to exercise judgement and authority. In other words, somebody capable of being led and leading 'conditions not only for the inevitable but also for the expedient' (Aristotle, *Politics I,* 1254, pp.18–19, lines 20–23). This citizenship constitutes an important part of ego-training in action, with the literal meaning of the words 'training' and 'action': a training community provides a great deal of opportunity for this (Tsegos 1996a).

STRUCTURAL-MATURATIONAL FACTORS: ALTERNATION WITH THE 'MESON'

It is interesting to consider the influence of the time that intervenes between two formal sessions: Aristotle calls the interval between two structured and boundaried activities the 'mean' or 'meson'. Foulkes was influenced by the psychology of Gestalt and the consideration of the ground against which the figure is defined, and this is close to Aristotle's way of thinking: the 'sense is a sort of mean between the relevant sensible extremes' (Aristotle, *On the Soul II,* 424a, lines 5–6). The sense for Aristotle is not a simple impression, but energy and drive which progresses to morphological classifications (Table 16.4).

Any structured activity of the community is followed or preceded by an unstructured interval (Figure 16.2). The importance of this inactive 'between while', 'mean' or 'meson', is an important factor not only for ego training in action (Table 16.4, column 4) but it is also critical as a learning factor (Table 16.4, column 5), particularly in the procedure of 'discerning'.

A flattering common illusion shared equally by teachers and therapists, is the belief that whatever insight or knowledge the student or the patient obtains during training or therapy – in other words whatever change occurs – is made within their office or classroom alone! But consider the meson: the rather neglected condition which intervenes between two teaching or therapy sessions. The main characteristic of this interlude is that it is unspecified, in terms of boundaried and structured qualities, and of identity, and of the role of the student or patient. After they have participated in a boundaried and

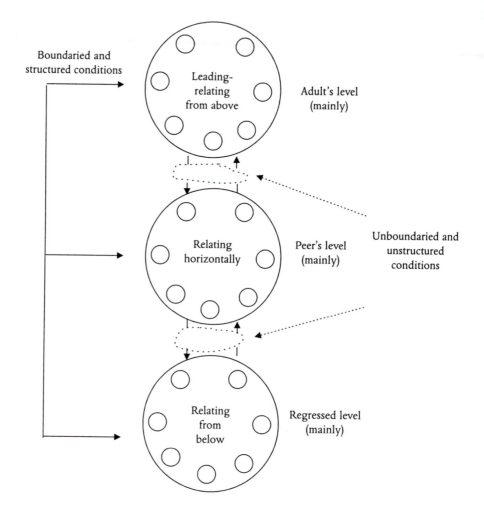

Figure 16.2 The 'up and down' or the 'elevator' process within the three developmental models and the boundaried-structured and unboundaried-unstructured conditions

structured situation, they remain for a while in a situation which is unboundaried and unstructured – a kind of vacuum experience (Figure 16.2). We can assume then, that during this condition, the person is somehow 'lost' and forced to become aware of his or her own strengthening elements: a procedure that fortifies the personality structure. If we accept that strength is what remains when power is lost, this is an experiential demonstration of it. We can conclude that some important qualities are acquired between the structured activities, and not during them! And perhaps it is later on, and in a structured situation, that we gain insight and become aware of these acquisitions.

LEARNING FACTORS AND CREATIVITY

As teachers and therapists, we expect patients or students to understand several things: ourselves, themselves, and many specific topics. This does not necessarily mean that in order to *understand* they always have to '*stand-under*' us! A community setting – for training or therapy – can provide both sides with a vast variety of enjoyments with a finer taste than those of domination and control, which after all are an indication of weakness.

Learning can be promoted not only by *regression* but also by *progression*, and the communal setting is very suitable to cultivate the learning–unlearning procedure with its constant movement between situations, experiences and roles (Tsegos 1995b). This repeated interchange between the structured and unstructured situation accentuates the meson situation, which as well as the strengthening process, cultivates the critical faculties. For this, we come back to Aristotle: 'it is the mean that has the power of discerning' (Aristotle, *On The Soul*).

Now a few words about *common* sense, for which there should be more respect, particularly as common sense is not so ... common. It can be cultivated and thrive best within a communal spirit and atmosphere – for apart from being an antidote to 'non-sense' – it could also be the best protection against the development of a mechanistic way of thinking. This mechanistic and reductionistic way of thinking is the doctrine of rationalism – which can too easily be cultivated in psychotherapy, and within all the helping professions.

CONCLUSION

Within all this 'technology' of the training community, I might have given the impression that the trainer's role is vanished completely; however, this is not so. The frequent participation on equal or equivalent levels does not imply that the personal qualities or abilities of the teacher are undervalued. It is exactly the opposite, for, as the trainers have been to some extent released from their roles, they can become more free to display or enrich their own strength, knowledge, experience and wisdom.

We, the teachers, usually know a lot, but most probably because of this we don't usually continue our learning! It's perhaps because of this that Oscar Wilde wrote his poisonous aphorism that 'everybody who is incapable of learning has taken to teaching' (1968).

The programme described is the outcome of several revisions which I hope will continue. Because of this process of continual reassessment and modification, which is close to the basic philosophy of therapeutic communities, this training scheme should be taken not as a model but only as a paradigm. This is particularly important for learning the art of this type of psychotherapy: it is not *applied to* other persons, but to a large extent it comes through the active participation of those on both 'sides'.

REFERENCES

Abercrombie, M.L.J. (1983) 'The application of some principles of group analytic psychotherapy to higher education.' In M. Pines (ed) *The Evolution of Group Analysis*. London: Routledge and Kegan Paul.

Aristotle (1995) *On the Soul II*, Trans. by W.S. Hett. Loeb Classical Library. Cambridge, MA: Harvard Univ. Press.

Aristotle (1990) *Politics I*. Trans. by H. Rackham. Loeb Classical Library. Cambridge, MA: Harvard University Press.

Foulkes, S.H. (1946) 'Principles and practice of group therapy.' *Therapeutic Communities*, Special Commemorative Issue, 17, 2, 1996.

Foulkes, S.H. (1964) *Therapeutic Group Analysis*. London: George Allen and Unwin.

Foulkes, S.H. (1969) 'Summary and conclusions.' In S.H. Foulkes and G. St. Prince (eds) *Psychiatry in a Changing Society*. London: Tavistock.

Foulkes, S.H. (1975) *Group Analytic Psychotherapy. Method and Principles*. London: Gordon and Breach. Reprinted London: Karnac, 1986.

Haddon, B. (1979) 'Political implications of therapeutic communities.' R.D. Hinshelwood and N. Manning (eds) *In Therapeutic Communities. Reflections and Progress*. London: Routledge and Kegan Paul 38–45.

Manning, N. (1989) *The Therapeutic Community Movement: Charisma and Routinization*. London: Routledge.

Tsegos, I.K. (1988) 'Three training communities: Comments and considerations.' Paper presented at the 1st Symposium in Therapeutic Communities. Athens: Open Psychotherapeutic Centre.

Tsegos, I.K. (1993) 'Strength, power and group analysis.' *Group Analysis 26*, 2, 131–137.

Tsegos, I.K. (1995a) 'A Greek model of supervision. The matrix as supervisor – a version of peer supervision developed at I.G.A. (Athens).' In M. Sharpe (ed.) *The Third Eye: Supervision of Analytic Groups*. London: Routledge 117–129.

Tsegos, I.K. (1995b) 'Further thoughts on group analytic training.' *Group Analysis 28*, 3, 313–326.

Tsegos, I.K. (1996a) 'Small, median and large groups in group analytic training.' *Proceedings of E.G.A.T.I.N. Study Days*, Ljubljana, October 1995, 77–97.

Tsegos, I.K. (1996b) 'To mix or not to mix. Uber die gruppen-analytische Therapie der KandidatInnen in Rahmen ihrer Ausbildung.' *Arbeitshefte Gruppenanalyse 1/96*, 65–78. Munster: Votum-Verl.

Tsegos, I.K. (1996c) 'Fifty years of an amateur enthusiasm (on the avoidance of training and of professional identity in TC).' *Therapeutic Communities 17*, 3, 159–165.

Tsegos, I.K. and Karaolidou, M. (1993). 'How to abstain ... via contact.' Proceedings of the 9th European Symposium in Group Analysis. Heidelberg, 402–411.

Tsegos, I.K. and Athitakis, M. (1997) 'Is the issue of TC training still in the shadow of the Quakers' inner light?' Paper presented at the Windsor Conference. Windsor, September.

Tsegos, I.K., Terlidou, C. and Yerasi, A. (1997) 'Why psychodrama in the training of a sociotherapist?' Paper presented at the Windsor Conference. Windsor, September.

Wilde, O. (1968) 'The decay of lying.' In *Complete Works of Oscar Wilde*. London and Glasgow: Harper Collins, 1997.

CHAPTER 17

Research
The Importance of Asking Questions
Janine Lees

EDITORS' INTRODUCTION

Jan Lees' long career in social work, counselling and research, has taken her in and out of TCs. On returning to Oxford to do her social work training (she had already graduated in history), she was introduced to TCs by her tutor, David Millard, whose interest and enthusiasm prompted her choice of dissertation and placement at the Maudsley on Ward 1, an experience she found both exciting and terrifying.

An ATC conference in Fulbourn was the romantic setting for her first meeting with Nick Manning (author of many books on TCs) and they now have four children! She moved to Kent, as a senior social worker, doing a PhD which involved field work at Henderson and later working as senior lecturer in social work at Mid Kent College.

She now lives in Nottingham, has a diploma in psychodynamic counselling and works at Francis Dixon Lodge as a researcher, where she struggles along feeling a bit of an outsider and longs to exercise her skills as a group therapist and be a full member of the community. She also chairs the ATC research group.

Her long involvement with TCs and working relationship with Nick Manning (they are working with Barbara Rawlings on an extensive review of TC literature for the High Security Psychiatric Commissioning Board) has produced an everything-you-need-to-know-about-research chapter, which should provide readers with a broad and comprehensive picture of the field and the many possibilities for further exploration. A future book in the TC series on research paradigms and methodologies is planned.

WHY DO RESEARCH?

In examining therapeutic communities in the 1990s, it is important to reflect on the relationship between therapeutic communities and research, and the current role and importance of research for them. Those involved, or interested, need to consider the following questions:

- Do we need to do research, and, if so, why?

- What research has been done in the past, and what, if anything, has it told us?

- What research is being done now?

- What sorts of questions do we want research to answer?

- What sorts of research methodology and tools are both available to us for, and appropriate to, addressing the sorts of questions we are asking?

- What are the pitfalls and shortfalls?

- What is the best way to proceed?

The relationship between therapeutic communities and research has been ambivalent in the past. However, there is now more certainty, both within and outside therapeutic communities, that research is a necessity and no longer a luxury or eccentricity. We need research for several reasons:

- to inform and improve practice, and make therapeutic community treatment more effective, and fit better with client need

- to provide a fundamental understanding of what therapeutic communities are all about, and how they work – and therefore how they can be replicated

- to meet the requirements of 'evidence-based practice', and provide information about cost-effectiveness for purchasers, and so to ensure therapeutic communities' continued survival, and expansion.

THERAPEUTIC COMMUNITY RESEARCH: THE PAST

Therapeutic communities have been in existence for over fifty years. However, the research tradition has not been as great as might be expected from such an innovative, and influential, 'therapeutic technique, and ... movement for social change' (Manning 1989, p.ix). The initial 'experiments' at Northfield and Mill Hill/Belmont would have provided ideal material for action research projects!

Research was an important part of early TC innovations. However, early therapeutic communities tended to prefer descriptive, qualitative and participant observation types of research, as these were more in keeping with the philosophy and practice of the therapeutic community. There was suspicion of quantitative research, in reducing people to numbers, and particularly unhappiness about the ethics of techniques, such as random allocation and control groups, which run counter to TC selection processes. This meant that there was little quantitative or evaluative research undertaken until the 1970s, when alliances with medicine and psychotherapy were becoming more important. During the 1980s, there were growing threats to funding and survival, and many TCs closed. More recently, there seems to be a revived interest in these treatment methods, and, there has been a concurrent increase in both the quantity and quality of research work.

The different types of therapeutic community have generated descriptive and evaluative writing, of differing amounts and quality. The *general TC approach*, or whole mental hospital as a therapeutic community, and the *educational TC* have produced very little research, mostly descriptive. The two other types of therapeutic community – the *democratic TC proper*, and the *concept-based (programmatic) TC* – have tended to dominate the research field. These are located mainly in the mental health, penal, and substance abuse rehabilitation fields. There has been a long, productive, evaluative tradition in the concept TCs – mainly on substance abuse programmes in USA and Canada – although it is of variable quality.

Perhaps the best piece of early research, on the democratic therapeutic community, is Rapoport's study of the Social Rehabilitation Unit at Belmont (later Henderson Hospital). His team looked primarily at ideology, social structure and processes, and reactions of patients to treatment, particularly through clinical judgements of 'improvement'. This study was important for several reasons. First, it described objectively and in detail the ideology of a therapeutic community, and its implementation in practice. Second, it identified three propositions, and the four cultural themes of democratization, permissiveness, communalism, and reality confrontation which underpinned therapeutic community practice (recently reworked and updated by Haigh 1996; also see Chapter 20), and the blurring, conflict, and contradictions between these. Finally, it highlighted conflicts within the unit between its treatment practices and the stated aim of rehabilitation (Rapoport 1960).

As a response to the Rapoport study, Henderson Hospital moved specifically towards dealing with 'psychopaths'; away from rehabilitation towards treatment; and to clarifying its technique. The study had a 'mixed reception' in 1960, but was re-issued in 1967, when Whiteley, the new consultant, brought the book back into use as a teaching guide, and turned attention again to the 'psychological and sociological dynamics of the therapeutic community' (Whiteley 1980). This provides an early example of research informing practice. The Henderson Hospital has continued the tradition of encouraging research into its practice by PhD students, by staff, and by outside researchers.

The Association of Therapeutic Communities (ATC) also recognised the need for research, and set up the ATC Research Group in the 1970s. This group undertook a small-scale research project to find ways of defining a therapeutic community, based on the use of groups. It found some correlation between the range and amount of time spent in groups, and the extent to which communities saw themselves as approximating an ideal therapeutic community (Crocket *et al.* 1978). The 1980s saw the demise of this group, at a time of waning interest in therapeutic communities. However, it was revived in 1995 and is now flourishing with intentions of setting up larger-scale, comparative and collaborative research projects.

THERAPEUTIC COMMUNITY RESEARCH: THE PRESENT

In the 1990s, research is seen as a necessary, and therefore accepted, part of therapeutic community life. Therapeutic community research has become more sophisticated in terms of research designs and methodologies, and our understanding of the complexity of the issues is greater. There is widespread emphasis on evidence-based practice, which has led to more outcome research and evaluations of the effectiveness of therapeutic community treatment. There have also been more sophisticated sociological and psychological analyses of input to therapeutic communities (e.g. in terms of diagnoses, symptomatology, co-morbidity of clients, and staff characteristics), and processes in therapeutic community treatment. The greater emphasis on evidence of treatment effectiveness and value for money, together with NHS reforms, has also led to therapeutic community research on funding and cost-effectiveness (see Chapter 18).

RESEARCH METHODOLOGIES
Levels of resolution of research

The sort of research undertaken will be determined by the level of resolution at which one wishes to examine the therapeutic community. 'levels of resolution' is a concept borrowed from microscopy, and systems theory (Kirk and Millard 1979). At a low level of resolution, the broad structure of an object can be observed and examined, but the fine detail cannot; at high levels of resolution, detail can be observed, but the general features are lost to view. At a low level of resolution, the therapeutic community field as a whole (for example, nationally) can be studied. At higher levels of resolution, groups of therapeutic communities can be examined, then individual communities, then the finer details of parts of therapeutic communities, such as treatment orientation, staff groups, resident groups, interpersonal interactions, and individual members. At the highest level of resolution, part-functions of individuals, such as intra-psychic processes, are studied.

These levels of resolution will also affect the sort of methodologies, assessment and measuring tools used. For example, if we want to look at the TC field as a whole, or groups of TCs, we need comparative and cross-institutional research designs. These will either use a number of communities, or compare some TCs with other institutions, across a range of dimensions. This will include process and outcome measures, with statistical techniques capable of dealing with the amount of information generated. At the other end, we need detailed psychometric and qualitative assessments of individuals' intra-psychic states and processes, and changes in them during treatment.

Research methods and tools

There have been, and still are, many debates within research about the relative merits of different types of research philosophies and methodologies, and these apply as much to TC research as elsewhere.

One of the first dichotomies in research is between *descriptive* and *evaluative* work. Descriptive research has value. It can be literary description, as, for example, in Parker's description of Grendon Underwood Prison's therapeutic community (1970). It can be descriptive of the principles and practice of therapeutic communities. It can also be theoretical, or exploratory, and involve the accumulation of reliable, factual information and evidence – for example, by survey or observation, which can provide the basis for informed discussion, and decision-making. For early therapeutic community work, both in Britain and the US, this often involved describing the process of change necessary to implement TC principles and practices in old mental health institutions.

However, evaluative research – meaning the assessment of the effectiveness of treatment programmes by determining whether they are producing the therapeutic gains expected – tends to be seen as providing more useful findings. There have been a few controlled trial experiments, there has been some cross-institutional research, but the majority of work has been done on single settings, and particularly on structures and processes within these settings, and their effects on specific aspects of residents' functioning.

Within the evaluative research tradition, there are also debates around the relative usefulness of *idiographic* (aimed at understanding and accounting for individual idiosyncrasies) versus *nomothetic* (aimed at developing general laws that apply to all) studies in helping us understand the mechanisms of change for residents, and the contribution of the treatment process to such changes. This debate is also about the relative value of in-depth analyses of *case studies* as against *empirical* (based on observation or experiment) and *numerical* studies; *qualitative* versus *quantitative* and *sociological* versus *psychological* methodologies; *hard* versus *soft* data; and *process* (what goes on, and how people change, in a TC) versus *outcome* studies (what changes have been effected and sustained after discharge).

In the past, these methodologies have usually been seen as mutually exclusive, but more recently there have been calls for research studies which combine both sociological and psychological, process and outcome, qualitative and quantitative methodologies and tools.

Experimental research and the randomised controlled trial technique

Much evaluative research in psychology, psychiatry and criminology developed from medical models, or modifications of them – because of the influence of the physical sciences, and the traditional association of evaluative research with medicine. The medical approach to evaluation is epitomised in the experimental drug trial, or randomised control trial (RCT), which is still regarded in many quarters as the research 'gold standard' for evidence-based practice (Seligman 1995). This experimental approach became increasingly popular through the 1960s and 1970s, but has more recently lost ground as a result of criticisms of the appropriateness and restrictiveness of its methodology, both for therapeutic communities and elsewhere (Evans, Carlyle and Dolan 1996).

One of the best known controlled trial experimental research studies for evaluating the effectiveness of therapeutic community treatment is that conducted at Kingswood Community Home with Education for 'delinquent' adolescent boys – best known, because it proved a large, and expensive, disaster in research terms (Cornish and Clarke 1975). Clarke and Cornish had several practical problems, including a drop in allocations during the research period, because referrers were anxious about the research, and 'contamination' between the different treatments because staff exchanged information, and discussed the respective regimes and work. The interpretative problems they highlighted were: disentangling the effects of regime from those of staff; measuring the effects of changes in the treatments; differential dropout rates between the randomly allocated treatments; difficulties in being able to generalise from the results; and no real possibility of being able to control for Hawthorne effects – the beneficial effects of experimental treatment which result simply because the people exposed to it know themselves to be the subject of special interest and concern (Clarke and Cornish 1972).

They observed that whilst the experimental design was appropriate for 'spot-the-winner', or 'does treatment X work better than treatment Y' research, knowing that one treatment has 'won' is of little use if it does not enable the identification of the factors that have made the difference between 'winning' and 'losing'. They did not find a winner, but felt they might have been able to extract some generalisable findings if the effective variables in the treatment situation could have been identified with precision.

They concluded that the controlled trial would only be of value when it is legitimate to regard the treatments being compared as '*molar*' (i.e. one large unit) variables, or when it is possible to manipulate only one variable, or interdependent set of variables, in the treatment situation, while holding the other variables constant. However, treatments such as the therapeutic community are multi-dimensional – in other words, the therapeutic community treatment consists of a great many '*molecular*' (i.e. single small unit) variables, which interact in a complex way, so that any one, or combination of them, might contribute to outcome. This makes it 'almost impossible' to link cause and effect unambiguously. They also argued that there are many variables, such as staff differences, which would be difficult to isolate and manipulate in an experimental situation.

These arguments have been taken up more recently by Seligman, in relation to psychotherapy research. He distinguishes between the *efficacy* study, as epitomised by the randomised control trial, and the *effectiveness* study – 'how patients fare under the actual conditions of treatment in the field'. Seligman expresses his disillusion with the 'gold standard' of the efficacy study (expensive in time and money) as 'the only, or even the best way of finding out what treatment actually works in the field'. He concludes that 'deciding whether one treatment, under highly controlled conditions, works better than another treatment or a control group is a different question from deciding what works in the field' (Seligman 1995, pp.1–2).

He suggests that some treatments are 'too cumbersome for the efficacy study paradigm' (Seligman 1995, p.3), particularly long-term therapies, especially if there is no fixed duration; where the therapy is self-correcting; where patients have multiple problems or psychiatric diagnoses; and where improvement is concerned with the general functioning of patients, as well as improvements in disorders, or specific presenting symptoms. He also suggests that random assignment 'may turn out to be worse than useless for the investigation of the actual treatment of mental illness in the field' (Seligman 1995, p.13). What Seligman suggests instead is naturalistic surveys of large numbers of people who have gone through any particular treatment, with multivariate measures of effectiveness, using sophisticated correlational methods. He also uses the molar–molecular distinction, but about outcome measures, suggesting questions should be more specific, e.g. 'how many times have you cut yourself in the last two weeks', rather than 'how much has treatment helped with your problems relating to self-harm?'

In addition, Evans *et al.* have offered a sophisticated critique of the statistical shortfalls of experimental and observational methods – here in relation to forensic psychotherapy. They argue that selecting from the complexity of therapy for research purposes must diminish it; that experimental research in the field is never as 'clean' as it is in laboratory conditions; that even very strong associations between variables still allow for many different explanations for that association, and that many other variables which were not controlled or manipulated could explain the association found between the variables studied (Evans *et al.* 1996).

They also raise important arguments about sample size and statistical significance, and the need for very large, 'sometimes logistically impossible' sample sizes of people, to have even 'a good chance' of detecting a realistic significant effect for psychotherapy (Evans *et al.* 1996, pp.523–524). Nevertheless, this has not curtailed the enthusiasm of funders for the RCT. The Cassel Hospital is undertaking a research project using methodology based on the RCT, to compare 12-month therapeutic community treatment with 6-month therapeutic community treatment, followed by 6-months out-patient group therapy, and psychiatric support/outreach nursing (Chiesa 1997).

The comparative, cross-institutional research design

One alternative method to the experimental design for evaluating therapeutic communities is that of exploiting the natural variations in them, by comparing large numbers of settings, and using their natural differences to explore relationships. This *cross-institutional* design can be both interpretative and exploratory, and include survey investigation in the design, both to facilitate exploration, and provide a basis for interpretation.

Interpretative research is perhaps best symbolised by the school of ethnography. It emphasises relying for explanation on the interpretations people themselves put on the reasons lying behind their actions. It also emphasises naturalistic observation of phenomena in the field, and seeks insights into social behaviour from data collected in a way which is as unadulterated as possible by the procedures and preconceptions of the researchers. An excellent example of this type of research is Bloor, McKeganey and Fonkert's sociological collection (1988, p.1) of 'ethnographies of therapeutic work in eight different therapeutic communities'.

More recently these cross-institutional, comparative designs have been adapted to be evaluative as well, sometimes by including methods used in randomised controlled trials, to make the results both interpretative and quantitative. This is done through the use of methods such as prediction, partial correlation and other statistical techniques. In this, the relative risks distributed in the populations of each setting are standardised, so that differences between predicted and observed outcomes will indicate the relative effectiveness of different institutions. In addition, measures of various aspects of the treatment process, or analyses of the treatment regime, are correlated with measures of effectiveness. Dunlop (1975, p.23) has suggested that the advantage of such a design is that it is capable of identifying small differences in regime effectiveness, and that, rather than using an artificial experimental situation, it can 'use, explore and, thus, help to explain the natural situation of the regime'.

This method of research is not without its problems. In the past, it has been assumed that treatments can be broken down into separately identifiable classes or units, but, as pointed out earlier, this involves regarding individual units or treatment regimes as molar, single variables, rather than molecular, multiple variables, and loses the subtleties of complexity. Second, there is the problem that correlations between measures of treatment process and measures of effects do not prove causation. Clarke and Sinclair pointed out that correlations are easier to interpret when there is a clearly causal dependent and independent variation and the direction of causality is only one way. However, this condition is not fulfilled, for example, in a TC where staff influence residents and vice versa. In addition, cross-institutional methods of research, like experimental methods, have sought to demonstrate and compare the gross effects of particular treatments, without making systematic attempts to describe the treatments, or to understand or explain how any results of treatment might be brought about and how any beneficial gross treatment effects could be replicated (Clarke and Sinclair 1973).

A more recent example of this methodology is that proposed by Moos, which attempts to address some of these issues. Moos has been working for some years on ways of characterising treatment environments in more sophisticated ways, in order to be able to relate these to treatment outcomes. Initially, Moos did this through the Ward Atmosphere Scale (WAS: Moos 1997), and later through the Multiphasic Environmental Assessment Procedure (MEAP: Moos and Lemke 1996). The WAS and its variants (e.g. COPES) have been used in therapeutic communities – occasionally in Britain (e.g. Trauer, Bouras and Watson 1987). MEAP has been used in a number of treatment settings in the USA, mainly for substance abuse programmes, but also psychiatric settings (Moos 1997), and was used in a study of Richmond Fellowship houses in Australia (Lees and Manning 1985). It has been little used in Britain, despite its potential usefulness for comparative, evaluative research.

MEAP evaluates the physical and social environments of treatment settings, and enables description, monitoring and comparison of such settings. It describes objective characteristics of the setting, such as the aggregate personal and social characteristics of residents and staff; the physical design of the setting; the programme's policies and services; the personal characteristics of those admitted to the programme, such as socio-demographic characteristics, health factors, and functioning; and the quality of the programme's social climate. The data obtained can be used to plot the direct and indirect effects of these key aspects of the treatment process and setting, in relation to resident outcome, both in-treatment and post-treatment, through path-analytic structural equation causal modelling (Moos and Lemke 1996, p.2). This provides a means of evaluating the effectiveness of treatment regimes, and a useful template for all therapeutic community data collection. Moos has now moved on to look at more sophisticated ways of measuring in-treatment outcomes, such as satisfaction and participation (Moos and King 1997).

It is important to note that one such study found that both social background and intake symptoms contributed substantially to the explained variance, and therefore are relatively strong predictors of outcome. Second, the unique variance accounted for by programme type was small, and most of that was due to either treatment experiences or perceptions of the environment.

However, the unique contribution of perceptions of the environment was almost as strong or stronger than any of the patient background variables, or any of the other variables of the model. The study concluded that apportioning variance between either client or programme may be too limited, and that the effects of certain combinations of client and programme-related variables may be more useful for understanding client outcomes, and therefore evaluating treatment effectiveness (Cronkite and Moos 1978). This interrelationship of key variables was also reported in a recent therapeutic community research review (Isohanni and Nieminen 1996).

Single community studies

There have been many more studies concentrating on the workings of single TCs, and describing and evaluating their treatment regimes. Some have concentrated on process, while others have concentrated on the more specific (rather than gross or overall) effects on resident outcomes. Some have considered factors such as psychiatric admission, or reconviction. The more psychological studies have tended to evaluate effectiveness, in relation to particular aspects of residents' behaviour, psychological states, or intellectual functioning, and some have combined both methodologies.

One example of studies of process is Sharp's sociologically based participant observation research in a Richmond Fellowship halfway house. He collected data on subcultural formation and processes within the therapeutic community, and this data was interpreted from a symbolic interactionist perspective. He highlighted the conflict for professionals working in therapeutic communities between their democratic ideologies and their function as agents of social control (Sharp 1975). A second example is Baron's sociological study of institutional dynamics, roles and rules, and particularly the use and misuse of power and social control, at Paddington Day Hospital, and the reasons for its subsequent downfall (Baron 1987). Genders and Player undertook a qualitative study of the stages of the therapeutic process, and derived a therapeutic career model, at Grendon Underwood Prison (Genders and Player 1994).

Of importance is the large-scale study and evaluation of Fraser House, a therapeutic community in Australia. Clark and Yeomans described the theory and practice of Fraser House, using social context theory, and a social systems analysis of social structure to identify roles and tasks, areas of conflict, and interdependence between component parts of the unit. Their quantitative, evaluative measures analysed psychological factors of social adjustment, community attitudes and patient improvement. While little difference was found between residents on admission, those who improved showed marked differences at discharge on factors such as satisfaction, acceptance of unit ideology and practices, participation, positions held, and mode of discharge

(Clark and Yeomans 1969). This study is particularly interesting because it attempts to use more than one criterion of unit effectiveness, or patient improvement, and attempts to relate these to several factors within the social environment of the therapeutic community, for it regards the treatment environment as molecular and not molar. It is one of very few attempts to do so.

Some single community studies have used simple outcome measures such as psychiatric readmission, or reconviction. Single community studies using reconviction as an outcome measure tend to be on prison therapeutic communities (e.g. Cullen 1994), while some studies combine both readmission and reconviction (e.g. Copas and Whiteley 1976). More recent single case studies of therapeutic community effectiveness include several conducted in American and Canadian prisons, using, and arguing for, recidivism *and* psychological variables as main outcome measures (e.g. Rice, Harris and Cormier 1992). Other studies have linked client characteristics to length of stay, treatment process and outcome (e.g. Kapur, Weir, McKevitt, Devine, Collins, Maxwell and Heaney 1997).

However, single community studies, whilst of value to the institution itself, are of limited generalisable value unless the findings are comparable – which most of them are not. These studies would be of more use if they clearly identified their populations, so that similarities and differences in client intake could be identified, and if they used the same measures of outcome as other units conducting similar research. The ATC is currently trying to devise such a research package to recommend to its members for use in their communities, which would then provide comparable data.

Psychologically oriented studies of outcome

Early examples of psychologically oriented studies of outcome in Britain include a series of evaluative studies at the Phoenix Unit at Oxford's Littlemore Hospital, and subsequently at the Ley Community, also in Oxford. These looked at social and medical changes in residents which could be linked to therapeutic community treatment, with particular reference to divergences between the perceptions of the patients, and their closest significant other person, and later to changes on the MMPI, and the 16PF personality questionnaires (e.g. Kennard and Wilson 1979). Other psychologically oriented studies have concentrated on in-treatment changes, such as in interpersonal relationships, depression, anxiety, hostility (e.g. Gunn, Robertson and Dell 1978).

Important examples of psychologically oriented studies of therapeutic community outcome, in the United States, are the work of De Leon and others. They have attempted to evaluate the effectiveness of concept-based therapeutic communities such as Phoenix House in changing the psychopathology of substance abusers over time, and to isolate the psychological variables which could predict success for therapeutic community treatment (e.g. De Leon 1984). In addition, there has been a continuing thread of research in the USA, again mostly in the substance abuse field, which first relates length of stay in therapeutic community treatment to other variables including outcome, and second explores the process of retention in treatment and the psychological variables which affect this (e.g. De Leon 1991). Recently, De Leon has published a collection of papers on the modified therapeutic community (residential and day) for special populations and settings – substance abusers – including mothers and their children, homeless people, adolescents, and in penal settings (De Leon 1997).

There were few other studies in Britain, using research methodologies concentrating in a rigorous way on the more specific psychological effects until the late 1980s. These are illustrated by the work of Dolan and others at the Henderson. For example, they used the 90 item Symptom Check List (SCL-90) questionnaire to measure changes in symptomatic distress following therapeutic community treatment and found significant reductions in neurotic symptomatology in residents followed up for 8 months after discharge (Dolan, Evans and Wilson 1992a).

In a related study, they examined the relationship between length of stay in therapeutic community treatment and improvements in neurotic symptom-atology, again using the SCL-90. They found that changes in symptomatology tended to occur in the first 3 months of treatment, and that there was an association between improvement at follow-up and length of stay, but these were not significantly related. However, they themselves commented that their study considered only one aspect of outcome, and that their residents had a wide range of behavioural, emotional and personality problems which would need also to be assessed for improvements following treatment, and that intervening life events between discharge and follow-up would also need to be taken into account (Dolan, Evans and Wilson 1992b).

More recently, Dolan, Warren and Norton (1997) have looked at changes in borderline symptomatology between referral and one year after discharge, using the Borderline Syndrome Index (BSI) and the Personality Diagnostic Questionnaire (PDQ). They found that reductions in BSI scores were significantly correlated with length of stay in treatment (Dolan et al. 1997). They also showed significantly more change in those admitted to Henderson, compared to those referred but not admitted, a group consisting of those turned down at assessment or turned down for funding. Since assessment involves evaluating the capacity to change, it is questionable whether this can be seen as a useful control group.

Cost-effectiveness studies

A more recent innovation in the types of research into therapeutic community effectiveness has been the cost-offset study. For example, Chiesa, Iacoponi and Morris (1996) assessed the impact of the Cassel Hospital TC treatment on patterns of patients' usage of health service resources. By comparing pre- and post-treatment usage, they found a reduction in the use of medical, surgical and psychiatric services in the year following discharge from the Cassel Hospital, although the compliance at follow-up was low. Dolan, Warren, Menzies and Norton (1996) compared the service usage (psychiatric and prison) of residents at the Henderson Hospital for one year pre- and post-treatment. They found reduced service usage following treatment, and a cost-offset which meant that the cost of therapeutic community treatment would be recouped within two years following treatment, and represent a saving after that. Davies and Campling (1997) have also shown similar reductions in patients' usage of psychiatric in-patient services following treatment at Francis Dixon Lodge. By comparing referrals from within and outside their own area, they also suggest that having an easily accessible therapeutic community, to which referrals are made earlier, offsets cost in the first place (also see Chapter 16).

THERAPEUTIC COMMUNITY RESEARCH: THE FUTURE

Manning pointed out as long ago as 1979 that 'research activity may enhance the status of a therapeutic community and hence be a vital ingredient in the battle for survival' (Manning 1979, p.295). What we need to decide is: *what* research activity? To this end, we have to know what questions to ask. The usual questions we get asked, especially by those purchasing or commissioning services, are 'Does it work?', or 'Does it work better than treatment X?' However, these are not necessarily the most helpful, and are beset by the problems described above.

Manning has pointed out that because of the conflicting goals and activities of therapeutic communities, the questions we need to ask will 'take a more disjointed, bitty, messy style' than these 'clean, clear-cut evaluations' (Manning 1979, p.294). He points out that we need to settle on an appropriate set of questions, and then the design and execution of the research should logically follow (Manning 1979).

It is pointless, however, searching for the perfect research design – we have to use the best we have now, and use improvements and refinements as they are developed. Evans *et al.* (1996) highlighted the usefulness of 'various imperfect research projects' in helping to prevent the closure of the Henderson Hospital (and now even in aiding its expansion!).

What we do need, and can implement, is more complexity and sophistication in identifying factors within the therapeutic community regime itself, and the relating of these to a more complex range of measures for identifying change in therapeutic community clients, both during and after treatment. We can then confidently state the contribution of therapeutic community treatment to client outcome. We need to acknowledge the differences between therapeutic community regimes, or to be able, as part of the research project, to tease out which aspects of the regime are affecting outcomes. There has been an increase in studies attempting to identify, describe and measure aspects of treatment settings, so that their differential impact on various clients can be evaluated. We need to build on these.

REFERENCES

Baron, C. (1987) *Asylum to Anarchy.* London: Free Association Books.

Bloor, M., McKeganey, N. and Fonkert, D. (1988) *One Foot in Eden. A Sociological Study of the Range of Therapeutic Community Practice.* London: Routledge.

Chiesa, M. (1997) 'A combined in-patient/out-patient programme for severe personality disorders.' *Therapeutic Communities 18,* 4, 297–309.

Chiesa, M., Iacoponi, E. and Morris, M. (1996) 'Changes in health service utilization by patients with severe personality disorders before and after inpatient psychosocial treatment.' *British Journal of Psychotherapy 12,* 4, 501–512.

Clark, A.W. and Yeomans, N.J. (1969) *Fraser House. Theory, Practice and Evaluation of a Therapeutic Community.* New York: Springer Publishing Co.

Clarke, R.V.G. and Cornish, D.B. (1972) *The Controlled Trial in Institutional Research.* London: HMSO.

Clarke, R.V.G. and Sinclair, I. (1973) *Towards More Effective Evaluation.* Strasbourg: Council of Europe.

Copas, J. and Whiteley, J.S. (1976) 'Predicting success in the treatment of psychopaths.' *British Journal of Psychiatry 129,* 388–392.

Cornish, D.B. and Clarke, R.V.G. (1975) *Residential Treatment and its Effect on Delinquency.* London: HMSO.

Crocket, R., Kirk, J., Manning, N. and Millard, D.W. (1978) 'Community time structure.' *Bulletin of the Association of Therapeutic Communities 25,* 12–17.

Cronkite, R.C. and Moos, R.H. (1978) 'Evaluating alcoholism treatment programs: an integrated approach.' *Journal of Consulting and Clinical Psychology 46,* 5, 1105–1119.

Cullen, E. (1994) 'Grendon: the therapeutic prison that works.' *Therapeutic Communities 15,* 4, 301–311.

Davies, S. and Campling, P. (1997) (In press) 'Therapeutic community provision at regional and district levels.' *Psychiatric Bulletin.*

De Leon, G. (1984) 'The therapeutic community: study of effectiveness: social and psychological adjustment of 400 dropouts and 100 graduates from the Phoenix House therapeutic community.' USA Department of Health and Human Services National Institute on Drug Abuse Treatment (NIDA) *Research Monograph.* No. (ADM) 85–1286. New York: US Department of Health and Human Services.

De Leon, G. (1991) 'Retention in drug-free therapeutic communities.' NIDA *Research Monograph 106,* 218–244.

De Leon, G. (ed) (1997) *Community as Method. Therapeutic Communities for Special Populations and Special Settings.'* Westport, CT: Praeger.

Dolan, B. M., Evans, C. and Wilson, J., (1992a) 'Therapeutic community treatment for personality disordered adults: Changes in neurotic symptomatology on follow-up.' *International Journal of Social Psychiatry 38,* 4, 243–250.

Dolan, B.M., Evans, C. and Wilson, J. (1992b) 'Neurotic symptomatology and length of stay in a therapeutic community.' *Therapeutic Communities 13,* 3, 171–177.

Dolan, B.M., Warren, F. M., Menzies, D. and Norton, K. (1996) Cost-offset following specialist treatment of severe personality disorders.' *Psychiatric Bulletin 20,* 1–5.

Dolan, B., Warren, F. and Norton, K. (1997) 'Change in borderline symptoms one year after therapeutic community treatment for severe personality disorder.' *British Journal of Psychiatry 171,* 274–279.

Dunlop, A.B. (1975) 'Experience of residential treatment and its effectiveness.' *Home Office Research Unit Research Bulletin.* Autumn, 2, 22–26. London HMSO.

Evans, C., Carlyle, J. and Dolan, B. (1996), 'Forensic psychotherapy research.' In M. Cox and C. Cordess (eds) *Forensic Psychotherapy,* Vol. 2. London: Jessica Kingsley, 509–542.

Genders, E. and Player, E. (1994) *The Therapeutic Prison: A Study of Grendon.* Oxford: Oxford University Press.

Gunn, J., Robertson, G. and Dell, S. (1978) *Psychiatric Aspects of Imprisonment.* London: Academic Press.

Haigh, R. (1996) 'The ghost in the machine: The matrix in the milieu. Principles, cultures and structures for modern TCs.' Paper read at ATC Windsor Conference, 10 September.

Isohanni, M. and Nieminen, P. (1996) 'A twenty-year programme of research on treatment (mainly) and variables (also): A response to Holman.' *Therapeutic Communities 17,* 3, 217–220.

Kapur, R., Weir, M.B., McKevitt, C., Devine, M., Collins, L., Maxwell, H. and Heaney, C. (1997) 'An evaluation of threshold therapeutic communities in Northern Ireland.' *Irish Journal of Psychological Medicine 14,* 2, 65–68.

Kennard, D. and Wilson, S. (1979) 'The modification of personality disturbance in a therapeutic community for drug abusers.' *British Journal of Medical Psychology 52,* 215–222.

Kirk, J.D. and Millard, D.W. (1979), 'Personal growth in the residential community.' In R.D. Hinshelwood and N. Manning (eds) *Therapeutic Communities: Reflections and Progress.* London: Routledge and Kegan Paul.

Lees, J. and Manning, N. (1985) *Australian Community Care: A Study of the Richmond Fellowship.* Canterbury: University of Kent.

Manning, N. (1979) 'The politics of survival; the role of research in the therapeutic community.' In R.D. Hinshelwood and N. Manning (eds) *Therapeutic Communities: Reflections and Progress.* London: Routledge and Kegan Paul.

Manning, N. (1989) *The Therapeutic Community Movement: Charisma and Routinization.* London: Routledge.

Moos, R.H. (1997) *Evaluating Treatment Environments. The Quality of Psychiatric and Substance Abuse Programs,* 2nd edition. New Brunswick: Transaction.

Moos, R.H. and Lemke, S. (1996) *Evaluating Residential Facilities. The Multiphasic Environmental Assessment Procedure.* Thousand Oaks: Sage.

Moos. R.H. and King, M.J. (1997) 'Participation in community residential treatment and substance abuse patients: outcomes at discharge.' *Journal of Substance Abuse Treatment, 14,* 1, 71–80.

Parker, T. (1970) *The Frying Pan. A Prison and Its Prisoners.* London: Hutchinson.

Rapoport, R. (1960) *Community as Doctor.* London: Tavistock Publications.

Rice, M.E., Harris, G.T. and Cormier, C.A. (1992) 'An evaluation of a maximum security therapeutic community for psychopaths and other mentally disordered offenders.' *Law and Human Behavior 16,* 4, 399–412.

Seligman, M.E.P. (1995) 'The effectiveness of psychotherapy.' *American Psychologist 50*, 12, 965–974.

Sharp, V. (1975) *Social Control in the Therapeutic Community*. Farnborough: Saxon House.

Trauer, T., Bouras, N. and Watson, J.P. (1987) 'The assessment of ward atmosphere in a psychiatric unit.' *International Journal of Therapeutic Communities 8*, 3, 199–205.

Whiteley, J.S. (1980) 'The Henderson Hospital.' *International Journal of Therapeutic Communities 1*, 1, 38–58.

ACKNOWLEDGEMENTS

Some of the work for this chapter was financed by a research grant from the High Security Psychiatric Services Commissioning Board. An extended version of this chapter, with full references, is available from the author on request.

CHAPTER 18

Survival and Growth in the Marketplace

Does Every District Need a TC?

Steffan Davies

EDITORS' INTRODUCTION

Steffan Davies is a senior registrar in Leicester, which is where he stumbled upon Francis Dixon Lodge and found that TC ideas resonated with his strong political views about the benefits of empowerment and co – operative action.

Particularly interested in organisational dynamics, he had been involved in a number of Royal College Committees and is presently studying for an MBA at Nottingham. He is currently working at Arnold Lodge, Medium Secure Unit and believes that the TC approach has much to offer rehabilitation and forensic psychiatry.

He relaxes from trying to change the world by playing with his baby daughter, learning Tai Chi, cooking good food and drinking real ale.

In this chapter, he looks at TCs as business ventures (in the widest and best sense) and uses managerial and economic arguments to persuade us of their value and efficiency.

This chapter will concentrate on the economic arguments for funding therapeutic communities in the UK National Health Service (NHS). Most economic analyses of British TCs have taken place in health service settings, although there is no reason why the arguments advanced in this chapter could not be applied to TCs in other sectors – public, private and voluntary. Indeed much outcome research, if framed in terms of service usage, whether that be hospitalisation, outpatient therapy, social services contacts or periods of imprisonment, lends itself to economic evaluation.

The introduction of the NHS internal market in the early 1990s led to much greater scrutiny of the costs of treatments. This emphasis on financial and market factors was alien to many in the NHS and to TC practitioners in particular. The conflict between the community values espoused by the TC movement and the individualist philosophy of Thatcherism and market economics has been discussed at length (Campling and Davies 1997). The result was that many TCs closed, but those that survived have become more cost conscious and managerially professional.

NHS management has traditionally been viewed with suspicion by many professionals, including TC practitioners. This was particularly so at the height of the internal market when 'macho management' and 'short termism' put managers in direct conflict with many clinicians. Management was ignored at peril and many of the TCs that survived the internal market did so by engaging constructively. Examples of this are the use of marketing, in its broader sense, to influence stakeholders such as referring clinicians, academic institutions and purchasers. The use of economic analyses of outcomes is another example of positive engagement. Clinicians, like myself, who have studied management as an academic discipline, have found many sympathetic ideas including the identification and engagement with stakeholders in marketing strategies (Davies 1996) and the philosophy of the 'soft' school of Human Resource Management which contains many ideas that are directly compatible with TC principles (Davies 1998).

The conflicts of the late 1980s and the 1990s were predicted by Menzies (1979):

> Scarcity of resources may make desirable the devotion of more resources to the best 'bets' and only limited objectives such as good custodial care for the others. Such discrimination is hard to face in the institutions concerned without society's support. The result is more ambitious objectives everywhere and the chronic inadequacy of resources to achieve them, unless management is very tough. (pp.199–200)

The failure to engage with higher order systems and understand their perspectives' was identified by Main (1989) as one of the reasons for the failure of Bion's first Northfield experiment. The lesson has been learnt again in the last decade: for many it has been a hard one.

Although the philosophy of the free market is antithetical to many TC principles, the ideas behind cost-effective treatments are to be found in the earliest origins of the TC movement. The Northfield and Belmont experiments (see Chapter 1) that launched the TC movement as we understand it today were strongly informed by economic considerations. The problem at the time was to treat large numbers of men traumatised by the experiences of war. This occurred in a situation where the main therapeutic resources – army psychiatric medical and nursing staff – were scarce, and with an economy and country which needed to rebuild itself after the devastation of the Second World War. The response at Northfield and Belmont was to use group therapies and for the 'patients' to become an integral part of their own therapy. 'The large outpatient population among the military could be more efficiently dealt with when treated in groups' (Bloch 1986) using the scarce resources available. A triumph of pragmatism over adversity.

There are other examples of what we would now regard as economic evaluations of treatment in the history of the TC movement. Tuke's Retreat was set up in response to the poor treatment received by one of the Quaker brethren at the York Asylum. The Retreat was funded by the Quakers as a charitable institution without public or Church finance. The reputation of the Retreat spread, not only for humanitarian treatment, but for its results in terms of reduced hospitalisation. Tuke's (1813) *Description of the Retreat* includes the annual statement of the finances for six months of 1797. His Practical Hints on the Construction and Economy of Pauper Lunatic Asylums (Tuke 1815) could be regarded as one of the first texts of mental health service management. In it (p.16) he compares outcomes, in terms of discharges, for the diagnostic groups 'violent' and 'melancholic', with those of the Bethlehem Hospital. A higher percentage of both were discharged from the Retreat and for admissions of over one year, 27 per cent were discharged from the Retreat and only 1 per cent from the Bethlehem. The economic argument here would be that the more expensive treatment at the Retreat (due to smaller patient numbers and higher staff ratios) was more cost effective as it produced far better results than the treatment at the Bethlehem.

More recent examples of resource use comparisons include Pullen's analysis of three admission wards at Fulborn Hospital in Cambridge (Pullen 1982; see also Chapter 12). Street ward, which was run on TC lines, had a substantially shorter length of average admission of 16.8 days in comparison with the other two wards' average length of admission of 34.9 and 38.1 days. There was little difference in the numbers of admissions or readmissions to account for this (Table 18.1).

The economic arguments for the Northfield experiment would appear self-evident as long as therapy was effective. There were effectively no other treatments available and the aim of rehabilitating returning soldiers was a desirable outcome. However, comparing wards at Fulbourn Hospital is more complex and problematic. The wards all served the same function, namely, to act as acute admission wards for defined populations in the Cambridge health district. The task comprised assessment, containment and treatment for a variety of psychotic, neurotic and personality disordered individuals in various degrees of crisis and distress. If the populations had been similar in terms of their mental health needs, and the outcome in terms of health and social functioning were comparable, then the method of treatment on Street ward, involving shorter admissions and probably greater patient satisfaction, could be judged superior on economic grounds. From this limited example we can see some of the economic principles and some of the methodological problems of economic evaluations in health services research.

	Street	Ward A	Ward B
Table 18.1 Admissions, re-admissions and patient numbers for street and other acute wards			
A. Number of admissions 1.7.78–30.9.78	77	73	65
B. Number of patients	69	63	58
C. Number of patients re-admitted during following 12 months	16	15	22
D. Number of admissions 1.10.78–30.9.79	300	277	232
E. Average length of stay in days for D	16.8	34.9	38.1

Source: Pullen 1982; see also Chapter 12, this volume.

Economic evaluations in health care usually fall into five groups (adapted from Ovretveit 1998): cost description; cost minimisation; cost benefit; cost effectiveness; and cost utility. The last three are of particular interest.

Cost effectiveness compares the costs of achieving a measured consequence. The consequence is assumed to be of value (for example, lives saved) but no value is placed on the output. It is therefore used to compare costs for achieving the same end result. The use of this methodology requires comparison of two or more defined comparison interventions and has many similarities with randomised controlled trials (RCTs) (see Chapter 17) for comparing different treatments. Many RCTs now include an economic element. The study above would have been an example if conducted as an economic evaluation. There were two treatments, standard acute inpatient and TC. The patient groups were likely to be similar and the output in terms of discharge (improved) a desirable one. The cost, easily calculated from inpatient days, is lower and the cost effectiveness demonstrable.

Cost utility is a more complex form of cost effectiveness study considering the utility of the end result for the patient. This methodology often uses weighted measures such as QALYs ('Quality Adjusted Life Years') – combining quality and length of life. There are obvious examples of utility to psychiatric patients in terms of improved social and psychological functioning, less reliance on psychiatric services and decreased levels of self-harm. No work has been done on weighting this in TC outcome studies.

Cost benefit includes an attempt to value the consequences of an intervention in monetary terms. There are a number of difficulties with cost benefit studies including the idea that benefits can be in initial costs saved as well as direct benefits. There is also a value to individuals in the improvement of their own health. This last benefit is often assessed as Willingness To Pay (WTP). How much would individuals be willing to pay for a treatment, in the same way as the willingness to pay for a new TV? This methodology is an attempt to value a healthcare intervention but should not be confused with charging (McCrone and Thornicroft 1997). There are a number of difficulties in applying this methodology to long-term psychiatric treatments: the capacity of patients to think long term; insight into their problems; the uncertainty of predicting outcomes and benefits in comparison with standardised surgical procedures such as hip replacement. In practice, many studies are only *partial evaluations* as they look at only one treatment and do not compare another controlled treatment with a standardised patient group.

To reach the standard of proof of superior cost benefit we require a measure of the benefits as well as the costs. Costs are in themselves difficult to derive and compare in the NHS. Costs for the same unit of service can vary widely for reasons other than the quality of the service provided; for example, in addition to the costs of mental health services, other health costs such as general practitioner services, casualty attendances and admission to medical and surgical units need to be considered. For a full economic evaluation, costs other than direct health costs need to be included. These may include social services, probation, police, prison service, benefit payments and revenues to the state in the form of taxation. The best outcome for TC treatment of personality disorder could be for an individual on a psychiatric intensive care unit with their children in local authority care to leave hospital, resume the care of their children and enter employment paying taxes. The cost versus benefit gain to society (and the individual) from the intervening treatment is obviously great.

In addition to the benefit of this treatment we need to demonstrate that it is superior to doing nothing (some conditions improve spontaneously), and also that it is superior, for appropriate subjects, to other available treatments. This is far easier to demonstrate for a simple treatment such as a drug, which can be double blinded to another drug or placebo and administered for relatively short periods to selected groups of patients. However, many such trials exclude large numbers of patients seen in normal clinical practice – such as those with co-morbid substance misuse problems, personality disorders, other psychiatric disorders, older age groups and non-standard presentations of illness. A recent paper examining the generalisability of an anti-manic drug treatment found only 17 per cent of patients who met initial inclusion criteria remained for randomisation, and there were substantial differences between the groups (Licht, Gouliaev, Vestergaard and Frydenberg 1997). It would be difficult to generalise benefits in such a small, unrepresentative sample to the clinical population using psychiatric services.

The majority, of NHS TCs treat individuals with severe personality disorders (SPD) (see Chapter 11). Much psychiatric debate has focused on whether or not SPDs are treatable rather than which treatments are effective. Many patients with SPD are under the care of NHS psychiatric services in spite of this debate. The Joint Home Office/Department of Health 'Review of Services for Mentally Disordered Offenders and Others with Similar Needs' (Reed Report) considered psychopathic disorder separately. This report concluded that there was evidence that TC treatment was effective and recommended funding further TC treatment for this group. Much of the economic evaluative work in the UK has therefore concentrated on the cost offsets to the NHS of TC treatments for patients already in the care of psychiatric services referred on to tertiary TCs. In the absence or failure of other services to treat this group, and the problems of diagnosis of SPDs and lack of widely used measurements of severity, no RCTs exist. A study at the Henderson was able to compare patients treated at the Henderson with others who had been accepted on clinical grounds but were not treated as their funding was refused (Dolan, Evans and Norton 1994). They found no clinical differences to justify the funding decision. The ethical problems of randomising to a no treatment group against a treatment one believed to be effective, could be overcome by purchasing authorities of the no treatment group refusing to pay.

Lees (see Chapter 17), Manning and Rawlings are currently reviewing the world literature on TC treatment for personality disorder for the High Security Psychiatric Services Commissioning Board. To date they have only discovered economic evaluations from three groups, all NHS inpatient TCs in the UK: the Henderson Hospital; the Cassel Hospital; and Francis Dixon Lodge, Leicester.

The economic evaluations of these British TCs are in the form of *cost offset* studies. These are partial evaluations as they look only at the costs of TC treatment without a control group. They compare service use in the period before and after TC treatment and produce the offset by calculating the difference in costs pre- and post-treatment. The assumption is made that service use would have continued at the same rate if the intervention had not been provided. Although this is an assumption, most referrals were made by consultant psychiatrists who would be providing the treatment as usual if patients were not treated at a TC. Referrers implicitly see a greater therapeutic value in TC treatment for these patients – or they would not refer. Due to the difficult process of getting funding for a referral from outside the district, they will have made a considerable investment in treatment before getting a patient into a TC. The cost offset argument for TC treatment of SPD has been made by two groups at the Henderson Hospital and by the author at Francis Dixon Lodge in Leicester. Further work has been carried out at the Cassel using a different methodology, and probably a different patient group.

HENDERSON

The original Henderson study examined a cohort of 29 admissions to the Henderson (Dolan, Warren, Menzies and Norton 1996). Data about previous psychiatric service usage was collected by questionnaire and case note examination at admission. One year after discharge questionnaires were sent to patients, their original referrers and current general practitioners. Twenty-four replies were received with information on service usage forming the group use for the cost-offset study. Twenty-three of the patients had completed the personality diagnostic questionnaire whilst at the Henderson. This gave self-report DSM-III-R diagnoses of personality disorder with patients scoring a mean of 6.04 personality disorders each, 74 per cent received a diagnosis of borderline personality disorder. Service usage was assessed for psychiatric inpatient, day-patient, out-patient and periods of imprisonment. Inpatient costs were calculated using Thames regions, average daily tariffs for acute inpatient and close supervision units; Henderson costs were their contract prices. Out patient and day patient costs were estimated as costs for a one-off assessment, and eight appointments for 'individual therapy', and average daily costs for day hospital treatment. Prison costs were from Home Office statistics.

The average cost of treatment at the Henderson was £25,641 per patient. Total psychiatric and prison costs for the year before treatment were £335,196 and for the year after treatment £31,390. This was calculated as an average cost-offset of £12,658 per patient. If this reduction in service was maintained, the treatment at the Henderson would pay for itself in just over two years (see Table 18.2).

There are inevitably a number of criticisms of this study. The cost-offset calculations make a number of assumptions about service usage. Service usage would need to continue at a steady rate over a prolonged period of time (at least three years) without intervention and after intervention would continue at the same rate as the year post-discharge for the cost offset to be valid. However, service usage is unlikely to be stable: the year before admission is likely to be one in which crises have led referrers to contact the Henderson: the year after discharge may be a particularly good one with a 'halo effect' that isn't maintained over further follow-up. This has been described as a 'ceiling–floor' effect, where by measuring the extremes, the difference before and after treatment are exaggerated. It is equally possible that the year before admission demonstrates a worsening of a condition that would have deteriorated further without intervention. Another criticism is the loss of 5 of the original series of 29, 17 per cent of the sample. If dropout had been selective (for example, not wanting to let the treatment team know how badly particular ex-residents were doing), this could have biased the sample towards a good outcome. Other weaknesses relate to the incompleteness of the information on service use, derivation of costs and the limitation of costs to psychiatric and prison services.

The importance of the study is in its adoption of the techniques of economic evaluation to TC treatment: it provides initial evidence of cost benefits, as well as improvements in behavioural and psychological terms. This study, despite its limitations, has been of immense value to other TCs when negotiating (or arguing!) with public health physicians about funding services (Campling 1997).

FRANCIS DIXON LODGE

The Francis Dixon Lodge (FDL) study (Davies, Campling and Ryan, in press) built on the methodology of the initial Henderson study, and tried to improve on it. FDL felt it had a similar treatment ethos to the Henderson – with all treatment taking place in group settings and a similar patient group, with a predominance of 'borderline' residents. The Henderson has a much greater reputation as a centre of excellence attracting referrals from the Thames regions and nationwide. FDL is more reliant on referrals from the district population (Leicestershire is the largest health district in the UK, with a population of 930,000), but attracts referrals from elsewhere in the Trent region and occasionally from further afield. The population at the Henderson usually contains a greater proportion of males who may have more extensive offending histories (Dolan, Evans and Norton 1994).

The FDL study looked at a series of 52 consecutive admissions between January 1993 and December 1995. Only one patient with a very short stay was excluded. It sought to examine histories of inpatient admission for three years before and three years after admission to FDL for all residents. For those living in Leicestershire at referral a much more extensive record of service contacts was sought. In addition to psychiatric contacts, general practice, social service, Accident and Emergency and general medical and surgical contacts were sought. Attempts to trace periods of imprisonment have so far been unsuccessful. As information was actively collected directly from services rather than ex-residents there have been no losses to follow up. To date, inpatient data for the entire sample for three years before admission and for the first year after admission has been analysed; other service contact data collection is continuing.

Some 87 per cent of the FDL sample had a diagnosis of emotionally unstable personality disorder (the ICD-10 equivalent of DSM-III-R borderline disorder, diagnosed in 74 per cent of Henderson patients). In addition, 40 per cent met criteria for harmful use or dependence on alcohol and/or drugs, 25 per cent for eating disorders and 13 per cent for recurrent depressive disorder or dysthimia. Diagnosis gives us little information on severity of personality disorders beyond meeting minimum diagnostic criteria, but concepts such as 'diffuse personality disorder' may be of use in the future (Tyrer and Johnson 1996). The Leicestershire district (District) (N = 40) and the outside

Leicestershire Extra Contractual Referrals (ECRs) (N = 12) formed two distinct groups in terms of previous inpatient usage but there were no significant differences in terms of diagnoses or historical items such as histories of sexual, physical or emotional abuse, or offending. The mean number of occupied bed days (OBDs) in the three years preceding admission was 56.3 for the district residents and 168 for the ECRs (independent sample t-test after data reduction (z-scores), 0.009).

In spite of very similar figures in terms of service usage to the Henderson group (see Table 18.2) the cost offset for FDL ECRs was less marked. This was for two reasons: first, FDL costs were higher (partly due to its being a smaller 16-bedded unit, in comparison to the Henderson's 29 beds; and partly through being in a trust with very high central management costs). Second, acute bed costs are much lower in the Trent region than in the Thames regions. Compared to the Henderson, the costs are therefore biased against FDL in both directions – and treatment would take around four years to fund itself.

This study seeks to improve on the Henderson study on which it was modelled in a number of ways. First, the sample is complete: reducing the possibility of selective biases in response. Second, the periods of pre- and post-treatment follow up are longer, reducing the possibility of ceiling–floor effects. Third, a more complete range of services will be examined, at least for the district patients (for the ECR group it is only practicable to study a more restricted range of services).

Already a number of interesting factors have emerged. For the ECR group, which is likely to be the most comparable to the Henderson sample, results were remarkably similar for OBDs. In terms of considering expansion of the numbers of TCs dealing with SPD patients, the ability of other TCs to replicate Henderson results is of great importance. The finding that 43 per cent of the ECRs three-year total OBDs occur in the year before admission argues against a substantial ceiling–floor effect. Although greater in the year before referral, substantial service usage has occurred in the preceding two years, and usage may well have continued to increase rather than spontaneously decrease without intervention. If this were the case, the cost offset could be an underestimate rather than an overestimate. Due to small numbers having completed the full three years of post-treatment follow-up, no information on the size of a floor effect is currently available. The other interesting finding is that the district group accounted for 63 per cent of their three-year occupancy in the year before treatment at FDL. One interpretation of this would be of a ceiling effect in the year before admission but a counter-argument would be that local referrers, having a better understanding of TC treatment for SPD, and easier access to treatment, may refer patients earlier on in their psychiatric career before they have prolonged, often untherapeutic, admissions to acute wards geared up to deal with acutely psychotic patients (Norton and Hinshelwood 1996).

An extension of this argument would be to claim that these patients may be less disturbed, certainly in terms of requiring less hospital admission, and that some or all of their treatment could be carried out in day TC services. This course of action would have a number of advantages. In economic terms, day services are much cheaper as they only require eight-hour staffing and have much reduced hotel costs (Haigh and Stegen, 1996). For the patients there is the possibility of maintaining closer contacts with supportive networks in the community and possibly an easier transition at the end of treatment. The disadvantages are in terms of the levels of disturbance that can be contained; a potential reluctance to confront difficulties when the patients are returning to isolated accommodation; and the restrictions in catchment area due to the need to travel each day. Further boundary issues about clinical responsibility and the management of out of hours crises also need addressing. Although there is literature on the clinical efficacy of TC day services (e.g. Vaglum *et al*. 1990), we are aware of no economic evaluations. One study 'Substituting 24-hour therapeutic communities by 8-hour day hospitals: a sensible alternative to accepting budgetary cuts?' (Kruisdijk 1994) was obviously inspired by economic considerations but contained no economic analysis.

CASSEL

The Cassel study (Chiesa *et al*. 1996) also took the form of a cost offset analysis. It used two samples, a series of 26 consecutive admissions from June 1993 to May 1994 and a post-treatment group comprising 26 out of 52 patients, who had been in-patients at the Cassel for at least a year, and discharged between

Unit	Cassel	FDL	Henderson
Number of patients: pre (post)	26 (26 of 52)	12 (12) ECR 40 (35) District	29 (25)
Mean OBDs year before admission	31	74 ECR 36 District	71
Mean OBDs year after admission	0.2	7.2 ECR 12.1 District	7.5
Borderline/emotionally unstable p.d.		86.5%	74%
Cost offset (£)	7423	8571 ECR	12,658

Table 18.2 Comparison of in-patient usage pre- and post-treatment at the Cassel, FDL and the Henderson

Sources: Chiesa *et al*. 1996, Dolan *et al*. 1996 and Davies *et al*. (in press).

May 1991 and December 1992. The post-treatment group were those who replied to requests for interview, a 50 per cent non-response rate. They examined a range of services including: psychiatric inpatient; out-patient; community psychiatric nursing; psychotherapy; A and E; general medical and surgical; and general practice. Service use information was only obtained from patient questionnaires and not independently corroborated. They estimated a cost offset of £7423 per patient. ICD or DSM diagnoses were not given, and the sample had a lower mean inpatient use of around 31 OBDs in the year before admission. The nature of the samples compared leaves the study open to serious methodological criticisms (see Table 18.2).

CONCLUSION

Although all economic evaluations of TC treatment are open to the criticism of lacking a control group, there is good evidence that TC treatment for severe personality disorder produces a cost offset. (As we have seen, the 'gold standard' of RCTs is not necessarily representative of clinical practice.) There is some evidence from FDL that this is not purely a ceiling-floor effect, but longer follow-up is needed to confirm this.

The process of engaging with the needs of higher order systems by providing economic evaluations of TC treatment has been very successful. The initial Henderson study in particular has been influential in arguing for the preservation of other NHS TCs and funding of extra-contractual referrals. This strategy has been taken further and, in combination with the recommendations of the Reed Report on Psychopathic Disorder, has enabled the Henderson to successfully bid for central funding to establish inpatient TCs in Birmingham and Salford. In the prison service there are also plans to expand TC provision (see Chapter 14). Further opportunities exist to develop cheaper day services at a more local level for patients with moderate to severe PD, or after initial inpatient treatment. The new political climate – advocating the values of collaboration and gaining better value from public money by removing the barriers between agencies – is one in which TCs, with the confidence gained by surviving and proving themselves in economic as well as clinical terms, may thrive.

REFERENCES

Bloch, S. (1986) 'Group psychotherapy.' In P. Hill, R. Murray and A. Thorley (eds) *Essentials of Postgraduate Psychiatry,* Second edition. London: Grune and Stratton, 739–757.

Campling, P. (1997) 'Suitable cases for treatment?' *Health Service Journal* 108, 5588, 22 January 1998, 34–35.

Campling, P. and Davies, S. (1997) 'Reflections on an English revolution.' *Therapeutic Communities 18*, 1, 63–73.

Chiesa, M., Iccoponi. E. and Morris. M. (1996) 'Changes in Health Service utilization by patients with severe personality disorders before and after inpatient psychosocial treatment.' *British Journal of Psychotherapy 12*, 4, 501–512.

Davies, S. and Campling, P. (1996) 'Market research – how a therapeutic community wins friends and influences people in the new NHS.' Presented at the ATC Windsor Conference, September 1996.

Davies, S. (In press) 'Therapeutic community treatment of personality disorder: is organisational culture a psychosocial treatment?' In *Clinician in Management.* BMJ Publishing.

Davies, S., Campling, P., Ryan, K. (In press) 'Therapeutic community provision at regional and district levels.' *Psychiatric Bulletin.*

Dolan, B., Evans, C. and Norton, K. (1994) 'Funding treatment of offender patients with severe personality disorder. Do financial considerations trump clinical need?' *Journal of Forensic Psychiatry 5,* 2, 263–274.

Dolan, B. and Norton, K. (1992) 'One year after the NHS Bill: the extra contractual referral system and the Henderson Hospital.' *Psychiatric Bulletin 16,* 745–747.

Dolan. B.M., Warren. F.M., Menzies. D. and Norton. K. (1996) 'Cost offset following specialist treatment of severe personality disorders.' *Psychiatric Bulletin 20,* 413–417.

Haigh, R., and Stengen, G. (1996) In-patient psychotherapy.' *British Journal of Psychiatry 168,* 524.

Kruisdijk, F. (1994) 'Substituting 24-hour therapeutic communities by 8-hour day hospitals: a sensible alternative to accepting budgetary cuts?' *Therapeutic Communities 15,* 3, 161-171.

Licht, R.W., Gouliaev, G., Vestergaard, P., Frydenberg, M. (1997) 'Generalisability of results from randomised drug trials.' *British Journal of Psychiatry 170,* 264–267.

McCrone, P., and Thornicroft, G. (1997) 'Reading about: health economics.' *British Journal of Psychiatry 171,* 191–193.

Main, T. (1989) 'The concept of the therapeutic community: Variations and vicissitudes.' In T. Main, *The Ailment and Other Essays.* London: Free Association Books.

Menzies, I., (1979) 'Staff support systems: task and anti-task in adolescent institutions.' In R.D. Hinshelwood and N. Manning (eds) *Therapeutic Communities: Reflections and Progress.* Routledge and Kegan Paul, London.

Norton, K., and Hinshelwood R.D. (1996). 'Severe personality disorder – treatment issues and selection for in-patient psychotherapy.' *British Journal of Psychiatry 168,* 723–731.

Ovretveit, J. (1998) *Evaluating Healthcare Interventions.* Buckingham: Open University Press.

Pullen, G.P. (1982) 'Street: the seventeen day community.' *International Journal of Therapeutic Communities 2,* 125–127.

Reed, J. (1994) 'A Review of Services for Mentally Disordered Offenders and Others with Similar Needs: Report of the Subcommittee on Psychopathic Disorder.' London: Department of Health/Home Office.

Tuke, S. (1813) *Description of the Retreat.* Reprinted 1996. London: Process Press.

Tuke, S. (1815) *Practical Hints on the Construction and Economy of Pauper Lunatic Asylums.* York: William Alexander.

Tyrer, P. and Johnson, T. (1996) 'Establishing the severity of personality disorders.' *American Journal of Psychiatry 153,* 12, 1593–1597.

Vaglum, P., Friis, S., Irion, T., Johns, S., Karterud, S., Larsen, F. and Vuglum S. (1990) 'Treatment response of severe and non severe personality disorders in a therapeutic community day unit.' *Journal of Personality Disorders 4,* 2, 161–172.

CHAPTER 19

Therapeutic Communities in Europe
One Modality with Different Models
David Kennard

EDITORS' INTRODUCTION

David Kennard trained as a clinical psychologist and group analyst. An early visit to Henderson Hospital was a formative influence, and he went on to work at Littlemore Hospital in Oxford, where he did research on the Phoenix Unit (a TC psychiatric admission ward) and helped to set up the Ley Community (a concept TC for ex-addicts). He began a series of visits to other therapeutic communities which eventually led to his writing Introduction to Therapeutic Communities. This was originally published in 1983, and he has recently rewritten it as the first book in the series of which this volume is the second.

In 1992, after working as regional tutor and at Rampton Special Hospital, he took on the challenge of helping to revitalise The Retreat in York – birthplace of moral treatment, which is one of the antecedents of therapeutic communities. He believes that therapeutic communities represent, at their best, the most optimistic and courageous view of human relationships, and particularly values his therapeutic community colleagues for being honest and unstuffy!

Like some others in the therapeutic community movement, he has an interest in and works as a consultant in Eastern Europe, where interest is developing but is still somewhat embryonic. In this chapter, he focuses largely on Western Europe and uses the links he has made as editor of the journal, Therapeutic Communities. *He describes the common themes and differences between established therapeutic communities in countries where they exist, places them in their political contexts, and speculates about free enterprise and survival.*

INTRODUCTION

The European Union has 15 member countries and, to the best of my knowledge, at least 11 of these have, or have had, therapeutic communities for people suffering from mental disorder. (This tally does not include those TCs solely for ex-drug addicts based on the concept house model.) This information comes partly from people I have met at the annual Windsor conference, for several years now a regular forum for therapeutic community workers from different parts of Europe, but mainly from papers submitted to the journal *Therapeutic Communities*, which I edited from 1992 to 1998. For the numerically minded reader it may be of interest to record the results of a small survey I undertook in preparing this chapter. In the 5 years from 1993 to 1997 the journal published 37 papers from countries in mainland Europe. In descending order of frequency these came from Holland (15), Finland (6), Italy (5), Greece (4), Germany (3), Belgium (1), France (1), Norway (1) and Slovenia (1). Of course, not every paper describes an active therapeutic community, but most do, and the others reflect an awareness of the TC field. The surprise here for British readers may be Finland since personal links have been fewer than between workers in the rest of Europe.

The spread of therapeutic communities in Europe really took off in the 1960s. The how and the why of this process are hard to pin down, but were probably a mixture of personal visits and training in England by European psychiatrists, visits to other countries by key figures like Maxwell Jones, and the influence of the writings of therapeutic community pioneers and the leaders of the anti-psychiatry movement, R.D. Laing and David Cooper. Coupled with these external influences there seems usually to have a been a combination of two significant local factors. One was the presence of one or more champions of the therapeutic community, people committed to the cause and sufficiently well placed in the academic or mental health field to make things happen; and the other was a profound dissatisfaction with the existing practice of psychiatry, especially the conditions of asylum care for the severely mentally ill. And in these two respects the pattern is remarkably similar to the early years of the TC movement in the UK.

What follows is a brief sketch of developments in six different countries, drawn largely from material published in *Therapeutic Communities*, supplemented where possible with more personal or direct knowledge. As the reader will find, the terms used vary. As well as therapeutic community they include psychotherapeutic community, group-analytic community, bi-polar inpatient psychotherapy and others. No doubt these do reflect real differences, but with an overlap of practice, ideas and values. I have not tried to define just what the overlap includes, the common core, although it almost certainly includes regular meetings of the whole community, membership responsibilities for patients/clients, therapeutic use of everyday tasks and social interactions, and closely examined staff team relations. Whether this is sufficient to mark something as a therapeutic community may be debated elsewhere. Inclusion in this chapter reflects a wish by the authors/practitioners to identify themselves with the therapeutic community field and its literature.

THE NETHERLANDS

From the 1960s up until the early 1990s therapeutic communities had become well established and accepted as part of the mainstream of psychiatry in the Netherlands. Leading figures included Lout van Eck, who was both a psychiatrist at Santpoort Mental Hospital and Professor of Psychotherapy at the University of Utrecht. The Dutch Association of Therapeutic Community Workers (VWPG) was formed in 1973 by six hospitals or hospital wards with the shared purpose 'to transform the large asylum-type institutions into places where human rights and dignity were recognised and respected... developing small communities in which staff and residents share responsibilities and patients are trusted and encouraged to take the initiative' (Montfoort and Verwaaijen 1994). These six created a rigorous accreditation procedure for therapeutic communities, involving a two day inspection visit, and eventually the six grew to become twenty accredited therapeutic communities. These were mainly small specialised hospitals calling themselves 'psychotherapeutic communities' providing 'residential psychotherapy' for homogeneous groups of patients with psychotic, borderline or neurotic disorders.

The Dutch therapeutic communities showed a strong commitment to training, empirical research and clinical investigation. Training along the lines of the experiential weekends started in Britain in the late 1970s was introduced in Holland soon after, and by 1996 over 750 professionals had taken part (Gerritsen 1997). During the 1970s eight of the communities collaborated in a major follow-up study of 1344 patients admitted over four years (Wagenborg *et al.* 1988), and for many years therapists from these twenty communities produced a string of thoughtful psychoanalytically based clinical and theoretical papers for the annual Windsor conference, which was until recently co-hosted by the British ATC and the Dutch VWPG.

All this is written in the past tense because in 1997 the VWPG was absorbed into the Foundation for Residential Psychotherapy. This followed a period during which therapeutic communities were suffering the impact of trends very similar to those in the UK – the closure of mental hospitals in favour of local community care, sheltered living accommodation rather than therapeutic environments and an emphasis on individualised treatment plans. Therapeutic communities were seen as offering a costly and rigidly standard form of residential treatment (Montfoort and Verwaijen 1994), although some were willing to experiment with cheaper day care and to integrate the psychodynamic approach with more focused or prescriptive techniques, including family therapy and cognitive restructuring (Kruisdijk 1994). At the same time as these external pressures gathered force, interest within the membership of VWPG seemed to fall off and a more eclectic and market oriented approach to residential psychotherapy gained the ascendancy. At the time of writing it is unclear how great the loss is. The knowledge, skills and dedication are still there, but the early champions and motivating forces seem to have gone.

FINLAND

Therapeutic communities are well established in Finland and have been influenced by a variety of outside sources. Kari Murto (1991) wrote that 'from the fifties onwards Maxwell Jones influenced the development of Finnish psychiatric care through his books and articles' (p.139). Matti Isohanni, a Professor in the Department of Psychiatry at the University of Oulu, noted that 'the first experiments with Finnish TCs were started in the early 1960s in some university clinics and small innovative mental hospitals following the visits of pioneers from the United States' (p.87). In Isohanni's view Finland has been at the forefront of TC applications in Europe, and he cites the Finnish national programme for the treatment and rehabilitation of schizophrenic patients carried out between 1981 and 1987 which 'stresses the importance of TC models in inpatient care' (Isohanni 1993, p.87).

Isohanni has been a significant champion of therapeutic communities in Finland. In 1975 he set up a 20-year programme of research in an acute psychiatric ward run on modified TC principles, and he has since been involved in developing and researching therapeutic community applications in a variety of settings. Some of these have taken TC principles into areas little tried elsewhere: an old peoples' home, a geriatric ward, a home for disabled war veterans, a prison for inmates with long criminal histories, as well as more familiar territory such as psychiatric rehabilitation centres, institutions for disturbed children and adolescents, and people with a mental handicap (Isohanni 1993; Isohanni, Winbald, Nieminen, Soini and Sakkinen 1994a, Isohanni Soini, Hannonen, Hakko, Karttunen and Mielonen 1994b).

As elsewhere, this activity has been supported by the forming of an association, the Finnish Milieu Therapy Association founded in 1983, and by professional training. There has been a particular emphasis on training nursing staff, who in addition to their basic teaching are offered specialised TC training in a number of centres. In 1992 a three-year education in TC methods was initiated. Finland has not escaped the economic climate of the times and in the 1990s has been subject to the pressures of cost containment and reduced lengths of hospital treatment. However as Isohanni (1993) points out, the therapeutic community movement is well suited to a country where 'real democracy has been an essential part of everyday life during the last century' and 'people do not tolerate intrusion, hierarchy... or inequality'. It seems there is little likelihood of the therapeutic community influence disappearing, although one can't help feeling it could be strengthened through increased contacts with fellow workers in other countries. Perhaps this lack of contact can be attributed to what Isohanni calls the Finns' 'deep ambivalence towards foreign influences', but let us hope this can be overcome in the future as we could learn a lot from each other.

GREECE

Unlike in northern Europe, therapeutic communities in Greece have largely been championed from outside the universities or public health services. A distinctive Greek therapeutic community model has been developed by the Open Psychotherapeutic Centre, a private non-profit-making organisation founded in Athens in 1980 (see Chapter 16). However, through its training programmes the centre has developed links with psychiatric hospitals in Ioannina in the north and Tripoli in the south. The OPC was very much the brainchild of its founder and present Director of Training and Research, Ioannis Tsegos, a psychiatrist who trained in group analysis in London in the 1970s and who subsequently founded the OPC, as well as the Institute of Group Analysis (Athens) and the European Group-Analytic Training Institutions Network (EGATIN).

The OPC is home to four different day therapeutic communities and to training programmes in group analysis, sociotherapy and psychodrama, family therapy and psychological testing. At any one time 50–70 patients attend the daily psychotherapeutic community and around 60 mental health professionals are working and/or training at the centre. Free of institutional constraints and able to 'do its own thing', the centre has developed some highly innovative approaches. These include two fortnightly psychotherapeutic communities that meet on alternate Fridays for patients who live a long way away or work shifts that prevent them attending more regularly; the opportunity for patients to pay some of their fees in kind – for example, a senior patient can move into the role of conducting a sociotherapeutic group; selection for community membership being the responsibility of the prospective member; all staff positions including leadership being for fixed terms; and a conscious amalgam of therapeutic community and group-analytic principles together with Aristotle's influence on ideas of public life and citizenship (Kokkinidis, Giftopoulo and Korfiatis 1997).

There appear to have been relatively few TC developments outside the OPC. One of these has been in the psychiatric inpatient unit of the University General Hospital at Ioannina, which since its inception in 1983 has been run on TC lines (Pappas, Yammitsi and Liakos 1997). Another was a valiant attempt to apply TC principles in a de-institutionalising unit for 25 long-term psychiatric patients in a traditional psychiatric hospital in Tripoli in the early 1990s (Kanellakis, Atchitakis, Paterakis and Tsegos 1995). This account is reminiscent of other attempts to use TC principles in large institutions without sufficient understanding or support from those in authority. The patients responded positively, staff morale improved, and things went well until a new hospital board of directors with a different agenda (and political affiliation) imposed a sudden change of regime. The story emphasises the need for consistent champions in positions of sufficient influence, and also underlines the reason why those who wished to see therapeutic communities flourish in Greece chose to establish themselves independently of government agencies. The emphasis on formal training for mental health professionals in TCs, which characterises the OPC and the views of its founder (Tsegos 1996), is intended to provide the professional recognition to sustain TC principles in the psychiatric field. While this is important, experience suggests that champions and defenders in the right political places are also needed. Part of the training at the OPC requires trainees to attend the annual Windsor conference, where reports of the centre's work are regularly presented: a simple idea that has facilitated continuing links and exchange of views between the OPC and TCs in other countries.

ITALY

Therapeutic communities have achieved two distinct generations in Italy, which might be termed pre- and post-Law 180. Law 180 was passed in 1978 to reform the psychiatric services at a stroke by banning any future admissions to psychiatric hospitals. (They weren't actually closed, but existing patients were thenceforth designated as guests.) In the ten years leading up to this event therapeutic communities and Franco Basaglia's Democratic Psychiatry Movement had developed as 'separate lines of assault on…biological psychiatry and its anachronistic practice in the asylum' (Pedriali 1997). This meant that unlike in most other European countries the main focus of TC efforts in Italy was on the position and treatment of the chronic psychotic patients. But interestingly, although inspired by the writings of Tom Main and Maxwell Jones, the other chief influence was not, as you might have thought, the work of David Clark and others who developed the 'therapeutic community approach' in the large English mental hospitals, but the anti-psychiatry movement led by Laing and Cooper. It was their much more theoretical, existential and political approach to psychosis that seemed to appeal to the Italians' search for a comprehensive ideological solution to the asylum problem, rather than the more pragmatic, piecemeal approach of the British hospital superintendents.

A number of therapeutic communities were set up in the 1960s and 1970s in Milan, Rome and Venice, but Pedriali (1997) notes that these were mostly 'experiments isolated from the general context: individual wards, de-centralised departments, private ventures' (p.6). But despite their anti-psychiatry leanings these therapeutic communities were viewed by Basaglia and his supporters as part of the problem, not part of the solution: simply another version of the unacceptable segregation of the mentally ill from society. Thus TCs found themselves at odds with both the reactionary forces of traditional psychiatry and the progressive forces seeking to dismantle the mental hospital system. Pedriali (1997) went on to note that 'they revealed themselves to be much more fragile than either their supporters' fervour or their founders' charisma led one to expect. They ended by withdrawing into themselves, depleted of their original significance or ceasing to exist, in a climate of burning polemic that created splits and sometimes mutual scorn between innovative enterprises' (p.8). Pedriali has carefully analysed the reasons for their failure, including an idealisation of the TC as a solution to all problems, unrealistic expectations of the abilities of the chronic mentally ill to share responsibility and an over-reliance on analytic interpretation. We might note, from the accounts of developments in other countries, that the absence of a professional association, of a training programme and of empirical research may also have played their part.

Now the second generation of Italian TCs are beginning to emerge in the context of what are called 'intermediate structures' that have developed to fill the huge gap in mental health services created by Law 180. Most of these, presently around ten, are in the private sector in the north and centre of the country. Some are already well established such as Il Porto in Turin and the Raymond Gledhill and Majeusis communities in Rome. Most are psychoanalytically oriented but some, like the recently established Crest (Centre for the Study and Treatment of Personality Disorders and Drug Addiction) near Milan are developing new integrations of social therapy, cognitive behavioural techniques and family interventions (Bertolli *et al.* 1998). At the time of writing Italian therapeutic communities are poised to create their own Association of Therapeutic Communities to promote research, training and public awareness (there is already an association for centres dealing exclusively with ex-drug addicts) and are considering launching their own edition of the journal *Therapeutic Communities*. In contrast to some other countries there has been no single champion, but today a core group exists around the development of the association which includes leaders and supervisors from some of the well established non-NHS TCs, Enrico Pedriali, Aldo Lombardo, Metello Corulli, and Luisa Brunori from the Department of Psychology at the University of Bologna.

GERMANY

In-patient psychotherapy units for neurotic and psychosomatic problems were started in Federal Republic of Germany at the same time as therapeutic communities were just getting started in Britain – in the 1940s and 50s. By the mid 1980s Paul Janssen (1986) wrote that there were around 60 hospitals with between 4000 and 5000 places for residential psychotherapy. This was remarkable and perhaps closer to the situation in the Unites States at the time than to other parts of Europe. Janssen (1986) surveyed these hospitals and identified six forms of organisation. These included those which offered various forms of psychotherapy without any attention to patients' social interactions; those which used a bi-polar model in which, like the Cassel Hospital, individual psychotherapy was provided alongside a separate therapeutic community function; and those in which the clinic with its patients and team members formed a structured large group integrating all facets of the therapeutic field. Janssen, who is Professor of Psychosomatic Medicine and Psychotherapy at the University of Bochum and Director of the Psychiatric Hospital of Dortmund, has remained a key figure in the development of a sophisticated model of in-patient therapy in Germany, which does not call itself a therapeutic community but appears to include most of the ingredients (Janssen 1994).

Separate, and perhaps better known in England through their journal publications and involvement in the Windsor conference, is the work of Andreas and Sylvia von Wallenberg Pachaly in Dusseldorf. In a series of publications they have described some highly innovative work and ideas such as the time limited (three weeks) psychoanalytic milieu therapeutic community which takes place twice a year in a country manor (Wallenberg 1992), and the concept of the large system group which links together all those involved in the care and treatment of former psychiatric in-patients living in a number of sheltered flats (Wallenberg 1997).

Another development which puts Germany ahead of therapeutic communities elsewhere in Europe and closer to the USA is the development of social-therapeutic prisons since the late 1960s. There are presently 15 settings with a total of 831 places (Losel and Egg 1997). Although not explicitly based on a therapeutic community model, or any other single therapeutic approach, the participation of inmates and staff in daily procedures and decisions is an important part of all the programmes.

NORWAY

In Norway therapeutic communities have been developed primarily in the context of psychiatric day hospitals for personality disorders. Karterud et al (1998) trace this development from the day unit at Ulleval Hospital in Oslo, established in 1978, that was linked with the Research Unit at the University of Oslo, where Karterud is a professor in the Department of Psychiatry. In 1993 the leaders of four similar units in southern Norway joined together to establish a network of psychotherapeutic day hospitals. They were able to obtain funding from the Norwegian Medical Association to set up a joint quality assurance system: a sophisticated package of symptom and other questionnaires for patients to complete on admission, discharge, and at one and five year follow up – in effect a system of routine outcome evaluation. Early results are beginning to be reported (Karterud et al. 1998). With approximately 180 patients a year being treated in the participating day units this represents a major source of future knowledge of the outcome of this treatment model.

As in Athens the non-residential day TC model is closely allied to group analysis, which is seen as the main form of training for staff in Norway. Karterud himself regards the day treatment programme as a group analytic community rather than a therapeutic community because it is time limited, because staff roles are precisely prescribed and only trained staff are employed (Karterud 1996; see also Chapter 4). Perhaps his definition of a therapeutic community is too closely wedded to Maxwell Jones' original model, for it seems to me that as a clearly articulated model for a targeted client group the Norwegian model is an example of how therapeutic communities can develop in the future.

COMMON THEMES AND CONCLUSIONS
How many models?

Perhaps we should not be surprised that what emerges from this brief tour of therapeutic communities in six European countries is that they each have their distinctive flavour. Those in northern Europe tend to have good academic and public health service links, with champions in university departments of psychiatry, and to be engaged in multi-centre research programmes. Those in southern Europe have tended to develop outside the public health services and have found their champions in independent-minded entrepreneurial therapy practitioners.

Likewise theoretical approaches vary. In Holland and Germany there are close links with models of in-patient psychoanalytic therapy. In Norway and Greece therapeutic communities have allied themselves closely to group analysis. In Finland there seems to be a more pragmatic, 'what works' social interaction approach, and the focus on nurse training is reminiscent of the collaboration in the UK with the Royal College of Nursing to develop a one year certificate. In Italy it is hard to know – there seems to be an emphasis on analysing the mistakes of the past, particularly the idealisation of the TC as a cure for the asylum and psychosis, but less information as yet on current practice.

Perhaps what is more useful than trying to pack all these into a single TC model is to see the therapeutic community as a modality of treatment, like individual, group or family work, into which a variety of theoretical models can be fitted: psychoanalytic, group analytic, social learning, systemic, cognitive, and others.

Free enterprise

One common set of issues has been the combination of financial cuts in public services and the pan-European movement to close mental hospitals in favour of care in the local community. In this, Enoch Powell and Franco Basaglia were – one presumes unwitting – bedfellows. Therapeutic communities within large mental hospitals have, as a result, probably died out in most places. In their place have come a range of environments for those with psychotic and personality disorders: sheltered housing, day centres, staffed hostels, small specialised hospitals, therapeutic prisons, as well as new private, independent residences. Each of these environments can be, and somewhere is, being developed as a therapeutic community. The scope for new ventures has never been greater, and the freedom to innovate is probably greatest in the voluntary/private/independent sector. While therapeutic communities have diminished in Holland where they have remained primarily within the public sector, in countries such as Greece, Germany, Italy, and to some extent in the UK too, private and voluntary sector TCs are developing new structures with new therapeutic amalgams. We should watch these and learn from them.

The keys to survival?

Perhaps the most significant lesson to be learnt from this tour is the way therapeutic communities have secured their position in each country through a combination of developing a recognised training for staff (Finland, Norway, Holland, Greece), organising programmes of research on therapeutic process and outcome (Finland, Norway, Holland) and developed Associations of professionals with a shared interest in therapeutic communities (Finland, Holland, Italy). We should be cautious about seeing these three as automatic guarantees of survival, sometimes there is no stopping an ideological/political sea change. But these three elements, combined with well placed active champions, seem about the best one can do.

If we want to answer the question, how can therapeutic communities across Europe collaborate to their mutual advantage, then it will surely be in these three areas: European standards of TC training; collaborative research using standard measures, and a European Association of Therapeutic Communities to promote public awareness of what TCs are and what they do.

REFERENCES

Bertolli, R., Mori-Ubaldini, M., Rancati, F., Reveraf and Spagnuolo, A. (1998) 'Crest: A protected residence in Vinago.' *Therapeutic Communities.* In press.

Gerritsen, M. (1997) 'On an island in the sun: the place of art therapy in training for therapeutic community practice.' *Therapeutic Communities 18,* 2, 133–43.

Isohanni, M. (1993) 'The therapeutic community movement in Finland – past, current and future views.' *Therapeutic Communities 14,* 2, 81–90.

Isohanni, M., Winblad, I. Nieminen, P., Soini, R. and Sakkinen, T. (1994a) 'Nurse resident relations in a therapeutic community for the elderly.' *Therapeutic Communities 15,* 1, 15–28.

Isohanni, M., Soini, R., Hannonen, K., Hakko, H., Karttunen, M., and Mielonen. M. (1994b) 'The organization of an innovative Finnish prison: Experiences of staff and prisoners.' *Therapeutic Communities 15,* 4 255–64.

Janssen, P.L. (1986) 'On integrative analytic-psychotherapeutic hospital treatment.' *International Journal of Therapeutic Communities 7,* 4, 225–41.

Janssen, Paul (1994) *Psychoanalytic Therapy in the Hospital Setting.* London: Routledge.

Kanellakis, K., Atchitakis, M., Paterakis, P. and Tsegos, I. (1995) 'Trying to apply TC principles within a traditional psychiatric hospital setting.' *Therapeutic Communities 16*, 1, 37–46.

Karterud, S. (1996) 'The hospital as a therapeutic text.' *Therapeutic Communities 17*, 2, 125–9.

Karterud, S., Pedersen, G., Friis, S., Urnes, O., Irion, T., Brabrand, J., Falkum, L.R. and Leirvag, H. (1998) 'The Norwegian network of psychotherapeutic day hospitals.' *Therapeutic Communities 19*, 1, 15–28.

Kokkinidis, A., Giftopoulou, E. and Korfiatis, K. (1997) 'The community meeting in a daily psychotherapeutic community.' *Therapeutic Communities 18*, 3, 183–94.

Kruisdijk, F. (1994) 'Substituting 24-hour therapeutic community by 8-hour day hospitals: a sensible alternative to accepting budgetary cuts?' *Therapeutic Communities 15*, 3, 161–71.

Losel, F. and Egg, R (1997) 'Social-therapeutic institutions in Germany: description and evaluation.' In E. Cullen, L. Jones and R. Woodward (eds) *Therapeutic Communities for Offenders.* Chichester: Wiley.

Montfoort, R.v. and Verwaaijen, A. (1994) 'The accreditation procedure for psychotherapeutic communities in Holland.' *Therapeutic Communities 15*, 3, 153–9.

Murto, K. (1991) 'Maxwell Jones as an organization developer.' *International Journal of Therapeutic Communities 12*, 2/3, 137–40.

Pappas, D., Yannitsi, S. and Liakos, A. (1997) 'Evaluation of in-patient groups in a general psychiatric unit.' *Therapeutic Communities 18*, 4, 285–96.

Pedriali, E. (1997) 'Italian therapeutic communities: from historical analysis to hypotheses for change.' *Therapeutic Communities 18*, 1, 3–13.

Tsegos, I. (1996) 'Fifty years of an amateur enthusiasm (on the avoidance of training and of professional identity in TC.)' *Therapeutic Communities 17*, 3, 159–65.

Wagenborg, J.E.A., Tremonti, G.W., Hesselink, A.J. and Koning, R.F. (1988) 'The follow-up project on psychotherapeutic communities: design and preliminary results.' *International Journal of Therapeutic Communities 9*, 3, 129–52.

Wallenberg Pachaly, A.v. (1992) 'The time-limited psychoanalytic milieutherapeutic community.' *Therapeutic Communities 13*, 4, 193–207.

Wallenberg Pachaly, A.v. (1997) 'The large group and the large system group.' *Therapeutic Communities 18*, 3, 223–39.

CHAPTER 20

The Quintessence of a Therapeutic Environment

Five Universal Qualities

Rex Haigh

EDITORS' INTRODUCTION

Something that irritates me is the way the word 'quality' is used as an adjective in its own right: for example, when busy working parents talk about having 'quality time' with their children. At work, individuals are designated as 'quality managers', health authorities do 'quality visits', and we are all compelled to move in the direction of uniformity, ticking endless boxes, and wasting our time on superfluous issues. 'Quality management' has thus become an imposed and rather persecutory managerial process with totalitarian overtones, rather than a creative striving for improvement.

Of course, there is fundamental disagreement about what constitutes good quality in mental health care. I first got an inkling of this when, as a rather naïve student, I was terrified to be interrogated by an intimidatingly large and manic man – in a circle of about forty people – as to what my own diagnosis was. This was the Phoenix Unit in Oxford, where as well as learning all the standard lists and skills that a medical student does, I learnt something more important about a 'quality' that was not on the routine curriculum. It was about being yourself and still being 'professional', being respectful and yet playful with 'patients', and about being part of a team where you never had to feel the need to take things entirely on your own. Years later, when I was appointed consultant at Winterbourne TC, it felt like I had found some of these mysterious ingredients once again.

This contribution is an attempt to pin them down, an attempt to define the qualities that make a TC, using the language I've learnt in my psychotherapy and group analytic training.

This chapter describes a simple way of looking at five ingredients of a therapeutic culture: the underlying principles, the subjective experience and some structures which establish and maintain them.

The five are presented as a developmental sequence: from the earliest experience of *attachment*, to maternal and paternal aspects of *containment*, and the task to make contact with others in a way which allows intimate and mutative *communication* to happen. Then on to the adolescent struggle of *involvement* and finding one's mutual responsibilities amongst others, and finally to an adult empowered position of *agency* – finding the self which is the seat of action and from which true personal power and effectiveness must come.

These principles are not new: they derive mostly from object relations theory, self-psychology and group analysis. Their particular use in therapeutic communities comes from how well they fit with what we all intuitively know about – the development of our own sense of self in relation to those around us. This chapter argues that these five principles are what lie behind the establishment and maintenance of a psychosocial environment which holds, and heals and empowers.

ATTACHMENT: A CULTURE OF BELONGING

All individuals start their lives attached: umbilically, within the mother and with the blood of one flowing right next to the blood of the other. At birth, this attachment is suddenly and irreversibly severed: the smooth and fairly tranquil life of swooshing around in a warm ocean that is your whole world, without ever needing to eat and breathe, is over. It is the first separation and loss, with many others to come later. The effortless existence is lost, and experience suddenly becomes bumpy: with good parts and bad parts, and if you are lucky, with people close enough to help you through it.

For the baby who is fortunate, the physical and physiological bond will be smoothly and seamlessly replaced with an emotional and nurturant one, which will grow and develop until various features of that too are invariably broken, lost and changed in the inevitability of development. This secure early attachment gives the infant a coherent experience of existence, and protects against being later overwhelmed by life's vicissitudes. This places loss – of contact, of relationship, of security, of hope – centre stage in the process of individuation: attachment must take place so that loss can happen. It is through the successful endurance of loss that we all have to survive and change to live on (see Bowlby 1969, 1973, 1980).

For a less fortunate baby, who might be born with greater needs, or for whom the process does not go well, the emotional bond is not secure. Attachment theory research clearly shows that if the bond is not secure for the infant, neither is the adult who grows from it. If the deficiency of emotional development is severe and incapacitating, psychiatrists will often come to a diagnosis of personality disorder when the person has reached adulthood, although many other diagnoses are also likely.

When disturbance is this fundamental, the first task of treatment is to reconstruct a secure attachment, and then use that to bring about changes in deeply ingrained expectations of relationships and patterns of behaviour. The culture in which this attachment needs to happen is one where community members can clearly feel a sense of belonging – where membership is valued and where members themselves are valued. This is harder than it sounds for people who come with a lifelong history of unsatisfactory relationships – expecting hostility, abuse, trauma or abandonment. This is further discussed in Chapter 11.

Often, attachment is powerfully sought but strongly feared: the struggle between desperate neediness and angry rejection. Not enough stable ground has developed between, and the demands of reality almost always meet the emotional responses of anger, shame, humiliation and pain. When this is played out as the ambivalence to attach or not, it is often the very meat of the therapeutic process: can intimacy be tolerated, perhaps even used and enjoyed, or is it just too terrifying? Many never join, or drop out, because the fear and shame of letting others know them is too great.

For those who fall into membership of a therapeutic community like a warm duvet, the natural course of development demands that their intra-uterine-like experience soon becomes more complex. Members of any society who stay under the duvet all day will soon start having their responsibilities to themselves and others pointed out: conflicts will arise and need to be resolved. Various elements of the community will become invested with different and complex feelings – the stage is set for the rough and tumble: love, hate, anger, frustration, sadness, attack, defence, comfort and all the other ingredients of relationships. Facilitating the disillusion from the symbiotic fusion fantasy of the early attachment is about growing up and leaving home.

For those who start by fighting against it all, the destructive feelings can involve a wide range of primitive mental mechanisms, predominantly using denial, splitting, projection and projective identification. They can represent a deeply unconscious need to spoil, steal or envy what is good. For some, working with this can be the main therapeutic task: staying is an achievement, and any work to actually look at what that attachment means is a bonus.

The structural requirements for this mean we need to pay great heed to joining and leaving (see also Chapter 7). The joining process is all about referral and assessment, and how prospective members of a community are dealt with. The very first contacts with people will have significant impact on how they feel about attaching to a community, and much of this will be in a complicated interplay with their deeply held expectations of relationships. However, a successful TC does need to believe in what it is doing and present itself as a place worth belonging to. Being realistic about difficulties and doubts is necessary, but an early alienating experience in joining a TC will trigger persecutory feelings and defensive actions.

The practicalities of leaving are just as important. Leaving represents loss of a very important attachment, and the successful negotiation of it is a crucial part of the whole process of being there in the first place. Communities often arrange it with rituals and gifts, but the real sense of sadness and loss needs to be experienced, for it is by being fully aware of the pain of detachment that the intensity and meaning of the attachment before can be understood and 'taken inside'. It usually involves a mixture of anger, desolation, yearning and hope: the end of something very important, but also the beginning of the rest of life starting in a different place.

CONTAINMENT: A CULTURE OF SAFETY

One of the earliest things that 'grown-ups' do for babies on their bumpy ride through infancy is to be there and accept their extreme feelings of primitive and boundless distress. This process is the template for containment, and for infants who get a satisfactory experience of it, it forms the basis of a safe world in which experience which feels intolerable can be survived.

Using the commonest family configuration, this could be characterised as a maternal element: safety and survival in the face of infantile pain, rage and despair. In a therapeutic community, these primitive feelings are often re-experienced, and survival without criticism or rejection may in itself be a mutative new experience for members, whose usual expectation will be to face hostility, rejection and isolation. Now they have the novel opportunity to have these powerful primitive feelings accepted and validated.

An aspect of safety which comes a little later for children could be called the paternal element: about limits, discipline and rules. This is the safety of knowing what is and is not possible and permitted – done through the task of enforcing boundaries. This is somewhat at odds with the view of *permissiveness* as a required quality of therapeutic communities: if the experience of containment is to be achieved through holding the boundaries as well as holding the distress, although the emotions may be boundless, the actions they precipitate are within agreed limits. Thus it is more fundamental for a place to feel safe than for anything to be allowed. And that safety is what is experienced in the culture of a community when it is well contained: it needs to tolerate severe disturbance so it can witness and then digest violent emotions, and still feel safe. However, the size of the stage on which the dramas are played is not limitless – and members need to know where those edges are to feel safe. This is considered in more detail in Chapter 8.

The relentless regressive pull of the community, by continual and inescapable deep involvement and challenge, will act as a 'pressure cooker' for feelings and the actions they precipitate, so the negotiation of 'disturbance' will commonly be at the forefront of members and staff experience. The community needs to provide the stability to contain these overwhelming and primordial anxieties. Then, when the high emotion and incapacity to think has subsided, can the digestion, understanding and healing happen.

The holding process also depends on the sensuous and nurturant qualities of the environment. These qualities will bridge the gap between the reality of holding and the experience of being held. It is the difference between 'containing' and 'holding' – one is mostly inside, and one is mostly outside (see Symington 1995). Both are weaker without the other: sympathetic and compassionate holding is unlikely to be usefully internalised without a deep and significant internal experience of containment of powerful emotion, and that containment at this intensity would be difficult and somewhat sterile without some grounding in the qualities of real relationships within a community.

Sooner or later, a gap opens up between container and contained and it is safe enough to explore, and start seeking a sense of autonomous identity (see Winnicott 1965). It is here that the infant plays with new emotions, relationships and ideas. The therapeutic community can recreate this 'play space' with a richness, intensity and variety that is much harder to create in other therapies (see Chapter 10). It contains a large variety of people with different experiences, views, expectations and attitudes. It is as if all human life is here – for relationships to be made with, to have fun with, and to get into trouble with. Much as it is for a secure infant on its early explorations.

The structural features which embody the principle of containment, and make a therapeutic environment feel safe, are about support, rules and holding the boundaries. Support systems are important in providing a way in which disturbance is tolerated, distress is held and people are not left isolated and rejected when they are feeling desperate.

Rules need to clearly establish what is permitted and what is not: considerable efforts will often be spent on bending, stretching and interpreting the rules and boundaries. The process by which rules are invented, changed and discarded also deserves attention: the sense of safety will be compromised if the rules are not sufficiently held and owned by the community.

COMMUNICATION: A CULTURE OF OPENNESS

Once the primitive and turbulent preverbal work is in hand, a major developmental task is to make contact with others, enjoy mutual understanding of common problems and find meaning through this connection. For children, this starts in earnest once they begin to talk – although of course there is very deep and rich communication in the primary intersubjectivity which starts growing in the primary bond immediately after birth. However, it is by striving to put it into words that symmetrical contact is made through symbolic representation, that existence and identity is confirmed through mirroring and that despair and distress can be articulated and made bearable.

For this to be possible for adults, particularly in large groups, requires a very specific and unusual culture. First, the attachment and containment need to be securely in place. Then, an intangible quality needs to be present in the atmosphere so that people experience some certainty that the community will accept and digest what they have to say, rather than defend against, patronise or reject it. It is the opposite of those primitive feelings of being persecuted or isolated, where others are seen through two-tone glasses which colour them either wholly menacing and malign, or angelic and all-giving.

Communalism was one of the original TC themes (Rapoport 1960), and was described as tight-knit, openly communicative and intimate sets of relationships – encouraged by sharing of amenities, general informality and an expectation of participation by all members. Elsewhere, the essential ingredient has been described as a *culture of enquiry*, a *culture of commentary* or a *culture of questioning*. These are useful descriptions, but they need amalgamating and widening to incorporate a sufficient sense of the internal experience to fully describe this sort of culture. Perhaps *enquiry* is rather dry and cerebral, *commentary* loses the importance of the subjective experience, and *questioning* is somewhat inquisitorial. Calling the culture one of *openness* concurs with the qualities of communalism, adds the opportunity for enquiry, commentary and questioning and conveys a subjective sense of freedom, movement and possibility of change.

In this sort of openness, it is difficult to feel paranoid: persecutory fantasies are immediately and deliberately reality-tested. If an individual – staff or community member – feels any anxiety about somebody or not knowing something, then there is a shared acceptance that it is reasonable to challenge others, and try to understand it through open communication and making contact. This openness is unusual in most adult situations: it refers to the exposure of interpersonal material which is usually left unspoken, or shut away – beyond scrutiny or question. Amongst other things, it includes the questioning of motives, the relentless challenging of defences, and inquisitiveness about observable relationships. The defining characteristic is the expectation and demand that communication is more open, more deep and more honest than happens in everyday situations. Through it, relational connections are deepened and personal meaning is found through contact with others (see Foulkes 1964).

This openness is unremarkable for time-limited therapeutic sessions, but much of the time in a therapeutic community does not give that protection. For a therapist, it is reasonable and relatively easy to have a 'therapeutic demeanour' in a group, but much harder to know just 'how to be' when sitting together at lunch, or playing a game together. When the rough and tumble of this everyday milieu is avoided by staff, the openness gets undermined by 'us and them' feelings, which although useful and workable within a therapeutic arena, need to be minimised in the overall experience. Expecting this degree of openness can be a considerable challenge to staff: therapeutic boundaries are much more complex than in once weekly therapy, and there are many strong pressures on them. Careful selection of staff, suitable training and reliable supervision are essential.

Within a community, this sort of communication also needs well-arranged structures in which to take place. Normally this means stable, dependable groups with clear membership, protected time and space, and mutual agreement of boundary issues such as confidentiality and expectation of attendance. Individual therapy sessions are not helpful as they undermine openness within a community, and reduce the impact, cohesiveness and power of the groups.

Clarity about communication with professionals outside needs to be established. This can be done by copies of all letters and reports being given to members and openly discussed, or by all those documents being written collaboratively.

Some of the structures to promote openness are in keeping with contemporary expectations of transparency and accountability. Therapeutic communities need to be honest about what they are doing, and willing to communicate that to whoever is interested: including referrers, those who pay or commission such services, potential members, and colleagues with overlapping interests. Inviting visitors into the community can be an important part of this. If this spirit of accessibility runs through the whole service, then openness is an expectation which people know about before they join.

Research and scrutiny should also be welcomed, and met with the same openmindedness as the clinical work requires. The quest for evidence is parallel to this: in a therapeutic community one is immersed in evidence of the power of relationships in promoting health; the harder task is to pin it down and communicate it openly.

INVOLVEMENT: A CULTURE OF PARTICIPATION AND CITIZENSHIP

So far, the three principles together – attachment, containment and communication – could apply to several forms of psychotherapy. The next two are more specific to therapeutic communities: perhaps they take the developmental sequence through adolescence into adulthood – and real life – in a way some other therapies do not.

The term *living-learning* experience was an early description of therapeutic communities, and that is part of what this principle represents (Jones, 1968). Everything that happens in the community – from the washing up, to the board games, to the requests for leave – can be used to therapeutic effect. A disagreement in the ward kitchen can be more important than a therapeutic exchange in a group; it is as much part of the working day for a junior doctor to go swimming with the community as it is for him to formally assess patients' mental states.

This goes beyond openness, in that it requires the sum of the experience of all the members all the time to come to bear in understanding ourselves in relation to the human environment. So the meaning of an individual's existence is as much in the minds of others as in the physiological or biochemical reality of an isolated person: we are mindful of others and they are mindful of us. One member of a community is held in mind by all the others, and they are all held in his mind. In a community where people are together for considerable time at considerable depth, and often with uncertain definition of where their edges are, this is an almost tangible realisation of how we are only meaningfully defined through a social process.

In a residential therapeutic community, this holding in mind is made utterly tangible: no longer a fantasy, but reality. For 24 hours a day, all interaction and interpersonal business conducted by members of the community belongs to everybody. In day TC units, other ways are used to bridge the gaps and ensure that out of sight does not mean out of mind (see Higgins 1997). The expectation will be to use all aspects of interaction and understand it as part of the material of therapy. Not in isolation, but in the real and 'live' context of interpersonal relationships all around.

In a normal therapy group, which might meet once a week, it is not normally possible to see so much of the 'ground' against which the 'figure' is defined, but in a therapeutic community it is literally impossible to get away from it. Involvement of all aspects of a group member's experience, or the living-learning culture, is another reflection of the surrounding and context being an indispensable part of the relevant material. This goes much further than the behavioural formulation of *reality confrontation*.

This discourse leads to a position where any separation of an individual from society or constitution from environment leaves the definitions empty and meaningless: the very opposite of an individualistic world-view. Social cohesion becomes the dominant aim; interdependence emerges through ethical responsibilities more than by demanding rights; fragmentation and alienation are reduced through finding meaning in relationship to others.

In some ways, we take this interdependence to the limit in therapeutic communities. Each has a different but vital contribution to make to the health of the whole. The group constitutes the norm from which each member may individually deviate and the aggregate of all the individual elements produces a thing with its own qualities and a whole that amounts to more than the sum of its parts. This richness and variety of the web of relationships between the members, with all the feelings and responsibilities that implies, is itself a creative and reparative force.

To come back to practicalities, involvement and the continuous effort of looking at the context in which things are happening, is hard work. 'Dragging in' much material which members would rather avoid will clearly meet resistance. Communities vary in how much structure they see as needed, how it is demanded, and how flexible that can be. This demand for involvement can be by peer pressure, by rules and procedures, or by staff intervention.

The community meetings are a vital part of this, for they are normally where the day's business is all brought together in everybody's mind. Their frequency, length, timing, structure and need for specific agenda items can all be arranged with this objective. In this way, all that happens within the day is part of the therapy – whether it is spoken or not, interpreted or not, analysed or not. Sometimes it just needs to be acknowledged and held.

AGENCY: A CULTURE OF EMPOWERMENT

In 1941 at Mill Hill Hospital, Maxwell Jones found that soldiers suffering from 'effort syndrome' were more useful than the staff at helping each other. At Northfield, Wilfred Bion was taken off his therapeutic rehabilitation wing after six weeks, probably because his experiment was unacceptable to the military hierarchy. These two locations were the start of therapeutic communities as we know them, and they both made fundamental challenges to the nature of authority. They were ahead of their time – and many social changes since have undermined our notion of traditional authority, and made us re-evaluate how it is now carried and administered. Postmodernism and the deconstruction of tradition are part of this.

But for therapeutic communities, this challenge to authority was there at the beginning. It is in keeping with the idea that the patient's unconscious knows better where to guide the therapy than does the analyst's expertise, and the commonly accepted notion that most therapeutic impact comes from work the patient does, rather than the therapist. It also has echoes with the teachings of the interpersonal theory and self-psychology, where labelling and reifcation are seen as authoritarian, distancing and inimical to the establishment of a satisfactory therapeutic space. In group therapy terms, it is at odds with the models where therapists do individual work in the group, or only offer group-level interpretations. In both of these there is an underlying assumption that the therapist 'knows best' or at least knows what is going on: information which the group members cannot know, or which is delivered to them under close control of the therapist.

In communities where members have agency, things are different. An asymmetry and difference between therapist and patient is accepted, but an automatic assumption of 'superiority' is rejected: members acknowledge that anybody in the group might have something valuable to contribute to any other member. This is the essence of therapy by the group. Authority is fluid and questionable – not fixed but negotiated. The culture is one in which responsibility for all that happens within specified limits is shared: members are empowered to take whatever action is decided.

In other circumstances, the role of doctor or therapist might demand obedience or dependence, with a 'false-self' quality where true affects concerning a relationship have little bearing on the conduct of both participants. In a therapeutic community this will soon be subject to an uncomfortable scrutiny and deconstructed – for staff–patient relationships need to be grounded on something deeper than etiquette, seniority or custom.

There are easy ways to do things, without thinking or feeling too much, which rely on ways of dealing with situations which have become almost automatic. It is much harder to think about what really needs doing and why (Main 1990). This means struggling to understand each others' experiences and actions, and of avoiding standard responses, which might be dismissive or punitive, or using a stock phrase like 'what do *you* think?'. It also means respect must be earned as much through qualities of 'being with' as of 'doing to'. Intrinsic authenticity and demeanour will come to weigh more heavily than extrinsic authoritarianism and rank. Only through this process of experiencing parts of *real* relationships, perhaps beyond the resolution of the transference neurosis, can agency develop. Then action and feeling can have a clear connection to a true core self, and they are not held by a role or prescribed behaviour.

When members of a community take responsibility for each other as part of a live and intense process or relationship that really makes a difference, it is worth infinitely more than a risk assessment, or a procedure, or a protocol (see Cox 1998). It demands that authority must always remain negotiable – authority is something that exists *between* people rather than *in* individuals or policies. Of course this is not anarchy or wholesale delegation of responsibility or an unreal world with no outside references. In reality, we all work within a framework in which we are accountable for what we do. This may be where Bion's experiment fell apart, for he challenged authority head on, and those in power would not tolerate it. Bridger, Main and Foulkes challenged it by quietly demonstrating a way in which they could survive, and they went on to sow the seeds for radical re-evaluation of the nature of authority in therapy, and the development of a whole field of creative group relations.

The principle of agency in modern therapeutic communities follows this approach. With empowerment in human relations as the aim, it is in opposition to regimes based on biological determinism, the empty core of bureaucratically imposed policies, and the binary tyranny of ticking boxes and unthinkingly following protocols. This goes much further than the original 'flattened hierarchy' of *democratisation* (Rapoport 1960). Rather than being a fashionable idea, or a policy which is imposed on a unit, it demands a deep recognition of the power of each individual. It is not a 'harmony theory' that says we simply have to find this effectiveness within people – for it includes powerfully destructive, envious and hateful dynamics which exist in all of us and are sometimes beyond reach. However, working towards establishing personal agency which is anchored in a solid sense of self does entail work needing a considerable degree of intimacy. It needs to be an intimacy which is safe, open and healing rather than frightening, dark and abusive.

The structures which support this type of culture are concerned with when votes are held, how decisions are made, and progression to positions of responsibility. Where the culture is developing, staff might often find themselves giving decisions back to the community to make – 'it's up to you' or 'it's your community'. It can seem much easier to accept the projections of dependency and make the simple decisions, but then no power would be given back, and the staff would be the agents of action in the community. It is this process of refusing to accept members' individual or group dependency which makes them empowered – through having to search for their own agency – both as a community and as individuals within it. Much of the time, it is uphill work – but there are plenty of occasions when the collective power of the community transcends what any one person could do. It is easy to forget what a radical and subversive idea it is to give real power to the people.

SUMMARY: PRIMARY AND SECONDARY EMOTIONAL DEVELOPMENT

This last section will consider what we are recreating by trying to set up an environment with these five qualities. They can be seen as a simplified sequence of the fundamental requirements for reasonable emotional health in anybody – through the process of *primary emotional development*. Although we all start with slightly differing needs and have them met to various extents, it is something that goes seriously wrong with these five things in a infant's or child's environment when it is abused, deprived, neglected, traumatised or suffers a severe loss. And that results in a multitude of different consequences with possible symptoms and diagnoses, which all have a *disturbed emotional development* as the primary causes.

So *secondary emotional development* is what we try to facilitate by recreating these conditions in a therapeutic community. We are trying to provide a psychic space in which the things that went wrong or got stuck in primary emotional development can be re-experienced and re-worked in this artificially created setting. It might never have quite the impact as it could in childhood, but the experience can at least make a difference to expectations of relationships and the way in which care is sought of others.

Table 20.1 shows the five principles, their origins in human development, corresponding TC cultures and structures, and where the original therapeutic community themes fit. Secondary emotional development can also happen in other settings – different therapies, and to various degrees anywhere people are emotionally engaged together in developmental tasks. Of course, any of these environments can also be anti-therapeutic: with a culture that discourages attachment, that does not feel safe or containing, with perverse and distorted communication, unspoken rules about what is and is not admissible, and power based on arbitrary criteria. This can be as true of a school, office, company, hospital ward or community team as of a family or therapeutic community. These principles are therefore not only concerned with specialised treatment units – they are about everyday life, and struggling to try to meet needs that we all have.

Table 20.1 Therapeutic community principles

Theoretical principle	Origin in development	Culture in a TC	Structures in a TC	Original TC themes*
Attachment	Primary bond, losses as growth	Belonging	Referral, joining, leaving	
Containment	Maternal and paternal holding	Safety	Support, rules, boundaries	Permissiveness
Communication	Play, speech, others as separate	Openness	Groups, ethos, visitors	Communalism
Involvement	Finding place amongst others	Living–learning	Community meeting: agenda and structure	Reality confrontation
Agency	Establishing self as seat of action	Empowerment	Votes, decisions, seniority	Democratisation

Note: * 'original TC themes' were described by Rapoport 1960.

REFERENCES

Bowlby, J. (1969, 1973, 1980) *Attachment and Loss*: Volume 1, *Attachment*; Volume 2, *Separation: Anxiety and Anger*; Volume 3, *Loss: Sadness and Depression*. London: Hogarth Press; New York: Basic Books; Harmondsworth: Penguin Books.

Cox, J. (1998) 'Contemporary community psychiatry.' *Psychiatric Bulletin 22*, 249–253.

Foulkes, S.H. (1964) *Therapeutic Group Analysis*. London: Allen and Unwin.

Higgins, B. (1997) 'Does anyone feel they need support tonight? Twenty-four hour care on a day unit.' *Therapeutic Communities 18*, 55–61.

Jones, M. (1968) *Social Psychiatry in Practice*. Harmondsworth: Penguin.

Main, T.F. (1990) 'Knowledge, learning and freedom from thought.' *Psychoanalytical Psychotherapy 5*, 59–78.

Rapoport, R.N. (1960) *Community as Doctor*. London: Tavistock.

Symington, J. and N. (1995) *The Clinical Thinking of Wilfred Bion*. London: Routledge.

Winnicott, D. (1965) *The Maturational Process and the Facilitating Environment*. London: Hogarth.

The Editors

Penelope Campling is Consultant and Clinical Director at Francis Dixon Lodge, Leicester. Brought up in a busy vicarage, she soon felt at home with the pace and hurly-burly of life in a therapeutic community, interspersed with times of reflective calm. She spent many a long student vacation working in the Christian Community on the isle of Iona in Scotland and believes that life can be experienced most fully when living as part of an involved community – involved both with each other and with the world at large.

Her passion for classical music and experience of being a rather mediocre singer in a very good choir, reminds her of the great creative potential when people work together in groups. This is useful at the odd times when creative interventions seem impossible within the large group at FDL!

Living in multicultural, multifaith Leicester with her large family, she is particularly concerned that therapeutic communities embrace the richly diverse society in which we live.

Rex Haigh is Consultant Psychotherapist at Winterbourne Therapeutic Community and lives in Berkshire with his wife and four children.

As a medical student in Cambridge his mind was blown off the straight and narrow by a lecturer who introduced him to the ideas of Laing, Freud and other radical thinkers. A few years later, as a clinical student, he was again confronted with a similar challenge: this time by working in a TC admission ward (the Phoenix Unit in Oxford) where any ideas he had of learning routine clinical skills were soon overshadowed by something much more uncontrollable and interesting.

A search for this sense of excitement and creativity in his working relationships led him to general practice in Cornwall, psychiatry back in Oxford, psychotherapy in Birmingham, group analytic training in London, and on to his current post as consultant to Winterbourne TC in Reading.

Subject Index

Author Index